EVERYDAY MYSTIC

FINDING THE EXTRAORDINARY
IN THE ORDINARY

Dear Ed,
Here's to exposing your
inner mystic!
With love,
Linda

By

THERESA JOSEPH

With Linda Fallo-Mitchell, Ph.D.

This book is dedicated to God.
You asked and I have given.

And to Mother Mary and Jesus,
who have always been there with me.

Table of Contents

DIVIDING GOD

The moon starts singing
When everyone is asleep
And the planets throw a bright robe
Around their shoulders and whirl up
Close to her side.

Once I asked the moon,
"Why do you and your sweet friends
Not perform so romantically like that
To a larger crowd?"

And the whole sky chorus resounded,

"The admission price to hear
The lofty minstrels
Speak of love

Is affordable only to those
Who have not exhausted themselves
Dividing God all day
And thus need rest.

The thrilled Tavern fiddlers
Who are perched on the roof

Do not want their notes to intrude
Upon the ears
Where an accountant lives
With sharp pencil
Keeping score of words
Another
In their great sorrow or sad anger
May have once said
To you."

Hafiz knows:
The sun will stand as your best man
And whistle

When you have found the courage
To marry forgiveness,

When you have found the courage
To marry

Love.

The Gift: Poems by Hafiz The Great Sufi Master
(Ladinsky, Daniel, Penguin 1999, p.136-137)

PREFACE

I wrote this book at the insistence of two close friends and two published authors. In addition to the messages, most of the text was given to me by direct revelation during my predawn meditations, not that I was looking to write a book. The Divine would show up, in one of the many forms He assumed and would start speaking. My job was, and still is, to listen and record what I heard.

This is where all my learning took place—in the quiet moments when it was just that all-knowing Source and me. I mentioned this in passing to my dear friend, Linda Fallo-Mitchell, thinking that she may want the numerous spiral notebooks in which I recorded the messages should anything ever happen to me. I figured that if my husband were to find them he'd probably just throw them out—likewise, my kids.

Years after learning about these journals, Linda received guidance that the messages I had received were to be compiled into a book. That seemed like an insurmountable task to me for two reasons: first, because I can't type; and second, in spite of their source, I thought a lot of what was in the journals might be a waste of most people's time. Linda was not having any of my protests, and her conviction led her to type almost all of my journal entries that summer. As she began typing she became more, not less, convinced that I had to write the book.

Drawing on her experience as a developmental psychologist, educator and researcher—and using years of puzzle solving skills—Linda took my random, chronologically ordered revelations and grouped them into topics that became the chapters you will read in this book. Linda would send me a series of journal entries on a particular topic and tell me to make them into a chapter, which I would do and send it back to her for further editing. The only writing I did that was not by divine revelation was to connect the dots of my story and to link otherwise random entries to help the story flow more smoothly. In this way, working in God-time, Linda and I eventually gave birth to *Everyday Mystic: Finding the Extraordinary in the Ordinary.*

The purpose of this book is to tell you that you have the power to live your life on what I call God's jet stream and to illustrate what a life lived on His jet stream can look like. Judging by my own experience, it can be a wild ride with results more glorious than anything you might have imagined for yourself. It will show you how to align yourself with the Divine, how to have God streaming live, and then how to follow Divine guidance. The title of this book, *Everyday Mystic,* is not meant to trivialize mysticism but to underscore the profound depth of who each of us is, as a part of, instead of apart from, the One, the Unity, God.

I write not as a learned person, a priest or an intellect. I am here to pass on to you what Jesus has shown and said to me. I was never religious, nor did I know what to believe about Jesus until he spoke to me. Although I use the word "spoke," it is inaccurate because initially, he communicated without actually speaking. His first message was crystal clear—that the meaning of our life is pure love. That's all he wants in its deepest, truest form—for this love, which is the Divine within each of us, to be extended to everyone without exception. Extend it as if the person opposite you were the son of God because he is. And no matter how he chooses to live his life here on earth, God loves him no more and no less than he loves you. Jesus gave to me the gift of knowing what these words meant and what it felt like to be truly embraced by, and incorporated into, that kind of love. He allowed me, for what may have been a moment on earth but an eternity in heaven, to exist in his love. It is a love that is so beautiful, so totally unconditional that I did not wish to return. Yet, I did return with the realization that life back here is not as easy as it is on the other side, or is it?

I am acutely aware that many will simply think I am crazy after reading about my experiences and the messages I have received. But I assure you I am not—wait, isn't the first sign of mental illness that you don't recognize your own condition? I was the first to wonder about my sanity after my earliest mystical experiences, which I was careful not to share with anyone. Looking back, I see how much resistance I had to them. I completely shut down the first two experiences and returned from the third one intrigued but beguiled as to how I would apply what I learned in my own life.

I was concerned about how I would defend the messages I received and then realized that it would be impossible, so I won't. I received them in states of elevated consciousness or union with, dare I say, God? Quite probably considered by some as the basis for quackery. But how can the messages be quackery when they brought inner peace, love and joy into my life? My journey, this book, is taken from private journal entries that were never meant to be shared; in fact, the journal entries themselves would never have been written, were it not for the insistence of my mother. It was she who encouraged me to document my revelations even though I was working full-time and taking care of my two children. Knowing that initially I wasn't following her instructions, my mom started writing a few notes whenever we spoke. Eventually, I relented and started scribbling notes myself.

Linda is convinced that the story lies in the ordinariness of my life and the extraordinariness of the revelations—the message being, as author and medical intuitive Caroline Myss describes, that we can be mystics without a monastery. My story is about how I began, in the course of my daily life, to see and hear God. My premise is that if I can see and hear Him, so can you. I am here to tell you that you already have a direct relationship with God, if that is what you want. You already have God communicating with you in many different ways—you just need to open yourself to the infinite possibilities. I wrote this book so that those of you who are already having mystical experiences, or would like to, don't have to go through the same resistance that I did.

I hope that through the example of my journey, this book will guide you onto a practical path that can lead to mystical experiences, while helping you to make living the messages a reality. Once you put the principles in this book into action, you will have taken the first steps to making your ordinary life heaven on earth.

I am a mother, a wife, a friend and a volunteer—all those things that many of us are, have been, or will be. I have an MBA in Banking and Finance and worked 60 hours a week at IBM for 18 years, which included most of my kids' childhood. In 1998, I walked away from half my salary to work part-time—30 hours a week. I worked part-time for a year until I finally quit, walking away from my salary and our family's only source of medical coverage. My husband was starting a new business and our financial future was less than certain. However, I felt that my path was leading me home—not only to my children but also to my life's purpose.

I have never had the luxury of experiencing the traditional life of a mystic or chanting the sacred OM on a mountaintop. Instead, I share my time, my love, joy and sorrow with my husband, children and friends. Many of my early revelations came when I was balancing family and corporate life. The revelations continued as my life evolved from corporate executive to homemaker and volunteer, to full-time Reiki practitioner and teacher, to founder of the *Global Peace Movement* and *Channeled Grace Healing Circles*. My list of responsibilities and activities is long, just like yours. In my social life, and in life in general, I believe in having fun and in laughter—lots of it. The only thing I may be doing differently is finding time each day to sit in quiet solitude to listen to what God has to say. Sometimes I have a question for God, but many times I don't; I simply listen to, or look at, what He chooses to reveal to me.

I know that you can do this too. Sharing the story of my path is not intended to highlight how I am different from you. This story is about all of us. What makes you and me special is our divinity and unity with each other and all that is. Years ago I was asked by a woman, let's call her Eloise, for advice on a relationship issue. I decided to meditate on it and received a message for her from God. I was excited to pass it along because, as is always the case with God's messages, it was a beautiful, simple solution in which everyone would win. Her response surprised me, but I suspect it may be the response of many others. It was an angry, demanding, "WHO ARE YOU TO THINK YOU CAN TALK TO GOD?" I responded that I was nobody—that's the whole point. I am nobody special and God is talking to me, so that must mean God is talking to everybody.

It is my hope that the messages I have received will help you on your journey of self-discovery and will lead you to a life of inner peace, love and joy; that they will help you to discover that *you are in Him and He is in you*; that you will learn to love yourself unconditionally because that is the way God loves you. All of the messages from God and His messengers have love at their core, an unconditional love of oneself and one another.

The Light burns within you—it **is** you. Begin to see yourself as the physical manifestation of the Divine. As such, direct revelation is already there for you. Make time to sit quietly and listen to and see what God chooses to reveal to you, and out of the ordinariness of life will come the extraordinariness of a relationship with the Divine in you.

With love and recognition of your Divinity,
Theresa Joseph

INTRODUCTION

This is a story about finding the extraordinary in the ordinariness of our lives. It is already there, woven into the fabric of our everyday lives. It is about surrendering to Divine will and about humility. I unknowingly started on this journey by taking a Reiki[1] energy healing class in my spare time, picking up a book on angels, and remaining open to the infinite possibilities that exist within the realm of consciousness. Jesus entered the fray and I followed what I thought were his signs, not knowing where they would lead. Today, I am still just following the breadcrumb trail that he leaves me, which, to date, has led me to pastures filled with more inner peace and love than any I would have found on my own.

From the time I took that first Reiki class over 15 years ago, until fairly recently, I was hesitant to refer to this energy that I experience as God. Instead, I was happy to adopt the Reiki nomenclature of "universal life force energy" since it lacked any religious connotation. As I became more intimate with this universal life force energy, I began to feel that it was more of an organizing force with a consciousness that we were all tapped into. I started calling it Energy, the Universe, Source, the Divine. Then, tired of explaining myself, I lapsed into calling it God, which to me meant that genderless, ineffable **Something** that is Everything and Nothing at the same time—that Consciousness that pervades our very being and connects us to all things, living and inanimate. To me, now, God is Love. I anthropomorphize that Love by using the traditional Judeo-Christian masculine pronoun "He" **solely** to facilitate the telling of this story.

God loves us so much that He created us in such a way that we are never separate from Him. As a part of Him, we embody those attributes we ascribe to God, and although I don't see the need for religion, I do understand how religion, or a philosophy that teaches one to love unconditionally can be useful. I see no difference between an atheist who loves unconditionally and a Christian, Jew or Muslim who loves unconditionally. The God, Energy, Everything and Nothing that I am familiar with transcends religion and defies our attempts to define It. Jesus is my teacher and you will find many messages from him in these pages, yet he has never appeared to me as a Christian or a Jew. He has never told me to go to church or to synagogue, but neither has he told me not to. Mother Mary has also delivered messages to me, as have the Catholic saints St. Thérèse of Lisieux, St. Teresa of Avila, St. Rita, and the energy I call God—yet I find myself outside the boundaries of traditional religious practice. Instead, when possible, I try to spend two hours a day in silence with these entities and with God. Their love for us all is as alive and well as if they were here among us.

I know I am not the only one who can sit in silence and receive messages from Jesus, Mary, saints and other spirits, but those who have seen the messages that have been revealed to me say that they must be shared with the world. As I started to include these messages in the book, I kept feeling that I had to edit them or to couch them in some way, which ended up diluting both the messages and the feelings I was asked to convey. This was happening because I was trying not to offend anyone, even atheists, to whom I have written a note in the appendix. But then I was left apologizing to God. Therefore, in an effort to be true to the God who speaks to me, I offer the messages unedited. The Source who has made Itself available to me and spoke to me with unconditional love and lack of judgment loves everything and everyone. It doesn't exclude anyone based on his or her belief system or his or her way of life. We need to follow this example and when we do, we too will know heaven while we are here on earth. Heaven leaves no one out. God loves everyone and is waiting for us to love one another.

So please, as you read, do not get caught up in the names of the messengers. For those of you who are uncomfortable with my messengers, please replace their names with ones of your choosing. They are not coming to convert you or to endorse a religious belief, and they have no ego. They endorse unconditional love and don't seem too concerned about how you get there. Do, however, allow yourself to get caught up in the messages, and you will see that they transcend the presence or absence of religion. As with all mystical truths, they defy characterization because they speak to the heart of every person regardless of cultural or religious background. As St. Thérèse of Lisieux said: *We must own the deeds.* I found that living life according to the messages in this book brings inner peace, love and joy. As you find that peace and love inside you, you will become the embodiment of peace and love, bringing heaven to earth.

I offer how I found the Extraordinary woven into the ordinariness of my life. I am not suggesting that this should be your life, as mine is full of wrong turns. I am saying that if you want to have an intimate relationship with the Divine, you can. This book tells you how. Based on my experience, I don't see anything that stands between you and the Divine or between you and your divinity. The messages are what I have heard and, sometimes, what I have had to translate from a feeling that I was immersed in while in "heaven." I have been convinced that making the messages public could make a difference in the world, but for that to happen the messages contained herein need to be put into practice.

From a practical perspective, to be an ordinary person on the spiritual path requires a combination of action and stillness. It may begin with, and be interspersed with, your quiet interactions with God. In between, it demands that you live your life. It demands you put one foot in front of the other to cross a street. It demands that you help yourself, and it asks that you help others. You can sit and pray all day for groceries to appear on your shelves, but my guess is that unless you get up and go to the grocery store, those shelves will remain empty. Please don't confuse this with the pilgrim's journey, in which he deliberately sets out fully trusting God to provide, and He does. That is a different level of awareness that is there for you too, but it may take some time to achieve. The first step is to help yourself and continue to ask for God's help and guidance. Trust that it will appear, but if it doesn't, go buy those groceries.

This brings up that fine line between trust in God and doing what you are asked as you co-create your life with God. What is your part? That is something you will work out with God, but it is also something I address in this book. There is no formula and no one-size-fits-all solution, so while you are working out that balance, live your life. There is no instruction manual to tell you when to get up, when to pray, when to listen for God's voice. So, as you are working it all out, help yourself and help others. Love yourself and love others. Forgive yourself and forgive others. Let love and forgiveness permeate your life every minute of every day. The rest will begin to fall into place, and as you evolve so will the lessons.

I start this book with a recent story about how I followed God's will for me, which was to move from my beloved home. It will take you through the struggles with, on the one hand, wanting to surrender to God's will and, on the other, wanting to live the life I had planned for myself. It isn't always, but in this case it was difficult obeying and trusting God's will for me. Should you find the story interesting and would like to know how in the course of your ordinary life you can recognize the extraordinariness that is a part of your daily life, then sit back and read on as I share with you what God has shared with me.

The book is organized into three parts. The first part is my journey or, more aptly, how a former-banking-relations-manager-ends-up-hearing-angels-Jesus-Mary-and-others. Part II is how, based on messages I received from the Divine, I feel we can all help to birth a new world in which love and, therefore, peace reigns within ourselves and throughout the world. Part III chronicles the messages I have received from God, Jesus, Mary and others. Part III can be read from beginning to end and can also be used as part of a daily meditative practice by simply opening to a message for inspiration or guidance.

Throughout the book, italics indicate the voice of the Divine, also known as Spirit or the Holy Spirit.[2] These words are meant to help you to create your own life of love and inner peace. Many of the messages from Spirit were meant for deep reflection over the course of weeks or even months. Likewise, this book is meant to be read in small sections, by reading and stopping to reflect on how the passages apply to your life. The first appendix provides you with an in-depth explanation of what it is like for me when I see, hear or feel the presence of divine beings. All client messages are shared with their permission and client names have been either omitted or changed to protect their privacy.

My story is included for the sole purpose of illustrating how un-special you need to be to hear God's voice, what I call God streaming live, and to ride on God's jet stream. God's jet stream is what you ride on once you start acting on His guidance. On the jet stream, synchronicity becomes the norm in your life and solutions to problems are presented, seemingly, out of nowhere. You will see evidence of this in the chapter entitled "Following Divine Will." The default setting for God is to love us unconditionally. God knows we are fallible, so it is a good time to stop thinking you must live up to some perfect ideal before God will interact with you. If God's love had to be earned, he would not be talking to me. So, please do not be like Eloise who chose to forego the Divine message and instead focused on being right about whom God does and does not talk to.

The words of Jesus and highly evolved spiritual teachers are living, dynamic words whose meaning evolves with changes in the reader. They are meant to be read and reread as you grow and change. They are not stakes in the ground but more like signs leading the way. It is up to you to take the steps and, ultimately, to make the journey into their deeper meaning. The meaning I glean from Divine messages depends on my level of consciousness at the time. The meaning changes as I grow and as my understanding deepens. Then I find that my earlier interpretations may not have been so much "wrong" as also part of my journey. This is an ongoing, spiritual awakening of which this book and the messages I share with you are only one part. Spirituality must be incorporated into your everyday life to make a difference. It is an attitude with which you approach every relationship beginning with the one you have with yourself. And so you will see that many of the messages revolve around the central theme of loving yourself unconditionally.

Jesus spoke in simple words because the message is simple. Love. Forgive. That's it. So what is so complicated about this and why would you read this book? Because you need help putting those two words into practice, and you need to know that ordinary people are capable of the extraordinary life that comes when you follow Divine guidance. The first time I heard St. Thérèse of Lisieux, she said: *Lay down your swords and pick up a broom to sweep away the obstacles to peace—misunderstanding, judgment, and a sense of lacking. You lack nothing.* I will show you what she means.

PART I: MY JOURNEY

We can learn about mysticism, or we can practice being mystics.

Rabbi David Cooper

God is a Verb:
Kabbalah and the
Practice of Mystical
Judaism

CHAPTER 1
Following Divine Will

And everyone who has left houses, or brothers and sisters, or mother and father or children, or property for my sake will receive a hundred times as much and inherit eternal life.

- Jesus *The Gospel according to Matthew* verse 19:29

We moved into town with everything we owned in the back of the pickup truck we borrowed from our friend's landscaping company. En route, our mattress and box spring flew off onto the interstate and were run over by a truck. The mattress survived, albeit with tire tracks, but the box spring was crushed. As anyone who has bought a house knows, there is very little money left over to replace things, so losing something as simple as a box spring can be stressful. Fortunately, in the years to follow, our lives grew more comfortable. I wasn't raised "comfortably." I grew up in an old draughty house on a lot of land with not a lot of money. My parents were ahead of their time, organically growing vegetables on 10 acres and maintaining a 250 year-old farm house. My siblings and I were the built-in child labor. With the exception of a lucky few, we all have our childhood horror stories, so I won't bore you with mine. Suffice it to say that majoring in economics and getting my MBA took me a long way from growing my own food to my new town, with no regrets.

So imagine my surprise when, after living happily in Fairfield County for 21 years, I heard a voice in the middle of the night say: *Sell your house now. I will find you something.* I knew that voice, as he has spoken to me many times before and mostly I am okay with what he has to say. But this time was different. This message was contrary to all I believed my life would be. I imagined myself living some version of my current life, in my house, well past the age when my children (ages 23 and 18 years) had their own children. I imagined myself walking my grandchildren the 100 yards from my house to the beach and looking out my windows to see the sun dancing on the Long Island Sound. There may be more beautiful places in the world but not within 45 minutes of New York City. I was in paradise, and Jesus was asking me to leave.

I did the only reasonable thing I could think of—I ignored him. Realizing that I couldn't do this forever, I took the bait and asked him where I should look for a new house. He directed me to the "middle of the state." Since I am no geography wizard, "the middle of the state" had no meaning to me. I pulled up a map and saw Hartford, Connecticut in the center but what really caught my eye was a town call Litchfield, spelled out in large bold type, seemingly just west of Hartford. In later investigations, I would not even see Litchfield on the map due to its microscopic size, but on this day, it appeared as the most prominent town close to the "middle of the state."

I contacted a local family who had bought property in Litchfield County and got the name of a realtor. I figured it couldn't hurt to look, even though my Jewish husband thought I was out of my mind; and he didn't even know that I started my search because Jesus told me it was time to move.

My husband, children and I spent a day with a lovely realtor in Litchfield County. On the way home, I tried to convince my husband to seriously consider buying property in Litchfield County. We had just looked at 10 farms, but we were not farmers. My husband, his voice rising to an angry shout, rightly pointed out that our life was in Fairfield County and New York City. He pointed to the lack of supermarkets and restaurants in Litchfield County. Of course, my daughter and I responded that we wouldn't need supermarkets because we could grow our own food. I had done it before as a "child laborer," I would do it again, but not in an old house. Having grown up in an old house, I hated them. What other people called charming, like sloping floors and low ceilings, I called annoying. I wanted to build an eco-friendly, energy-efficient home. If I had to move to Litchfield County I wanted to get off the grid. This is not something Jesus was asking. I had always wanted a self-sustaining place in addition to, not instead of, my Fairfield County residence. I figured this was a better rationale to use with my husband than the truth, although that would eventually come out. Like any sane person, especially one who is in real estate, he wasn't buying into my rationale of wanting to be self-sufficient. We made a few more excursions with the realtor, and then I thought I had done my part. Jesus spoke. I looked at real estate; my husband was not buying into the plan. I let the issue drop.

Then on December 14, 2011, 30 days after Jesus told me to sell my house, I sat down to dinner by myself and decided to say grace, thanking Jesus for my meal and my home, which is something I don't usually do. That was a mistake. I had barely put my hands together in prayer when I heard Jesus say: *Listen to me; the road ahead is not easy. You have to plan.* All I wanted to do was to eat my dinner and say a little blessing over my food. I did not want a lecture. I burst into tears because I knew what he meant. I knew all at once that this was about the move, which I thought I had successfully evaded. The following conversation ensued:

> Jesus: ...*Do what I ask. I am asking you to move.*
> Me: I will.
> Jesus: ...*to the middle of the state. It doesn't matter where* (I wasn't too clear on that); *things are going to happen fast.*
> Me: Send me a buyer.
> Jesus: *It is done.*
> Me: I need my husband on board.
> Jesus: *It is done.*

Shortly thereafter, a friend of mine, who does business with my husband, called to say she was having, in her words, a "sucky" day until she had visited my husband's office and found out that I was looking at farmland. From that point on, all she could do was laugh. She called immediately to ask if I'd lost my mind. "Do you know it's cold in upstate Connecticut?" she asked. She knows me. I'm no farmer and I hate the cold. So after she and I stopped laughing, I told her my reason: Jesus told me I had to move, and I had to look in the middle of the state. So by now she was laughing so hard she could barely breathe, and so was I. I was hearing how utterly ridiculous it sounded to say, out loud, that I was following guidance from Jesus. It sounds as absurd as you think it sounds and worse. It sounds like a joke. My friend responded, through gasps for air, that she was going to tell her husband that Jesus told her to buy an island in the Caribbean. Then I described my son's response when I told him my orders from Jesus, "Good thing he didn't tell you to burn down the house." The words from Jesus sounded ridiculous when said out loud, especially when they go against everything you are and everything your friends know you to be. I go to farmers' markets and make a beeline for the farmer who has turned his crop into some sort of prepared food. I have little interest in the raw ingredients.

A Tale of Two Properties

A week or so later, my husband called me to say that he had just heard about a price reduction on a property in Washington, Connecticut. We should drop everything and go see it with a builder. What? How did he know what was going on with real estate in Litchfield County? Was he getting email updates? When Jesus said he would get my husband on board, he wasn't kidding. So we looked at that property, as well as one that we had seen on our very first trip with our broker. Now we needed to decide between the two properties, and we had to act fast due to the activity generated by the price reduction on the Washington property. I wasn't prepared for this. I may hear Jesus talking to me but that doesn't mean I am always ready to act on his commands. He had done what he said he would and had gotten my husband on board, so now the ball was in my court.

I did what I always do in these cases—I went into meditation. I heard Jesus say to me: *I'm bringing you home.* I didn't want to hear that. And which home did he mean anyway? How was I to choose between these two properties? His response prompted me to think about the **feelings** I had had when I visited each property and how easy it is to miss a feeling. When I had visited the Litchfield County property, tears of knowing filled my eyes as I stepped from the main house, a 1760 farmhouse that I hated, into the herb garden. Why did I have tears there? They were the same tears, accompanied by the same feelings I had when I visited the colleges that my son and daughter would eventually attend. I knew during the visits that those were the schools that were right for my children and sure enough those were the colleges to which they applied, were accepted and happily attended. This feeling was curiously absent when I had visited the Washington property. Washington is the "better" town. The property was gorgeous and it had all the elements I was looking for, including a stream, a pond and open pastures. The literature even described it as a sanctuary that would be good for writers and artists. The owners had crucifixes (not a symbol that speaks to me but a symbol of Jesus nonetheless) in every bedroom and pictures of Mother Mary on the fridge. "Signs" at the Litchfield County property were the presence of two apple orchards and a snakeskin reminiscent of the Garden of Eden. Mmmm, this was interesting. Were these signs at all, and if so, what is the difference between a sign and a feeling? Should one take precedence over the other? Author Gregg Braden says that **feelings** are the language of the universe. I asked Jesus these questions and he told me: *You are to follow your heart.*

I started to examine my feelings and realized that they can be so fleeting. They come and go so quickly that if one is not paying attention, one can easily miss them. Then it occurred to me that there was a feeling I'd almost missed regarding the Washington property. Although it had all the right features and it was in the right town, there was a fleeting feeling as I walked the property of "too much water." I had felt it rise up from my heart to the base of my throat. I had wanted to ignore it because I thought it was absurd. How could there be too much water? I pushed aside the feeling and forgot about it until it came back to me during a meditation. I was shocked to remember it. The property was being sold at a rock-bottom price because the owners were ready to move on. My eyes and my brain told me this was the place, and my heart and my intuition told me it wasn't. But there were all those signs—the words in the brochures and the crucifixes. I consulted with my daughter whose answer was brilliant. She simply said, "Mom, signs speak to your mind. Feelings are of the heart."

A Tug-of-War: Me vs. God

We had decided on the Litchfield County property, but I still did not want to move, so I meditated a lot in the days to follow, hoping each time to hear that this was all some sort of a test to see if I was listening and that I didn't actually have to go through with it. In one of those meditations I had this brief conversation with Mother Mary:

> Me: I love living where I live.
> Mary: *We're not giving you a choice.*

Much later, my mother told me that there is a Lourdes of Litchfield Shrine in Litchfield County. As it turned out, it is close to the property we were thinking of buying. So on a cold day, en route to make a deposit on the Litchfield County house, we happened upon the shrine. The place was empty so I sat by myself in the freezing cold and closed my eyes. I immediately saw Mary—she was carrying a wedding dress, which made no sense to me. She said: *With this move you become a bride of Christ.*[3] I knew it was true because I burst out crying. I didn't want to be a bride of Christ. I wanted to go back to living my normal life. I didn't even know what a bride of Christ was. I tried to make Mary say something different like, "tear up the deposit check and go back home." Instead I got: *Now go buy that house!* I gave up. I consented to be a guest at God's table, as was suggested to me a year earlier when Jesus said: *Someone has to be a guest at my table. I prepare a feast, and*

15

everyone thinks they have to prepare their own feasts. Be a guest, Theresa, and learn to feast at my table. It is always bountiful, and there are so many empty chairs around my table because so few choose to respond to my invitation. Don't be one of those people, Theresa. Respond with open arms, an empty stomach and an open heart. For at my table you feast on love. You feast on so much more than what you see on the table (in the vision I could see foods of all kinds and so many empty chairs). God[4] was exhausting me. He truly never gives up and my resistance was making me tired. We met the seller's agent at the house and handed over the deposit check. About two weeks later, in a predawn meditation, Spirit gave me a phrase that kept repeating in my head throughout the hour-long meditation: *To be a bride of Christ means to be married to his ways.*

In another predawn meditation I asked why I was resisting this move. Jesus responded: *Because you want to be in control. You have asked to surrender. Now surrender and follow me. When you stop resisting you will not suffer. Your resistance is hurting you. This is causing you pain…the road ahead is not easy.* Meaning, as Jesus explained to me, I will be asked to follow him more and more.

It was so hard to let go of my home in Fairfield County. My life and the lives of my family were so good there and, in that way, I know I have been fortunate. Sometimes, I wondered if maybe I had heard wrong—maybe I had made a mistake and God hadn't really asked me to move after all. I couldn't help thinking what an enormous mistake I would have made by selling my house, uprooting my husband and myself, leaving my friends and the life I knew, if I had simply heard wrong. The way I felt, you'd think Jesus was asking me to leave the continent or walk away with just the clothes on my back. I kept hoping that the deal we made on the house would somehow fall through. I gave it to Jesus and said, if such and such happens, let it fall through. Yet, such and such never happened. In fact, things moved ahead flawlessly.

Our bid was quite a bit lower than the asking price and was nonnegotiable. On the day we made the offer, my best friend Donna, whom I hadn't spoken to in quite a long time, called me to see what I was up to. The following day I spoke to her again, this time to say that we'd walked away from the deal because the seller countered at a higher number and we were not willing to negotiate. Later that night, the seller reduced his price significantly and before we had a chance to get back to him,

Donna called to say she'd finally received the photos of the property and loved it! Her overwhelming enthusiasm seemed to be another well-placed nudge from God.

The seller's new counter offer was within spitting distance of our offer, which so shocked us that we agreed to his price, and the next thing we knew we had signed a binder agreement. I felt sick with worry, interspersed with brief moments of peace. Friends were excited. Everyone I told confirmed that this was the right thing to do. They seemed to believe that having land to grow food was important, as was living a sustainable lifestyle. It was all a great idea, as long as you were not the one being asked to give up your life to do it. To my suburban and city friends, it was a very romantic life and when they saw the photos of the land, they swooned. But being the one who was asked to say goodbye to her entire way of life to follow Jesus to Litchfield County was not so romantic. Sometimes, I wish it were God who had to get aligned with my will and not me who had to get aligned with His. I would have been leading me in an entirely different direction. Like my friend who was having the "sucky" day, I'd have chosen the Caribbean location with a big ocean view, a few palm trees and bougainvillea climbing up the walls of my white stucco house. I would not have been looking for views of pastures, paddocks, chickens, horses, trees, trees and more trees. But God never asked me. Ever since I started to listen, all God does is direct me. Years ago God asked: *Do you really think the decisions I make will be worse than the ones you've made for yourself?* Well, I think in the past I might have made worse decisions than God, but this move was questionable.

Months before, thinking that I would be much better off leaving Fairfield County for a warmer climate, I had been inquiring about a property in North Carolina. It was a completely self-sufficient house and property with fruit trees, a water source, and privacy and was only minutes from a well-established town. Okay, so it wasn't an island with palm trees and bougainvillea, but I know that is not sustainable so this was a close second. We traded phone calls with the owner but never connected, and then I forgot about it, until one morning when she called again to see if we were still interested. After telling her we had an accepted offer on a property in upstate Connecticut, I laughed at myself. Once again, God was right. Could He really have made a worse decision than I would have made for myself? I was having anxiety and sleepless nights over moving one hour away from my friends, my clients and all that was familiar to me. I laughed at the wreck I would have been had I moved to North Carolina, much less to the Caribbean. In case you are keeping score: God 1. Me 0.

Regardless, I needed constant reassurances from God that I was on the right track. Not a bad thing, given the impact on my life and family, and God was only too happy to accommodate me. One night I asked God for a sign that I was making the right decision in buying this property. Now this is different from just any sign in that I was specifically asking God to help me to follow His will. He knew that I was having trouble, and I knew that He would help me. So the next morning the soil scientist (I had to talk to soil scientists now that I was in contract to buy a farm) whom I'd called and had not heard back from for five days returned my call. He and I spoke briefly about soil quality, but before he hung up, he mentioned that he recognized the first three digits of my phone number as being the same as those of the town in which he grew up. Well, you guessed it, he grew up in the town I was leaving but not only that—he had lived just around the corner from me, and his best friend had lived on my street. My current street was his old stomping ground. It turned out that he had left Fairfield County for college the same year I had moved in. He now lives in Litchfield County. He told me that once I left, I wouldn't even miss it. He knew because he had already done it, and he goes out of his way not to travel through the Fairfield County area.

This is only one example of many reassurances God gave me throughout the process. Yet, in spite of all the messages I had received, I was still hoping that I had heard wrong and I looked for any reason **not** to move. Maybe, at a minimum, I could delay the pain of moving by backing out of the deal before we signed the contract. With all the contingencies I had built in, there had to be an out somewhere. With the contract signing two days away, I anxiously awaited reports from an engineer on the state of the 250 year-old house, a chimney expert, two soil scientists, a well recovery expert, a water analysis laboratory and even a shaman[5] whom I had asked to check on the energy of the land. Surely the contingencies I had built in would outsmart God's plan to move me.

I felt alternatingly angry, sad and excited but mostly sad to be asked to leave a community that had been extraordinarily good to me, with too many friends to count and with the geographic beauty of living near the coast. Not to mention that I was being asked to leave the house God had brought me to in the first place. By now you will have ascertained that I have moved, but I am telling you that following God's will is not always easy. He told me He would take care of me, and there is the part of me that trusts and the part of me that still thinks I know better. I know it's laughable, but I think you need to know what this feels like so that when you try to follow

God's will you'll understand that sometimes it is a tug-of-war between you and God. Even when you know you should surrender, you might fight it. Sometimes He asks you to do things that are so great you'll be kicking up your heels and yahooing. Other times, like this one, it can be really, really hard. So I guess it becomes evident how fallible I am, and I hope that will demonstrate that if God doesn't give up pursuing me, He will not give up pursuing you. God is knocking on your door. All you have to do is get up and answer it. Don't worry, though, as it is not likely that as you begin your conversation that He is going to ask you to move.

So here is how my plan to back out of the contract turned out:

The house, built in 1760, had almost nothing fundamentally wrong with it other than a small piece of rotten wood on one window ledge and a few cracked panes of glass. The chimneys were in excellent health. The land, with its three apple orchards and hay field, was found to be completely free of pesticides and arsenic. Yes, I tested for arsenic. I had learned that in the 1920's and 30's arsenic was a common pesticide used on apple trees—not on mine. The well, it turned out, yields some ridiculously substantial amount of water although it did contain radon. But wait. That was easily remedied with a filtration system. The water was considered "hard," but once again that had already been taken care of by a water filtration system preinstalled by the seller. Okay, so my last hope lay with the shaman. I had heard the trepidation in her voice, which led me to believe some bad news was forthcoming. But that was not the case. The hesitation I had heard was due to an experience she'd never had before—as she journeyed to the underworld to meet her power animal and begin her process, she "saw the Hand of God reach down" to pick up her and her power animal and place them on my land. In her vision, she then walked the land with the spirit of a Native American guide. She saw this as a very good omen for the land I was about to buy. There was no longer a question. I was going to sign the contract to buy the land. All the contingences I'd built in to void the contract failed to materialize.

But wait! I had had one more chance. Just before the contract signing, the lead-in-soil tests came back showing high levels of lead in the herb garden outside the house. We promptly got a remediation estimate and asked that it be deducted from the purchase price. The sellers flat out refused because they'd already agreed to price reductions for other items. Great! I'd written a contingency into the contract stating that I had to be satisfied with the lead test results. I wasn't and they were not going to pay for remediation. So now I didn't have to buy the farm. Not so. The realtors delivered the sellers' refusal to reduce the purchase price along with their own proposal: they would split the remediation fee and take it out of their commissions. I never even had a chance to back out. My friend Linda laughed and said, "Did you really think you'd beat God?"

I was so sad. I shut my eyes, tears streamed down my face. These were not the tears of "being all choked up." These were tears of sadness, plain and simple. I connected with Jesus as we drove away from my beautiful coastal home and the life I loved, to close on a farm in the country. With my eyes closed, I could see Jesus clearly. In the vision, he took me with him as he walked through the Garden of Gethsemane. I saw the apostles sleeping while the sun was shining onto the golden fields and hillsides. *He showed me that the apostles were not only physically asleep at that time but also metaphorically asleep.* In this vision, I walked with Jesus through the garden gently awakening each sleeping apostle so that they may see the Light of the Sun. *This time there will be no need for a cross. One by one they are awakened by my touch, and then they start to awaken each other by tapping each other gently on the shoulder. They awaken from the deep slumber to the knowledge that the Sun has always been shining, even while they slept.* I don't know why Jesus had to ask me to walk with him in this vision and wake up people. Had this task not been assigned, and had I not followed Jesus' message to move, I would not now be driving away from the home I love. And I would not be so sad.

An Obedient Vessel—Not By Choice

In response to my announcement that I was moving, internationally acclaimed spiritual intuitive, speaker and author Roland Comtois said: *Beautiful. I am so proud that you are an obedient vessel of holiness. The land will flourish, bringing blessings to all. Many will come…Give yourself time to accept the blessings. The barn holds sacred energy that will bring healing to those who visit. Water will be found running across the land…The water has been blessed by Mary. It will take time to build… Be patient. Your husband has an equal role…he will be asked to be the caretaker of the place, overseeing the growth of the property. In the days ahead, a light will shine through the trees and a collection of color will be found…Let the journey begin…*

The next day proved him right. We met with the shaman, Luciana (Lucy) Walker, on our new property so that she could continue the work she had started remotely, checking on the energy of the land. She was brought to tears by the compassion and gratitude she felt from the Native American spirits who were thanking us for coming to live on this land. *They honor us for coming.* Lucy found that, historically, the Native Americans travelled across our land following a ley line[6] from north to south then turned and followed another from west to east. We walked these lines to a brook at the eastern edge of our property. I had a vague recollection that someone had mentioned a brook during discussion of the property, but being the skeptic I am, I had envisioned it as some sort of dried up, seasonal rain ditch. Instead, we found a magical babbling brook surrounded by moss-covered stones. Walking through the woods we passed stone walls interspersed with white quartz crystal. Those same crystals were strewn about the forest floor. We blessed the brook and continued back to the stable, which we now know is situated at the inside corner of an ancient migratory path. It is where the Native Americans would make their turn while traveling from north to east.

I think most people walk the land before they buy it. We hadn't. Once I had surrendered to God's will, I trusted that buying the property was the right thing to do and, as is the case with Him, the gift far exceeded my wildest expectations. Finding that magical brook and the quartz crystals strewn about the forest floor was far more than I would ever have asked. Lucy's presence made the discoveries possible. Without her we would never have known we were walking past quartz crystals nor would we have known that the turkey feather my daughter found was a symbol of abundance. We would not have seen the hawk glide in and land in one of our trees the moment Lucy arrived—a symbol, according to shamanism, of leading one to his or her life's purpose.

Lucy's original findings were confirmed. The land, the house and the barns were all energetically clear. She had felt that the only structure on the property that was in need of energetic clearing was the dairy barn because, sometime in the past, the cows it contained may not have been treated as well as they could have been. This required that Lucy, my daughter, my husband and I had to do some very loud drumming and rattling around the interior and exterior of the barn. The booming drums and rattling echoed in the vast emptiness of the barn. Being on 55 acres, we are not very close to neighbors, except for this dairy barn.

The elderly woman who lives next door marched over, wearing an angry expression and demanded to know what all the noise was. She first ran into my daughter, drumming. My daughter, with a big smile introduced herself as the new neighbor and then, seeing the look of worry on the woman's face, very calmly explained that this was a one-time event. Next, my husband emerged from the barn carrying a rattle made from the leg of a deer, hoof and all, topped with a turtle shell and wolf fur. He introduced himself and made conversation as if what he was doing was the most natural thing in the world. Then, I walked out of the barn. As I came upon this threesome my husband and daughter turned and pointed to me saying in unison, "She can explain!"

My appearance was no better than that of my daughter or my husband. I was wearing an ankle length fur coat, turned inside out so the fur would not offend anyone, a camera dangling from my neck, a baseball cap, backwards because the brim was impairing my vision, and I was shaking yet another rattle topped with some sort of seed pods. I smiled and introduced myself. I told the neighbor about the cows, which hadn't occupied the barn for maybe 65 years, and she said, "The prior owners treated their horses very well." Huh? I felt badly as the sight of us, on top of all the loud noise, must really have startled her. I tried another explanation, saying, "We are blessing the land and honoring the Native Americans who once lived here." She became animated, maybe feeling at last like she had a foothold in this otherwise bizarre conversation, so she asked if I was Native American. I said no, I am Italian. Once again she looked completely confused. I asked her a few questions to shift the conversation and then told her we were from Fairfield County hoping that would sound very conservative, as if that could offset this peculiar scene. I'm not sure that it worked. I was fairly certain that before we moved in, she warned all the neighbors about the crackpots moving onto their street.

Sell Now: A Contract with Christ

On November 14, 2011 Jesus said: *Sell now, I will find you something.* I didn't act immediately because I always thought they had no sense of time on the other side. I thought we could listen to the message then act whenever we wanted to. Not the case here. What I have learned is that when they say "*now*" they mean *now*. They don't recognize a linear time line. They recognize God-time and that is the present moment. This lesson cost me dearly.

I waited three and a half months between the time I received the message and the time I listed my house for sale, and even then the listing was prompted by a dream in which I was shown many houses on my street coming up for sale. The dream was prophetic, in that after my house sold, a historically unprecedented five houses on my street came on the market. What I came to realize is that had I put the house on the market the day Jesus told me to, I might actually have gotten the number he had promised. At that time there was very little inventory and a glut of buyers. By the time I came to terms with selling my house, the inventory had grown. Then, as bidding started, a "green act" was passed further restricting the square footage that could be built on town lots. My lot was adversely impacted and was scaring away would-be purchasers. Both my husband and our realtor suggested to me that we drop the price of our house. I meditated.

I was out of time with my husband. He felt that we were going to miss all of our opportunities to sell if we didn't lower the price. Jesus had asked me to move so I now turned to him for guidance, yet again. Was I meant to have faith and keep the price where it was or to have faith and lower the price? I couldn't hear Jesus' guidance clearly, so we lowered the price to put the house into play. When that didn't work, there was again pressure from both my realtor and my husband to shave more off the price. I meditated and I asked God to bring me a buyer quickly. Not one but **two** buyers appeared and bid on the house eliminating the need to drop the price a second time. The winning bid came in on March 30—my husband's birthday.

I will never know for sure if I would have gotten the original price if I'd listed the house the very morning Jesus told me to. What I do know is that when Jesus says jump, I need to jump, not doubt what I am hearing. It took faith to uproot my family, but it would have taken a faith I clearly didn't have to sell the house out from under them the minute Jesus told me to. As Linda always tells me and I still have trouble believing, I know what I know— meaning I hear clearly and must trust what I hear.

Jesus asks me to have a faith so deep and so grounded in his reality that no matter the circumstances, I must do as he tells me. In one of his many implorations Jesus said: *Listen to me. You need to move. Even if you see no changes (after looking back over the years to where you lived in Fairfield County), you need to move. You are still too strong willed.* It is as if part of the move was just to break my will. I know it is not the only reason—in my experience God never has just one reason. The reason will be infinitely dimensional and, if I am lucky, I will get a peek at a few of the underlying reasons before I die. It seems from my vantage point that two additional reasons were to teach me to have faith and to trust that God will provide me with everything I need. This time I was able to calculate in dollars how much my doubt cost me. The next time may not be as clear, but I am certain it will be more costly, and maybe not just in terms of money. It is time to listen. It is time to live in accordance with God's timing, or as I call it, in God-time.

Timeline of Events

11-14-11: Jesus said to me in the middle of the night: *Sell now, I will find you something.*

12-14-11: Jesus said to me while I was alone at dinner: *The road ahead is not easy...I am asking you to move...Things are going to happen fast...*

Me: I need my husband on board. Jesus: *It is done.*

1-3-12: Me to Jesus: Bring me a buyer and bring me a piece of property, land or a house.

1-29-12: We signed a binder to buy a house in Litchfield County.

2-28-12: I listed my house for sale prompted by a "dream" in which I saw many houses on my street come up for sale. After my house sold, five houses on my street were listed for sale.

3-20-12: We lowered the sale price on my Fairfield County house.

3-24-12: My realtor and husband wanted to lower the price a second time. Instead, I prayed for Jesus to move up the sale.

3-30-12: We accepted an offer on our Fairfield County house.

Expect the Miraculous

Our Litchfield County house renovations were not going to be done until mid-July, three months after the date the buyers of our Fairfield County property had signed the binder. Since synchronicities and miracles are the norm when aligned with God's will, it should come as no surprise that the three-month delay was no problem for the buyer. They were renting and were under no pressure to move out. God-time.

The renovations started and with them came the first bill. Because the closing sale of our house was three months away, we had a lot more money going out than was coming in. So, one Sunday morning I prayed to Jesus to help my husband, Peter, find the money to pay for the renovations and the bills that were coming due. Peter called me a few hours later to tell me that a large sum of money was just wired into his account. On a Sunday? He thought it was an error and I had to refrain from thinking the same. Monday proved it was no error. Money he had lent out was paid back much earlier than he had expected. Jesus answered my prayer. I suspect Peter, in addition to his daily hard work, prayed too. This kept happening—every time we had a large payment to make to the builder, and we didn't have the money, some big deal unexpectedly paid off early. Peter did his part and God did His.

Construction delays? No Problem. I was told that our new house would not be ready for our mid-July move-in date. In fact, it wouldn't be ready until at least mid-September. I heard the news with complete neutrality and stopped myself from writing, even in jest, to my friends about the two-month period when I would be without a place to live. Instead, I decided, for some unknown reason, to check an old email account I no longer used. There, sitting in my inbox, was an email from an acquaintance with this message:

"Hi Friends,

Know anyone looking for an apartment this summer?

I have a Fairfield County apartment (furnished). I am looking to sublet to a friend, or friend of a friend…It is a one bedroom, with a living room, small kitchen with a dishwasher (laundry is downstairs). It has a porch, and it is in a housing complex… It is within walking distance to the rail station. It has one window a/c unit, as well as a phone, Internet; all utilities included…Available early June 'til just after Labor Day…"

Well, I had yet to see it, but it sounded like God, my realtor, was already at work finding me temporary housing. I believe that this opportunity would not have arisen, or I would have missed it, had I gone into a place of fear and anger at my new house not being ready. If I had spent my time railing against the builder or emailing my girlfriends about the injustice of it all, I would never have checked the mail in this old account. This brought me back to Jesus' first message about selling my house. He said: *Sell now, I will find you something.* Not buy new house, sell old house and then move into a fully renovated house. I had altered his plan and he was putting me back on his track. He always wins, or as he once told me: *When I surrender, I win.* It is true, I felt oddly free knowing that all of my belongings would be inaccessibly stored, and I was renting an apartment.

I had a dream that my husband crashed his car into a deer and that in the process his car hit mine. Mmmm, sounds like losing control. Maybe we had undertaken too much. Not to mention that as a totem, the deer is a signal to be gentle with yourself and to allow yourself to be lured on new adventures, like Sir Gawain in *King Arthur and His Knights.* In the story, Sir Gawain is led deep into the woods and becomes lost but ultimately opened to new adventures while following a deer. Interestingly, just before having this dream, I had decided to book a vacation for my husband and me to go to England with Dr. Jude Currivan[7] to visit some of the sites of the mystical King Arthur. I wasn't aware of the significance deer played in the archetypal journey described in *King Arthur and His Knights* when I booked the trip. Of course, it is not lost on me that in my dream, the deer was hit by my husband's car, which may mean he was moving a bit too fast and pushing too hard. We don't want to kill our animal totem.

Mother Mary said to me: *The strongest trees in a storm are those that bend with the wind.* We were now bending in God's direction as He has seen to it that we must. The only reason we had time for this vacation was because of the delay in our renovation. It is always our choice whether to bend or not. We could have dug our heels in and yelled and screamed at the builder and done whatever one does in such cases. Going where God blew us the first time would have avoided some of the issues like tight finances we were facing. It may have brought other challenges as well. We can only accept what is given and know that with each challenge comes the opportunity to dig deeper into ourselves to find a strength that we did not yet know existed. We are forced to pull it up from the depths of our being and to use it. Until we do this, we don't even know we have that strength, and there is no other way to find it. You can't find that strength by reading about it in someone else. You can't find it by pretending to be in someone else's position. You have to be in the position to know what you would do. In finance, it is like buying or selling an asset. You can talk all you want about when you would buy or sell, but until you have real money in the game, you really don't know how you will behave.

I should have sold my house when told, but I didn't; and God was there to make sure I had an opportunity to learn whatever lessons were to come from being without a home. Don't get me wrong, I was not homeless; and that is one of the points of this story and how it differs from so many others. I don't believe that our lives have to fall apart; we don't have to get divorced or be penniless to live God's will. That may be the path for some, but it would be a mistake to think that is the only path.

There are a lot of people eligible for enlightenment without the requisite near death experience, suicidal thoughts and the like. Those experiences may put some people on the fast track—the Advanced Placement course—but the rest of us can still get there. We can still do the laundry and pick up the kids and take care of elderly parents or go grocery shopping, not to mention earn a living and have fun. Try to skip out on your responsibilities (unless doing so is your particular path) and you will likely not get much enlightenment or anything else for that matter. And, if you hear God say chuck it all and go buy a house in the Caribbean, call me because the wires may have gotten crossed. That is my message!

There is some plan in place. Some say we wrote it and that there are critical junctures along the way. I have seen that we wrote it and that we wrote in every wrong turn. We are playing out the script we wrote and learning the lessons we carefully wove into the tapestry of our lives. It doesn't matter whether you think this is destiny, fate, free will or whatever. You have to live and learn. Acceptance is the key.

When my daughter was in college, she was planning to stay in a less-than-desirable area of San Francisco because that was what she and her friends could afford during their college break. My daughter told me at the time that if she were meant to learn some lesson by being in that part of San Francisco, then all I was doing by paying for a hotel room for her and her friends, in a better part of town, was postponing the inevitable[8]. She, like most children, if we choose to listen, is wiser than her years. She is right. We can postpone our lessons to a later date in this lifetime or delay them into the next lifetime, or the one after that. You can delay indefinitely, but if you really want to learn, ask to be taught in every situation now and you will find the lesson.

Prior to one of my meditations, I was contemplating love, faith and Jesus' famous phrase "faith the size of a mustard seed can move mountains." My faith in Jesus made me move from my beloved home, but that, it seemed, was far inferior to moving mountains with faith. Then an aura photographer,[9] after viewing my aura, told me that my move will have a profound effect on humanity. So, maybe it is the case that one's faith in God really does move mountains, even if that faith is exhibited in a seemingly unrelated way. Is it possible that when each of us surrenders to God and has the faith to carry out His will that, in fact, we move mountains unseen? Maybe our job is to have the faith to follow that path that God sets before us so that mountains can be moved, seas can be parted, human consciousness can be shifted to a higher level—one in which we learn unconditional love of all, for all. Stay open to the possibility. Stay open to the miracles to come.

I don't believe the aura photographer was saying that I have a role in humanity's shift to a higher level of consciousness that is more important or bigger than anyone else's. I am saying that each of us has his or her role in the coming shift. Each of us is asked to follow God's will, or your higher Self, and to have faith. In so doing, we are all part of the movement to a new world in which love prevails over hatred. With faith we can move that mountain of hatred and intolerance and replace it with a mountain of loving-kindness.

No One Left Behind

I invited Lucy, the shaman, to my Fairfield County home to do a closing ceremony before we moved out. I wanted to ensure that we didn't leave behind any soul fragments.[10] Here I give my family a lot of credit because even though they may have thought it was weird, they honored my request and did as the shaman told them when they were asked to walk through each room of our house drumming or shaking a rattle. My daughter and my husband had been through this once before on the farm, but my son was new to it.

For me, the most interesting part of the ceremony came when we journeyed with our power animal. I was guided to the base of the beam of white light that led me to buy the house nine years before. I had always seen the beam shining through the living room and up into the heavens. I knew also that it extended into the basement below. What I hadn't realized until this closing ceremony was that the beam also extended downward into the earth. With my power animal, I walked around the interior perimeter of the beam over and over. As I completed each rotation, the beam got smaller and smaller until it disappeared. Now my house was just a house. I was distraught. Wasn't this beam of light supposed to be here for the next family? The answer was *No*. The implications were profound. It meant that the Divine Light appeared specifically to bring me to the house. It was meant to embrace, nurture and do whatever that Divine Light did for my family, friends, neighbors, relations, students, contractors, everyone who ever entered the house and, of course, me. Lucy explained that shamans always close off their sacred energy before leaving a place. Well, I am no shaman, but I was undoubtedly guided to close off that energy. I trusted that the next family would find the Divine in the house as well—all they have to do is look and they will see.

Following Guidance

No matter how hard I tried to convey the wrenching anxiety of dismantling my life in Fairfield County in order to follow God's will, my friends, as they looked in from the outside, still thought it was easy to follow guidance. They reasoned that if you have guidance then it must be easy because all you have to do is follow it. That is only half true. It is easy when the guidance is what you want to hear. It is not at all easy when, as in the case of my move, the guidance is at odds with what you want to hear. I touch on this later in the book, but it cannot be overemphasized. There is nothing easy about this. In the beginning it is not easy to know what is real guidance and what isn't. Then to say out loud that you are listening to Jesus or God or your higher Self, and that is the basis for a decision, sounds completely insane. Not every encounter with God or His servants is an apparition experience. So, practice with small things first. Ask if you should turn left or right; ask if you should drink coffee or tea today; ask if you should sleep that extra five minutes or get up. Learn to hear the voice of God or the Christ within you. Don't start with the big stuff, unless you feel confident in your ability to hear what is true. Be ready to be laughed at or to take the heat from your angry spouse when you tell him or her, "…because Jesus said so."

For many, if you choose to follow this path of aligning your will with the will of God, the first thing that will happen is that you will not be open to guidance because you will be afraid of what you might hear. That was true of me in my journey early on when I thought God would ask me to build a life-sized cross and drag it across the country. Next you will open up to the guidance but only tentatively because you want to make sure that only the stuff you want to hear gets through. And that is exactly what will happen because God will honor your choice. You will not be fully aligned with God's will until you surrender—until you are not afraid of what His will would have you do. Funny, as I type this, I pulled a card from the *Wisdom From A Course in Miracles* card deck, which read: "If you knew Who walks beside you on the way that you have chosen, fear would be impossible." Well, I know who walks beside me but I will tell you that sometimes, when this world's problems start to swirl around me, and my husband is angry because I am talking about uprooting him from the home and life he loves, it is hard not to be afraid.

I am not trying to encourage people to eliminate reason from their lives but to reintroduce the Divine. I am suggesting living your life in accordance with Divine Will but this CANNOT BE DONE WITHOUT A COMMITTED SPIRITUAL

PRACTICE. To me, **that means at least one to two hours per day**, if not more, spent in communion with God. Start with less and build up to that level using the form most in keeping with your religious tradition. I know you are saying you don't have that kind of time, so you might begin by trading in some TV or computer time for meditation or contemplative prayer.

To hear God and to allow God's will to be done through you, you must be available and fearless. That's what trust is after all. When you really trust God, you have no fear about where He'll lead you. That doesn't mean you can't question. Go right ahead. Make sure that you are hearing Him correctly. Then, as scared as you might be while you follow, know that He is leading you to Heaven on Earth. How else would you alone know the way?

I am having experiences now that I would never have had if I had chosen to ignore God's voice and those almost imperceptible feelings at the beginning of this process. And yes, I still worry about this move and the unknown at times, but less so than ever. And yes, had I had my way, I'd have chosen to stay in the security of everything I knew, but I never grew by staying in my comfort zone. I grow when I am forced beyond the edges of that space in which I feel so safe and confident; and God has a habit of pushing me past those boundaries. I don't like being outside my comfort zone any more than the next person, but if I am not willing to go there, if I am not willing to throw out all I think I know and put myself in the hands of God, how can I hope to know if God is there at all? How can I know if it is true that God can be trusted and that miracles abound when we put our life in His hands? I could certainly imagine a voice in the middle of the night, but I do not have the power to create the synchronistic events or miracles that ensue when following such a voice.

When you get to the point where you are not afraid to fully surrender to God's will, you will lose yourself. That is when the "you" that you think you are, disappears into the vastness that is God. And you will never actually get there because you will always be asked to surrender just a little bit more because you can always become even more immersed into the oneness that is God; into the supreme Nothingness and Everythingness that is this thing I call God. That is when the fun starts. That is when you will start to grow into everything He would have you become.

CHAPTER 2

How It All Began

How can others be what you yourself do not yet believe you to be?

- Jesus 9-15-06

I look back at the odyssey into the awareness of my own consciousness and wonder if it had a start date. Although I can't point to a specific time, I can recall several events that, in retrospect, seem significant.

The first was in my early 20s when I attended the funeral of a teenaged girl. I fought with my mother, who was making me attend the funeral. She explained that it wasn't about what I wanted but about supporting those left behind. I begrudgingly attended. The funeral home was packed with mourners, so all I could see was a sea of people—and the spirit of the deceased floating above them. Could other people see this? Is it appropriate to say, "She's not dead, she is right here with us?" I could see her so clearly. She seemed happy and I had the sense that everything was as it should be. I had never encountered death nor attended a funeral before, and if anybody else besides me was wondering what it means to die or what happens when we die, the presence of her spirit was proof that we go on living in a different form. Looking in on the deceased in the casket confirmed what I saw upon entering the room, which was that her spirit was no longer in her body. Oddly, it was by witnessing death that I understood what gave us life; and it was not just the science of a beating heart. It was that beating heart combined with the presence of a life force energy some call a spirit or maybe even a soul. I wasn't sure what to call it but I was certain that it was no longer in her body and that it did go on living.

I lacked the prerequisites, like religious piety or reverence, which one might deem necessary to see a spirit. The little I remember from my brief encounter with religion, while attending Catholic school from kindergarten to third grade, was that they had gotten Jesus' messages all wrong. I don't know what gave me the audacity to think I knew what Jesus' message was, but as a grade-schooler I remember two glaring misconceptions. First, it was not possible that Jesus loved only Christians and second, it was not possible that we were born with "original sin." Maybe it was the naiveté of a child, but I believed that God loved us all no matter what religion we practiced. If God made me, as the nuns claimed, then He didn't make me with original sin. I rejected all the teachings and grew up with not much more to guide me on matters of God than my internal compass. The one thing I did carry with me from those early years was the practice of saying, in rapid succession, the three prayers I'd been taught. I would say the prayers so fast that anyone eavesdropping on my nightly routine would think that each prayer was one long word. The rest of my time and energy was spent on more fun endeavors, which, in my teens and 20s, inevitably resulted in my having to ask for help from those same Beings to whom I directed my one-long-word prayers. When I wasn't asking to be rescued, I was focused on materialistic goals. I didn't have time for spirits and never gave the one I saw a second thought after the funeral ended. I worked hard and did not always make the smartest or safest choices in my personal life. It was my less than stellar personal decisions that gave me reason to have a direct line to God. And, contrary to fire and brimstone teachings, no matter how many times I messed up, He saved me and, seemingly, forgave me.

I was forever driving too fast, which lead to countless car accidents—one in which the car rolled over, and another where I hydroplaned backward down an interstate highway before coming to rest perpendicular to oncoming traffic on the opposite side of the highway. These are only two of many; and what I remember most clearly about each and every one is the feeling that I was safe. No harm ever came to me.

Then there was the boyfriend who I feared might kill me when he showed up in the middle of the night at my apartment, a third-floor space above the ballroom of a remote, dilapidated estate. I had to decide on the spot whether to let him in or call the police. I was trying to extricate myself from the relationship, but his constant pursuit was reaching a crescendo and I knew, that in the absence of 24-hour police protection, a call to them would only aggravate the situation. My intuition was telling me to let him in. He fell asleep on my bed after a long talk but I didn't feel safe following suit. I was trying to stay awake when the Virgin Mary appeared. She stood above my soon-to-be ex-boyfriend, arms outstretched and said: *Have mercy on him. He is a child of God.* Have mercy on **him**? I was the one whose life was in danger! I was not someone to whom you'd expect the Virgin Mary to appear, much less speak to. At twenty-seven I was working in finance and mostly agnostic. I was certainly not compassionate enough to **have mercy** (not language in my lexicon) for this **child of God** (more language I didn't use). Even if I were the compassionate type, I would likely not have it for someone who frightened me. Of course, I told no one of this encounter with Mary, thinking it must have been the result of exhaustion.

It was 1996, 13 years later, when I had my next significant experience. This time I wasn't tired. Jesus appeared to me clear as day, with his heart visibly surrounded by a crown of thorns, and pulled me across the veil separating my world from his. He showed me, and more importantly allowed me to feel, how beautiful and simple life is. In his presence I was completely unaware of the other people around me; I saw and felt an ethereal white light fill, and then emanate from my body as tears filled my eyes. At that moment, although I was **not** having a near-death experience, I knew what it was like to die, and I wished I could stay surrounded by and infused with that unconditional love. That is when Jesus "spoke" to me. He communicated without words: *It is so simple. It is all about love.* He was talking about the meaning of life.

The reality of the above experience not withstanding, I looked back over my various encounters and began to wonder if I had all my marbles. Being in the presence of Jesus was a profound experience, and although the encounter cured a stomach illness I had had for several weeks, I still wondered if I could have imagined the whole thing. Why would Jesus speak to me, and what was this about love? When not in that ethereal state created by his presence, my life as a full-time working mother certainly seemed infinitely more complicated. Why would he speak to me who has made so many mistakes in her life, who has no religion, and who does not believe in the messages of fear, guilt and sin that were taught to her in Catholic school?

Finally, I shared my experiences with my religious aunt. She told me that the message associated with the sacred heart of Jesus, the name given to the image of his heart surrounded by the crown of thorns, is one of love. As doubtful as I was, I knew I was not capable of imagining a vision and a message that would correspond in such a way. I began to accept that, perhaps, what I had seen and heard might have some validity, and I tentatively opened to the possibility that this sort of seeing and hearing was always there for me. Certainly, I was no one special; if I could see and hear Mary or Jesus, others could too.[11] It was a slow process, but once I let go of my resistance, I had many visions of Jesus and Mary. As it turns out, Jesus is my constant companion in good times and in bad. He told me: *I am in you and you are in me*. I had trouble believing this at first but I believe this to be true now and I don't question when he appears or speaks to me.[12]

I did, however, begin to question my role in finance at IBM.

A Turtle without a Shell

I began reading about the difference between the ego self and the spiritual Self. The concept, which was completely new to me, came from a book entitled *A Course in Miracles*. I began to understand that the role of the ego was to keep me separate from all others and, of course, to make me special in some way. Ultimately, it prevented me from seeing my unity with all others and with God. As I began to earnestly work on peeling away the layers of my own ego, I felt like a turtle without a shell. How was I to operate in finance at IBM without my ego for protection? I felt completely vulnerable. I needed to think that I was important and that the job I was doing was important in order to go in to work day after day and give 110 percent of myself. I realized how difficult it was to be in the world of finance and in the orbit of Wall Street without the ego self. As I began to identify more with my spiritual nature, that same nature that resides in us all and makes us equal to one another and to God, I began to feel more and more uncomfortable at work. I felt unprotected in a world where the ego was my armor. I intuitively felt that this spiritual work was important for me and that it would be very difficult to do it while working where I did. I decided it was a good time for me to leave work.

You may be saying that leaving work is a luxury, and it is, but it wasn't that easy. I don't take financial security for granted. I put myself through college while working at Sears, Roebuck and Company. With no money to spare, living at home and commuting to college was my only option. I did not go on vacations during spring and summer break but instead worked more hours. I pushed down my impractical passion for photography and followed the money into economics. I liked economics, probably because it was logical, but I particularly enjoyed a class on foreign currency exchange. So when IBM, with its large overseas business offered me a job, I took it. I started in accounting, which as a liberal arts student, I was not prepared for, and I hated it. Regardless, the job paid the bills and IBM paid for my graduate degree. I had no intention of getting a graduate degree, but it seemed silly not to get a degree that someone else was paying for, so I enrolled in an MBA program, at night. I set my sights on IBM's Corporate Treasury group, where they handled all foreign exchange exposures and was transferred into an entry-level job in Cash Management. I continued getting my MBA at night and eventually got the foreign currency exposure management job I'd strived for. I was offered, and took advantage of, many other wonderful opportunities with the company over the 18 years I spent with them. It was financially and psychologically difficult leaving the safety and security of a job, salary and our family's only medical coverage. Adding a bit more risk to the equation, my husband was starting a new business at exactly the same time, but I felt strongly that, at this point, my work was at home.

St. Thérèse of Lisieux told me that the ego is *insidious* and I learned that peeling back its many layers can be a never-ending and exhausting job, but nonetheless I was ready to get started.

Sign Me Up

Before leaving my job completely, I reduced my workweek from 60 to 30 hours. Never having experienced the luxury of free time the 30-hour workweek afforded me, I decided first to make myself available to pick up my children from school. Now I got to stand in the schoolyard and to talk to the other moms. I discovered that in their "extra time" some of the stay-at-home moms took yoga classes, so I promptly signed up. I also signed up for piano lessons, which I'd longed for as a child, but the lack of a piano and money to pay for lessons made them unattainable. After almost a year of piano lessons and not having made much progress, I decided it was a good thing that my parents didn't have the money when I was young. Yoga was another story—not that I was any better at yoga but my instructor and one of the other students in the class did something called Reiki. At the time I didn't know what that was, but since I had time, I signed up. I was used to making intuitive decisions, so it really didn't matter that I didn't understand Reiki. My intuition told me to go for it.

I sat in Reiki class for five long hours. The teacher kept throwing out words like "energy" and "healing." The word "energy" was never defined, it was just thrown about as if everybody had this energy thing and it could be used for healing. It was appealing on a fairy godmother kind of level, but I wasn't convinced that there was any real substance to it. There was nothing in my educational background, work experience or sensibility that would allow me to believe what I was being taught. By the fourth hour, I simply concluded that I had wasted $300 and most of my day. Thank goodness I was still working part-time and would be able to make the money back. It was like doing a bad trade. Every once in a while you make a wrong decision. I remember thinking that the class would end soon and I'd be on my way, but the strangest part of the class was just beginning.

I was told that I was about to receive a Reiki "attunement" during which time I would be aligned with this mysterious energy. The teacher walked me into a candle lit room, sat me on a chair and stood behind me waving her hands above my head. I am not one for rituals, so for me, the class had crossed a line into the absurd. Then, all of a sudden, I felt and saw a whoosh of white and purple light cascade down through the crown of my head, filling my body down to my stomach. The teacher told me that she also saw purple and white light and that the attunement had opened me to receive universal life force energy from God. Okay, now God, the Universe, or whatever one called it had my attention. I figured, if a skeptic like me can see and feel this thing my instructor called energy, then there must be something to it.

Although I wasn't too diligent about yoga and showed no aptitude for the piano, I did start practicing Reiki. It seemed bizarre to charge a fee for "universal life force energy," so I practiced mostly on friends and one or two brave souls in the trading room at work, for free. It would be seven years before I would finally charge for my services and then only to stem the flow of gifts that people felt compelled to bring. In 2003, with my practice well under way, I decided to take my Reiki Master training with Heather Cumming, prominent Reiki Master, shaman, John of God trip leader and co-author of *John of God, the Brazilian Healer Who's Touched the Lives of Millions*.

In the class were three other women with whom I had no relationship. On the last day of class, while I was putting on my coat and hat, I turned to the other women and asked if they wanted to meet weekly, at my house, to practice what we had learned. It was purely self-serving. I was not looking for friends or some kind of affinity group. I was already seeing Reiki clients, but I wanted to practice some of the skills I had learned in the Master class with people who had had the same training as I. We exchanged phone numbers and I set up our first Reiki Master Exchange. Only two of the other three women ever came to practice.

As time went by one of those two stopped coming, and I was left practicing with Linda Fallo-Mitchell, who would go on to become one of my closest and dearest friends. Linda was a great student and remembered everything we were taught in our Master class. Keeping their identities confidential, I would call Linda to share new experiences I was having while working on clients. She would confirm that what I was experiencing fit with what Heather had taught us. I preferred to learn by doing, but for Linda, putting her knowledge into action wasn't so easy. To her credit, in spite of being outside her comfort zone, Linda kept coming to our weekly Reiki Master Exchanges and in this way we developed what has now become a consistent weekly exchange since 2003. Through my practice and the exchange with Linda, I have been able to live what I have learned.

We all must **practice** what we are taught if we want the teachings to change our lives. Our lives are not going to change by listening to someone else's story or even by learning their particular technique or method, unless we take the pieces that resonate with us and put them into practice. Take the examples of learning to ice skate, type or drive a car. Or imagine that you need transportation so you read all about bicycles and how to ride them. Then you watch the Tour de France on television and you purchase a bike for yourself. That bike cannot change your life unless you get on it and ride. Only by putting all of your knowledge into the practice of **riding** that bicycle can you move forward. The practice seems to be the hardest part for many people.

After taking the Reiki Master training and being told numerous times, by several different people that I was a "healer," I decided to start a full-time Reiki practice. I set my intentions down on paper stating my mission, how many clients I would see and how much I would charge.[13] I then cleared my calendar of all my volunteer responsibilities and gave my plan over to the Universe. And so it was that, without advertising, my practice grew until clients had to book appointments three weeks in advance. In addition, I started teaching Reiki classes and other workshops with Linda, which along with my journal entries and our Reiki Master Exchange sessions provided the breeding ground for this book.[14]

There were many things I experienced while practicing Reiki, which were inexplicable, yet which intrigued me. Although Reiki is not about Jesus or about hearing messages, from the first time I laid my hands on someone, I could see angels and see and feel Jesus' presence—I would hear messages for my clients. It interested me enough to take it to the next level, which in my case, was setting up my practice. Without being intrigued by the experiences, or wanting to know more, it could easily have gone the way of the yoga classes and piano lessons, but it didn't. At the time of my decision, I had no idea that it would become such a meaningful part of, not just my life, but who I was to become.

Yet, the only way I would find that out was to keep taking Reiki to the next step. Sometimes we make choices that take us further and further along a given path, and other times they bring us to new and divergent paths. If you don't start on your journey, you will never know where it will lead you. Everyone has a different threshold for the risk/reward analysis needed before they can risk moving forward on a path. I will tell you that if all you do is the **analysis,** you will never get anywhere, no matter how smart you are, or how many classes you take, or how many degrees you hang on your wall. For me, the risk was that Reiki was a dead end street, that people would laugh at me and that I had wasted my time and money. In this case, however, the reward far outweighed the risks. Sometimes you just need to sign up and see where the journey takes you.

When You Ask, Plan to Listen: Conversations with Angels

As with Reiki, once intrigued by a new experience, I like to jump in and move forward quickly, so I purchased two books, which had been suggested by my Reiki teacher. *A Course in Miracles* caused me to dig deep within myself and ask the hard questions about who I was at the core of my being; *Angelspeake* by Trudy Griswold suggested that I talk to angels—and that they would talk back. At IBM we didn't spend any time talking to angels, so this was new territory. I had no idea who my angels were, but I figured I had nothing to lose by trying to communicate with them. I would take any help I could get. The first time I queried my angels, they woke me up in the middle of the night to respond. I thought it was my imagination but, if these were in fact angels talking to me, they must have had some sense of humor depriving me of the little sleep I got as a working mother. In the morning, I had trouble remembering all they'd said so I learned to keep a pad of paper and a pen next to my bedside to be prepared for their 3 a.m. "conference calls."

Sometimes they would give me only a word at a time. On other occasions, whole sentences or whole thoughts would somehow be transferred into my consciousness, and I would have to scribble very fast so as not to lose them. It is quite embarrassing to pass along some of the earliest conversations, as they are not very deep, and they revolve more around my personal life than global issues. Yet, awkward as they are, I am sharing two of them so that you can bear witness to the beginning stages of this sort of mystical communication. You will see in the course of this book how, over time and with a dedicated practice, the messages grow in depth and move from the personal to the global.

> 10-31-96 3:35 a.m. Message from my angels: *The children are angels. You can see their aura. They were sent here to make your life better. They were sent here to help you see us. You are not ready to see us.*

> 12-16-96 Message from the angels: *Dear Theresa, we are here to help you. Pick up the pen! God has sent us to find you. You will help the children. You will teach…You will teach them how to live and love You will not work (at your current job) more than three years.*[15]

After a few months of these clumsy messages, I decided to make an appointment with the book's author, Trudy Griswold. Maybe she could tell me about my life's purpose, my children, our finances, where we should live—minor stuff like that. Griswold was able to "channel," meaning she would listen to my angels and relay the messages to me. I had no idea what to make of a channeler, but I figured I had received enough messages from my angels to know if what she was saying rang true to me.

Her messages that day confirmed some things about my life and my children that I had been feeling for a long time. What I took away from the hour-long session was that my kids were okay and that what I was hearing was, in fact, my angels speaking. I told her nothing about my children, or myself yet she shared details about all of our past lives that metaphorically helped explain my children's personalities and some of my life circumstances. I thought little about past lives then, as I was struggling to deal with the present: working, raising kids, doing laundry, picking up dry cleaning, cooking and—you know the drill. But I got what I went for, which was validation of my own communication with the angels.

The rest of her messages I had forgotten about until now, 14 years later, when I serendipitously rediscovered the audio recording of the session. If you are at all like my husband, you would have said after initially reading these messages, "You paid her. She is going to tell you what you want to hear." I have to admit to having had that same bias, which is probably why I shoved the audio recording into a cupboard and forgot about it. I was careful never to tell my children what Griswold had channeled about them, so that her messages would not become self-fulfilling prophecies. Being concerned about self-fulfilling prophecies, I also pushed the messages about myself out of my mind and never listened to the recording of the session again until now. It is only in hindsight that I am able to listen and realize that many of the messages proved to be accurate.

Once I became aware of the angels' presence, I saw them everywhere. In one instance, I saw an enormous angel over my close friend's newborn baby. The angel filled the space above the hospital basinet so that it seemed to stretch 15 feet high and spanned maybe eight feet wide. It was hard to tell, as the figure was smoke-like. The feeling, however, was not hard to decipher at all. This child would be well protected and cared for by a very powerful angel. I have also seen two people with wings walking this earth. On one occasion, my husband and I were dining in a New York City restaurant when, all at once, I could see everyone's angel; many people had more than one. Then, the spirit of my husband's deceased grandfather showed up, standing just off my husband's left shoulder. If you've been to New York City you know how many people there are, so you can image the scene in a crowded res-taurant where the population, thanks to the angels was now tripled. It was so beau-tiful. Everyone went about their business, but all about them were white, angelic beings watching and loving them.

After dinner we went to a Broadway play and there on the stage were all the actors and each of their angels. I tried to watch the play but found that I was completely overwhelmed trying to separate the actors from the angels hovering nearby. It became completely chaotic and my need for order won out. My feelings must have been instantly communicated to the heavens because, after that day, my ability to see everyone's angels stopped. I could still see angels from time to time, like Archangel Michael, who oftentimes helps me in healing sessions. There was also the time, when in response to my anxiety over my daughter's severe asthma, Archangel Michael left a slip of paper on my desk that read: "Our minds are so powerful our fears can easily manifest into reality. During difficult situations in your life and those around you, replace negative thoughts or worries with **ARCHANGEL MICHAEL'S ILLUSION PRAYER:**

I will not allow this illusion to separate me from my peace. Archangel Michael, intervene and dissolve this situation in divine right order. Under God's Law of

Grace IT IS DONE. Keep this card with you until you memorize it and expect your miracle. (Katierussell.com)"

I did memorize the prayer and it did help to relieve my severe, middle of the night anxiety as I prayed for my daughter to be able to take her next breath. It has also helped many of the people I have shared it with.

Today, I can still talk to and receive messages and help from my own angels, but I was not cut out for the commotion of seeing what God sees. To Him, it is order. To me, it was chaos.

More Questions, More Answers

After meeting with Griswold, my angels continued to wake me up at all hours of the night to answer my questions or just to tell me things they thought I should know.

3-16-97 Conversation with angels:

> I sensed my messages were coming from angels other than the ones named by Griswold, so I asked:
> Will Anya and Oliver ever talk to me directly?
>
> *Yes. When you are ready. They are extremely powerful angels. You are not ready. You need to cleanse your soul. You need to be free, clear of mind and solidly grounded.*
> Will they give up on me?
> *No. They've been waiting for centuries.*
> Will they talk to me in this lifetime?
> *It's up to you.*
>
> Amy,[16] can you and the angels help me to prepare?
> *Yes.*
> How?
> *Let go. Let go of everything that drags you down.*
> Will I ever have inner peace in this lifetime?
> *No.*
> In the next?
> *No. It will take many more lifetimes. You are heavily burdened with thoughts and questions. You want to know the answers. What is right and wrong. There is no right and wrong. There is only what you do. You live as you were meant to live.*
> Can I become free in this lifetime?
> *Yes, if you work hard.*

Will you help me?

Yes, you have a long way to go. Don't give up. It can happen.

What's the first step?

Let go of all your notions and be happy.

What is (my job in this lifetime)?

It is to help a lot of people—it is not clear.

When?

When you are ready.

How will I know?

You will feel it.

What else should I know?

You are on the right track. Stay with it. Do not be deceived. Everything will become clearer. Life will get easier. These are our thoughts. We are close to God. You will be happy. Life will be good. It is coming. All those around you are children of God. They are in need. Help them. You know how. You can do it. We have given you the resources. Don't worry. Everything will be taken care of. That is why we are here. You have work to do. Don't delay. We are here to help. We love you and support you every day. Your spirit will start to shine. Go, and bring peace to all you meet.

My angels explained that, *we are all filled with the light and love of God. We need but to share it to recognize it in ourselves.*

Bring It On

I was horrified to hear my angels tell me that it would take many more lifetimes for me to find inner peace. There is no way I wanted to come back again and again, stumbling around learning the same lessons. I could not imagine going through those teen years again. My angels said if I worked really hard, it was possible to learn my lessons and find inner peace in **this** lifetime. I was determined to do that. So, I had a little conversation with the Universe, God, my angels, and whoever else was listening and I said, "Bring it on! I am not coming back, so give me all my lessons now, in this lifetime. I am determined to learn them and to move forward. You said it could be done and I am ready to do it!"

I asked for them, and the lessons came. I examined everything that happened to me both literally and metaphorically to tease out the underlying lesson. I worked on the premise that there was nothing that was not a lesson in some way. In between work and mothering, I diligently worked at my spiritual practice. I tried to keep my mind open as to how I might learn my lessons and find inner peace. If I went to a channel like Griswold, I took what resonated with me and pursued it. If it was a book, I read it. If it was a recommendation to see some other healer, I made an appointment. What I found interesting was that, especially in the case of written material, each book I read tended to corroborate the messages I had already gotten from Spirit. I am not suggesting that my path to inner peace and ultimately, to unconditional love, is the right path, nor that it should be your path. I am suggesting that you get on a path and start walking.

One night after moving to Litchfield County and before going to bed, I decided to ask my angels to touch me, so I would know they were with me. I waited and had some sensations but, ever the skeptic, decided that they weren't concrete enough—things like muscle twitches happen, so that didn't count. Feeling something brush near my forehead didn't count either; it could have been a hair. So I waited. Then, I felt something I could not make an excuse for. As I lay there in the dark, I felt as if someone were taking a pencil and very slowly drawing a crooked line down my forehead. It went on for about a minute. Okay, that was the proof I needed. But what did they look like? Were they the two angels that Trudy Griswold had seen so many years ago standing, like bookends, on either side of me? I had no more clues from my angels that night, so I meditated and went to sleep. The next morning I had a dream; or perhaps I should say it was partially a dream and partially a visitation from my angels.

In my dream, which in this case is another way in which my angels communicated with me, I turned my handbag upside down to empty out the contents, which I expected to go all over the floor. Instead, what came out was a circle of angelic beings. Their arms were around each other, with their heads bowed toward the center of the circle so that I could see only the backs of their heads. Like synchronized dancers they all splayed up at the same time. It was magical. Circles and more circles of angels were inside and, as each circle opened, like petals of a flower, sparkling lights emanated up in between them. Finally, one angel spoke, saying "hello" to me. Then, the head angel spoke (they seemed all to be female), saying "hello" to me as if she and I had met a million times before. It was a, "Heeeellllloooo Theeerrrrreeessssa," as if she were saying, "Yes, it is me again. It has always been me. I am always here." I am not sure who all those other angels were but there were maybe 90 to 100 all together. I must need a lot of saving.

Awakening to Consciousness

The work I was doing on myself and with my Reiki clients was having the unintended effect of making me aware of my own consciousness. What is consciousness anyway? There are entire institutes (some of which I refer to in Appendix II) with brilliant scientists, trying to answer that question, and since I may not be as smart as even the pets of these geniuses, I'm going to give you the layman's answer. The best way to describe it is through the question my son asked me when he was four years old: "Mom, if your brain does the thinking, then what is it that tells your brain to think?" The answer to the question, as well as the reason a 4-year old even conceives of the question, is **consciousness**. It is the essence of what makes you, you. The nonscientific term might be soul, Spirit, God, the Unmanifest, the All That Is, the I Am. Whatever the nomenclature, the effect is the same; it is the field you interact with moment by moment. It is the energy system that is within you and surrounds you at the same time. If you are open to it at any level, then you are conscious, albeit to varying degrees.

How was I to become more conscious? I received the answer to this question from Spirit in May 2007. The first step was to recognize that I am made up of mind, body and spirit. Western society has acknowledged the need to extensively develop the mind and body. In the United States, to nurture the mind, parents voluntarily enroll children in preschool, followed by mandatory kindergarten and 12 years of grade school. After that many students themselves choose vocational school, college, and graduate programs. Adults continue exercising their brains with adult education, seminars, bridge classes, etc.

Utilizing gross and fine motor skills develop the physical body. We know that physical exercise has to be done regularly, or we lose muscle. So daily athletic activities, whether it be walking, running, swimming or weight lifting, are considered important. To maintain peak physical condition requires a daily exercise. Musicians and artists, in addition to honing their craft, need to develop the physical coordination necessary to play instruments or to paint. To maintain and improve, they must repeat the technique by practicing it over and over.

So what about growing spiritually or reaching higher levels of consciousness? Is it so unlike nurturing the mind and body that it can, at best, be developed by attending a religious service one hour a week or, at worst, through complete neglect? Would spiritual development occur on its own, with no effort from me? I found that some effort is needed to become spiritually aware; it is spiritual awareness that expands consciousness.

Jung refers to the collective unconscious because it is just that, **un**conscious until you tap into it. Once you access it, it becomes consciousness in you. So how do you access it and how often? Is it like the education of the mind, which requires practice at least five days per week, six to eight hours per day for nine months of the year? Is it like physical development, which ideally requires a daily regimen? The answer is that it may be somewhere in between, but it surely is not one hour per week of passive listening. It may require that you continue your traditional weekly religious service, but it requires more. How much more is up to you. How conscious do you want to become? Do you want a kindergarten level of consciousness, fifth grade level, high school level or graduate level?

To attain the higher levels of consciousness requires a daily practice; a time during which you put your mental and physical needs aside and focus solely on connecting with the energy matrix, God, or whatever you feel a part of—the Source of consciousness. Just as when you study or sit in class, you do not simultaneously exercise your body. Spiritual practice requires single focus. Focus on connecting with the Divine or your higher Self. Do not engage your mind, other than to "listen" and "see" what the universe has to say to your spirit. If you are always doing the talking, how can you hear what God has to say? Prayer can be used to achieve a meditative state but, at some point, you must quiet your mind and LISTEN—this is how you start becoming aware of your consciousness, thereby becoming more fully conscious.

Beginning and Maintaining a Spiritual Practice

I try to meditate for an hour every morning. I find the best time to do this is at 4:00 a.m., which means I have to go to bed by 8:00 p.m., much to the thinly veiled disapproval of my husband. I stumbled upon this schedule as a result of medication I am taking for my migraines. The medication makes me sleepy and takes 14 hours to get out of my system. So to wake up refreshed at 6:00 a.m. with my son, I had to take the medicine at 4:00 p.m. Four hours later I got drowsy, and I had to go to sleep—a schedule more suited to a monastery than a social suburb of New York City. And my husband loves to socialize, as do I, just not nearly as much as my husband. To accommodate our social schedule, I do end up going out many weekends but it takes me a good four to five days to recover, which in turn, causes more migraines.

I do not have the luxury of being in a monastery, so I have to balance my needs with those of my family.

I start my meditation with three prayers: *The Lord's Prayer*, the *Hail Mary* and a prayer that was given to me by the Divine one night as I was trying to go to sleep. As I collapsed onto my bed, exhausted from a long day, the Divine told me to get a pen and a piece of paper. As is my way, I first replied that I was too tired—please don't make me get up. God repeated His request and again, like a child, I resisted. He asked a few more times before I relented. As soon as I had put the requested pen and paper on my bedside table, the Divine started to dictate the following prayer. I have been saying it ever since:

> *God I love You.*
> *God I trust You.*
> *God I find You in my heart.*
> *God, when I am lost find me; when I am blind help me to see.*
> *God, I am Yours to do with as You please.*
> *May it please You to have me serve You; for without Your love, I am nothing.*

I do not get out of bed to say these prayers. I stay where I am comfortable and warm. As I have not chosen a life of an ascetic, I do not see any reason to make myself uncomfortable, and my praying while lying down with one hand over my heart, in bed doesn't seem to adversely affect my relationship with God. You should do what suits you the best. I start by asking God to send me grace. Then, I say my prayers with complete and total focus on God, creating a sacred space that enables me to drop into a deep meditative state following my last prayer. In that meditative state, I can feel the presence of God in every cell of my body. It is a process that starts by quieting my mind, but it is not limited to my mind. My entire body becomes the prayer; it becomes one with God. And yes, there are times when I am too worried or too distracted to meditate. On those occasions, I do my best, and get up and start my day. God does not expect me to mull over my inability to meditate that day. The only loser in that case is me—He knows it, and I know it. Sometimes, I am so busy that I forget to pray, and I feel negligent but not guilty.

I taught myself how to meditate using *Meditation: Achieving Inner Peace and Tranquility in Your Life* by Brian Weiss, M.D. The CD is a guided meditation, which I used for a few months until I realized I was meditating as soon as the music started to play and I didn't need to listen to the words. Of course, there are many schools of meditation (some of which are listed in Appendix III) and, as always, you should choose the one that is right for you.

If I count the time I spend with clients, on a busy day, I can be in a meditative state, communing with God, three to four hours per day. If you are not particularly religious or comfortable with the concept of God, but feel at peace in nature, then use nature as your door to higher consciousness. Commit to regular time spent in nature by yourself. Empty your mind as you take in the sights, sounds and smells that surround you. For a structured practice that does not involve God or nature, try mindfulness meditation.

The key is to find a practice and a schedule that works for you then repeat it daily. Whatever path you choose, you must listen and act on those things that resonate with you. And so it was with this in mind that I attended a healing arts class hosted by the Maryknoll Sisters Mission.

CHAPTER 3

Prove It to Me

Listen to the Universe when it speaks to you! Your mind is too limited to imagine all the possible outcomes. Even if you don't get what you hoped for, the Universe has something better in store for you. Believe, trust, love.

- Holy Spirit, 2005

Maryknoll Sisters

My close friend Kim had invited Linda and me to join her for a class on the Healing Art of Sat Nam Rasayan at the Maryknoll Sisters Mission Institute in Ossining, New York. Intellectually, I was telling myself that it would be good to attend in an effort to expand my knowledge of healing; my intuition, however, was telling me to go just because it was at the Maryknoll Mission and that I needed to be with the nuns. I had experienced very few nuns in my short stint at Catholic school, and what I did experience was not particularly pleasant. Add to that my natural skepticism of everything related to the church, and the feeling that I needed to be with the nuns made no sense. I questioned my judgment, again, when we discovered that the class was in the Maryknoll Mission nursing home. We walked into class and sat among 40 or so elderly women, all of whom looked like lay people. Maybe my intuition was wrong. Where were the nuns? Halfway through the class we learned that these women were the nuns—they no longer wore habits. I plotted with myself that if we were asked to break up into pairs for some sort of exercise, instead of linking up with Kim or Linda, I would pair up with a nun. Sure enough, that opportunity was presented, and I slid over to the nun who was sitting a few seats off to my left. She and I immediately held hands, and after introducing ourselves, Sister said she was sure that God put us together. So was I.

In the first exercise, I was supposed to be the "healer" and Sister was to be the "client." This was ironic—that I would have anything to offer, or that I could be a channel for healing energy for this elderly nun. The holiness just oozed off of her. In spite of my earlier nun encounters, it was obvious that this woman embodied holiness and loving-kindness. As the "healer," I had to ask Sister what she wanted healed. With tremendous humility, she said she yearned to be more present with God. Although it was so glaringly apparent to me that she was already in the presence of God, I proceeded with the "healing" but not as instructed by our teacher. Instead, I did what Jesus had taught me. I surrendered myself to God and asked that He do for Sister whatever was for her greatest good. God allowed me to see and feel His presence in and around Sister. God's presence was so beautiful, powerful and gentle it made me cry. I told her that she was already filled with the presence of God and that I was crying because I could feel His presence in her. I explained that I had sensed that God is with her all of the time. She said again, with humility, "You have no idea how important that was for me to hear. I never know if He is here with me." Now I was blubbering. She was so humble. How could she devote her life to serving God without the proof that He was here? My faith is a joke compared to hers. I always need—and thankfully—am always receiving proof of His existence. At this point my tears prevented me from speaking. And then she added that she wasn't sure if she was worthy. Worthy? She truly had no idea how worthy she was. If it had to be earned, it was me who was unworthy to even be in her presence, much less "heal" her or be in the presence of God. What lessons God was giving me through His servant! I was sitting in front of a crystal clear incarnation of God.

Next, it was Sister's turn to heal me. In this case, there are no quotation marks around heal because her presence and her grace were truly healing. She was and is a true channel of God's grace. She held my hands, and I told her that I wanted to be more humble. Once again, with all the grace of God, she told me I seemed so humble, but began her healing anyway. When I left she hugged me and said she was grateful to God that she made a friend today. A friend? She enabled me to see and feel God as if He were standing right in front of me. She showed me, through the example of who she was, what we look and act like when we are Divine and human at the same time. In her humility and grace, I saw and felt the Presence of God. Furthermore, while she healed me, I saw her transform into Christ. I made a mental note to see her again.

The day after my experience with Sister, I felt as if my need to see results had vanished. I was at peace doing whatever God directed me to do and living in obscurity. Sister, in those few precious minutes during which she held my hands, had transferred to me the grace of humility. I now know it and feel it at a deeper level. I am sure I am not "there yet," but Sister helped me to bypass many smaller (and if the past is any indicator, painful) steps, bringing to me deep peace with what is. I felt, at that moment, content to do the work God asked of me. I never did learn the healing art of Sat Nam Rasayan.

A Visit with Sister

I arrived for my first post-class visit with Sister at the appointed time of 10:00 a.m. She was paged but could not be found, so I asked the receptionist to keep paging her while I prayed in the chapel. I sat in the chapel, with my eyes closed, and immediately saw a vision of Mother Mary. Her love consumed me. When I returned to the receptionist, 45 minutes had passed and still there was no sign of Sister. A lovely nun waiting for a visit from her family took me under her wing and walked with me in search of Sister. By the time we found her, Sister had just sat down for 11:30 a.m. Mass.

I have always hated Mass, so I have not attended one for possibly 45 years. Yet, there I was, seated alongside my new friend, bracing myself for the torture that was sure to follow. To my surprise, the time passed quickly, and I was repeatedly moved to tears by the profound sincerity and faith of the sisters. They prayed The Lord's Prayer aloud. They prayed aloud for all the world leaders and for all the people on earth. That they would need a male priest to deliver the Mass baffled me. The priest walked up to each nun to deliver communion, as most were in wheelchairs and could not get up. I did not feel prepared to accept communion—I remembered very little from my third grade religious education except that one had to go confession before communion. I had not been to confession for longer than I had not been to church. I am not prone to follow all rules, but I felt that in the presence of these nuns, in the presence of such holiness, I shouldn't mess around. As I tried hard to be pious, an absurd childhood memory ran through my head—communion meant the end of the church service, and that wafer was my appetizer before Sunday dinner. And so it was, with these ridiculous thoughts in mind that at the last minute, I accepted the wafer that represents the body of Christ for Catholics. I placed the wafer into my mouth and, once again, burst into tears. For the first time in my life,

I felt the communion with Jesus that this sacrament represents. I was overwhelmed with its significance and with the love of Christ, which unwittingly caused tears to pour from my eyes. It always amazes me how God (in this instance, through Jesus) loves us so much that He never stops trying to find us. God never passes up an opportunity to love us no matter how weak we are, no matter what foolish thoughts are going through our heads. I may offend your sensibilities, but I can't offend God. He is always forgiving and never judging. And as long as we are not repressing the emotion, we will feel His love.

Mass ended and Sister and I went to lunch. Afterward, we sat for a half hour, and I did some healing work on her arm to alleviate the pain from a fall she had taken the night before. Once again, I was overcome by her grace, holiness and humility. She expressed how much it meant to her for us to be together. She also repeated that although she didn't feel worthy of God, she was blessed with the constant feeling of gratitude. We hugged, and I wept some more. I am not much of a crier, but she must think I am completely feeble and inarticulate with all the crying I do around her. All I seem to be able to do around her is nod my head.

As I drove away, it dawned on me that I was the one who had a healing, along with a cleansing and purification. I realized that the time I had spent in the chapel was needed to allow Mother Mary to purify me before I met with Sister. While sitting with Sister, she, in her holiness and humility, had surrounded me with the grace of God—something she is completely unaware of. I tried a few more times to get together with Sister, but she was impossible to reach by phone and never answered her email. I think we both got what we were meant to from our meeting, and I look forward to seeing her on the other side—that is as long as I don't end up in one of Dante's lower rings of hell as a result of taking communion without going to confession.

Faith of the Blind

In bed with the lights off, I had just finished praying and sending healing energy to a friend. My husband was in bed beside me working on his computer. After praying, I turned onto my side to sleep, but my mind wandered to the subject of faith. I thought of Sister and how she had faith even though she didn't seem to see or hear God. Then I thought about myself—how I never had faith. I had to hear God. I had to see and hear Jesus and Mary numerous times to believe they were real. One of my friends describes my type of faith as "faith of the blind." I had never intended to have faith in someone or something I couldn't prove was there. Some part of me always thought faith in the unprovable was a cop-out, a convenient way of excusing reason. As I was apologizing to God for my weakness, but at the same time acknowledging that there was nothing I could do about it, I saw from behind my closed eyes a quick bright flash of light. I jumped up and asked my husband, who was still sitting up working, what had happened. He explained that the bulb in the lamp on my nightstand, which had been off for an hour, suddenly illuminated, then went out. He said it was as if there was only enough energy to make the filament glow and that the light had almost an orange tinge. It was very quick, like lightning. I reached up and checked to see if I had completely turned off the light switch; I had. I turned it on and off a few times to see if it was working and, yes, the bulb turned on and off as it should. I guess God hears me loud and clear when I say I need proof. I am in awe of Sister and her faith in the absence of all the signs I seem to need to keep my faith.

Signs from God

I have never understood faith and probably still don't. It is a complex internal struggle—on the one hand, I need proof and then, on the other hand, I have tremendous faith in God's infinite, unconditional love and the endless miracles available to us all, simply for the asking. I knew Jesus was there when I was in my teens and in my 20s because he was the only one capable of helping me out of the jams I got myself into. But because I didn't record those moments, I have no accurate record to share with you. However, beginning in 1998, at the urging of my mother, I did track my slow awakening to God's attempts to help me accept His miraculous existence. I don't know why God puts up with me. Because I am in no way special, I am certain that if God is hounding me, God is hounding you too. It may help you to see how God is trying to get your attention if I share with you examples of how, in the early years, He got mine. So here, in humble gratitude for God's never-ending patience with me, are some of the earlier journal entries I made as He helped me to see, hear and feel His presence. Similar to my early angel messages, some of these entries, in retrospect, seem quiet naïve, but everyone has to start somewhere; in reading them, you may find that you too have already had direct experiences of God.

God Speaking Through Our Physical World
The Wave 1-6-98

Lately, when I draw certain conclusions based on information received, as after reading passages in *A Course in Miracles*, a feeling washes over me that runs over my entire body like an internal wave. I asked God if that's His way of telling me that my conclusion is correct, and I immediately received another wave feeling.

Call is Impossible 2005

My sister forwarded me a particularly disturbing email she'd received from her soon-to-be-ex boyfriend and asked that I call her to discuss it. I decided to call her from my cell phone as I was on my way to run errands. I had a nagging feeling as I dialed her number that I should really give some thought to what was written before reacting to the abusive nature of the email. I ignored my intuition and continued to dial. Each time I began to dial, my cell phone would say "Call Ended" before I'd finished typing in the phone numbers. Of course, not being deterred, I kept redialing. I got the same message: "Call Ended." Still not deterred, I dialed again and got #$?/@^*…Now I was angry that I couldn't get through, and for the ninth or tenth time, tried to dial my sister's number. This time my cell phone flashed the message, "CALL IS IMPOSSIBLE." Naturally, I started to laugh at myself and at my determination to ignore the more subtle messages from the universe. In the end, I was grateful for the universe's persistence and clarity, because when my sister and I finally did speak, it was after I had received a channeled message from the Universe that was much clearer and more helpful than my ranting would have been.

God Speaking Through Revelations and the Books We Read
Validation 2-10-01

As I was doing Reiki on my daughter, I had a revelation (when I had the revelation, I got that wave of energy that comes over me when I get something right) that maybe what Reiki does is solve the emotional problems, which then allows the body to heal its own physical problems. The premise being that every physical problem is associated with an emotional problem. When I finished Reiki, I came upstairs and opened Caroline Myss' *Anatomy of the Spirit,* at page 204. I read the following: "Jesus always first healed his patient's emotional sufferings; the physical healing then followed naturally."

The Sun 6-9-04

While Linda did Reiki on me, I saw Moses parting the Red Sea. In the vision I was a young girl and Moses told me to walk in the path of the parted sea toward the light (sun). The sun was the focal point; it was enormous on the horizon. There were no other people with me. Each step I took caused the water in front of me to part. Moses was teaching me about co-creation. When I finally reached the sun, I saw Jesus. I started to kneel and he told me not to because we are equals. Not just he and I but he and each of us. (Jesus explained this further when he said to a client I was doing Reiki on: *The first mistake of mankind was thinking he was special. The second mistake of mankind was forgetting his (own) Divinity.*) He walked with me back across the sea floor and told me I was to lead by example.

I read later that in the West, there are countless testimonies like that of St. Teresa of Avila: "When the soul looks upon this Divine Sun the brightness dazzles…" I thought it was odd that on 6-9-04 the sun figured so prominently in my vision. In fact, I thought it had no significance. I now see that it is an ancient symbol of the Divine Presence.

God Speaking through Our Dreams
So What are the Chances? 12-5-08 2:05 a.m.

St. John of the Cross appeared to me in a semi–dream state, accompanied by orbs of light. They (the orbs) worked in my energy field, repairing it. Then they opened an energetic layer as if unzipping a full length "coat" with a zipper down the back. They communicated to me that this is what has been "holding me back." I still need to "walk" out of it. St. John and St. Thomas Aquinas were standing together watching over me. St. John said: *We've been waiting for your awakening. Step out of the coat. Give us the coat. You now have no boundaries.* I know I have held back my power because Linda tells me so in almost every Reiki session we have together—It is time to shine; to be who I am. Next, I could see the suit I came out of, and it was the size of a layette onesie. How did I ever fit into it? It was impossibly small. Then St. John said: *Be the super nova. Don't be afraid of your Light…Honor what God has made you. Honor your journey. Show the way.* How? *That will come. Get used to your new "skin."*

Over two years later, I read these words from St. John's book, *Dark Night of the Soul:* "Just as Abraham made a great feast when his son Isaac was weaned, so there is rejoicing in heaven when God removes the baby clothes from the soul."[17] So what are the chances that I would have a dream that matched something St. John of the Cross actually wrote or said when I didn't know anything about him? I knew he existed, but I had no idea what he said until I picked up this book more than two years after having the dream. The fact that St. John makes reference, in his famous *Dark Night of The Soul,* to God's removing our soul from its baby clothes confirms for me the validity of the vision and the message.

God Speaking through Spirit, Songs, Radio, Fax Machines: You Name It, He Uses It

At 12:30 p.m. on December 11, 2005, I was driving to my mother's house knowing that my grandfather lay there in his last hours. I hit the scan button on my radio three times, but it wouldn't move off the station it was on, so I decided to listen. *Silent Night* was playing and it made me think of Grandpa when they sang "… around yon virgin mother and child…" and I began to cry for our loss. When I arrived at my mother's house, I was told that Grandpa had died at about the same time my radio was stuck on *Silent Night.*

Driving back home that night, three things happened. First, Grandpa spoke to me and said he was in the "inner most chamber" and that it was more beautiful than I know. I knew he was referring to St. Teresa of Avila's teachings but I had never heard her use the term "chamber." I had been reading the *Interior Castle* and was up to the third mansion. When I got home, I picked up the book and flipped to the seventh mansion. There I read that when one is in the seventh mansion, they are in the Presence **chamber.** Second, I was once again flipping radio stations and settled on some rock music. I heard Grandpa's voice saying, "Don't listen to that. Listen to something I would listen to." Not knowing what that would be, since I'd never heard my grandfather listening to music, I started scanning the stations again. I settled on something that sounded like opera. There was a bit of static but soon I heard them sing the words "Ave Maria." The announcer said it was by Shubert and then played another version of *Ave Maria.* I was going to call mom to tell her that I thought Grandpa wanted this played at his funeral, but Grandpa said, "wait until the song is over." I did as he asked, and found out that the second version was by Bach. I phoned mom and told her that Grandpa wanted *Ave Maria* **by Bach** played at his funeral. Mom said she had been thinking for three days that she wanted to play that song at her father's funeral. Lastly, an extremely bright star, the only one in the sky, followed me most of the way home. I thought that maybe it was my grandfather but then brushed it off as my imagination. Seconds after I brushed off that "thought," a shooting star emanated from just below that bright star. I guess that wasn't a thought but a feeling that I shouldn't have ignored; it was a representation of Grandpa after all.

The night before Grandpa's memorial church service, the priest received a fax with no cover letter and no originating phone number. It was the music and words to an Italian song called *Tu Scendi Dalle Stelle*. He decided to give it to the organist who, as it turned out, knew the song and played it at Grandpa's service. It turned out to be a song that Grandpa's wife, my grandmother, had requested her granddaughter, Rachel, play on the piano every year at Christmastime. Grandpa was 99 years old when he died and had only his family (12 of us including his wife) and two friends left in this world, none of whom had sent the fax. The whole family understood the fax to be a gift from Grandpa to Grandma. The opening line of the song is, "You come down from the **stars**, O King of the sky..."

The Proof is in the Listening

I was asked how God chooses to whom He is going to speak. I believe He chooses **all** of us. The question is, "Who chooses to listen when God speaks?" He is always there speaking to all of us. He communicates in words, visions, signs, even the radio, and in some cases, via the fax machine. He communicates by putting up roadblocks to your dreams and opening other avenues. Once one stops defining how the communication should take place and becomes open to all possibilities, the communication is received. Take the story of the fax to the priest. That was a communication from the spirit world. Whether from God, Grandpa or Grandpa unified with God, we don't know, and it doesn't matter. When I asked the priest if that sort of thing happens often at his church, he said it didn't until he became open to them; now they happen all the time. Would we expect God to talk to us via a fax? No. Give up the expectations and listen. The messages and the "proof" are there for us all.

CHAPTER 4
Faith

Come children to the hem of my garment. No one who comes unto me will be lost. (Your) faith should come as easily as (your) breath. Fear not. What comes will come. Always know that I am here to guide you. You will never be lost.

- Jesus 4-28-10

Faith has been defined as the complete trust in someone or something and trust as the belief in the reliability, truth or strength of someone or something. In addition to my struggles with faith, I seem to have an issue with trust. From the first moment I did Reiki on people beginning in 1996, I saw images and received messages from angels and Jesus. I thought, however, that it was my imagination. Being distrustful, I never shared the messages with my clients unless, at the end of a session, they happened to tell me what was bothering them. Only then did I realize that the messages and visions I had received during their session actually had meaning. And even then, I hesitantly shared what I had seen and heard. To further test the veracity of these images and messages, I would ask new clients not to tell me anything about themselves or why they had come. I practiced this way for years before becoming even mildly convinced that what I saw and heard was real and not the result of my imagination. Many times, the images were metaphorical, but my client always knew the link to his or her current life. Even when I shared the images and messages more freely, I would explain to the client that she or he should ignore the messages if they were not relevant. They were not supposed to force fit them.

It wasn't a steady ascent from receiving messages, to having them confirmed, to learning to trust my ability, to receiving them clearly and then to sharing them. This was a rocky road with twists and turns, ups and downs. I would glide along effortlessly for a long time and then bam, run smack into a crisis of faith. How does one go from "faith of the blind" to "blind faith?" Does faith develop over time? Is one born having faith? Was it fear that prevented me from trusting myself or having faith in God and the messages I was receiving?

Very early on in this journey, in October 2005, I entreated God: "Please help me to trust, to have faith, to release my fear of speaking the truth as you convey it to me." Around this time, I received some messages while sending Reiki to a friend of a friend. The messages were about her needing to resolve long-standing issues with her husband in order to avoid becoming physically ill. In the message, she was told that she had two choices: she could leave her husband to avoid the illness, or she could create a new order within the marriage. What if I was wrong? This was her marriage at stake. What if I was right? This was her health at stake. I didn't want to deliver the messages, in spite of the fact that I was told by Spirit: *You deliver the message; we will take care of you.* I didn't trust Spirit. Who is the "we" who was supposedly going to take care of me? I had no faith. I was scared, almost sick to my stomach. I spent the next two days teaching a Reiki II class and thinking, "What if this is all crap? What if we're nuts?" My ego-self was fighting hard to take control. I even received an email from an old business colleague whom I hadn't seen in almost ten years. There it was, my entry back into the concrete world of finance and the ego. The timing of the Universe is impeccable—always a choice.

Grasping for straws, I asked for guidance by pulling a card from a deck of angel cards, which read, "I am bringing you esoteric information and symbols, and helping you understand spiritual truths." That didn't help. So later that night, I asked for guidance about which book to read to help me with this situation, and I was led to *A Course in Miracles.* I asked "which page" and I was led to page 363. It dealt with a crisis of faith. I never delivered the messages. I clearly lacked the kind of trust, faith and courage I needed to move forward, even though I didn't yet know what I was moving toward.

A year later, I was still struggling with faith and trust when Linda received the following message for me from Spirit: *What is it, my child? What is it that you fear about the messages? About being a messenger? You are a messenger of peace and hope. Have trust that what we ask you to deliver will only be for the greatest good. Fear not the ways of this world, for you are being divinely guided. Seek only the Truth and know that the Truth lies within. Honor your ways of knowing and teach others to do the same.*

And now, many, many years later, I still needed support releasing my fears around disseminating the messages through *Everyday Mystic*. I silently asked for reassurance at the start of a yoga class when we were asked to draw a card from a deck of angel cards I was not familiar with. My card read: "Gabrielle…the feminine expression of Archangel Gabriel—the chief revealer of divine mysteries to humanity…In Revelation, it is Gabriel who blows the trumpet of rebirth, asking human beings to rise out of their antipathy and embrace each other in selfless love and compassion. The name Gabriel actually means "hero of God." Gabriel impregnates the human soul with a vision of divine wisdom, hoping to stir the personality into a life of greater devotion and service. Gabriel helps human beings unite their spirits and bodies through heart-centered revelations and insights." So, there it was, another nudge urging me to move forward.

The Seven Stages of Faith

As is my habit, I was in meditation at 4:30 a.m. when I received the following *Seven Stages of Faith*. I was not being told that every one of us goes through each stage to get to faith, although some will. It is more common that, like me, you have gone through or will go through some and not other stages on your journey into faith. And to be honest, with as much as God has shown me, and as far as I have come since my earlier crises in faith, I still have a lot of work to do to reach what anyone would consider deep faith. Here is what I heard on March 10, 2011:

There are seven stages of faith:

> *1. Doubt*
> *2. Betrayal*
> *3. Anger*
> *4. Bargaining*
> *5. Resignation*
> *6. Surrender*
> *7. Faith*

Stage 1: Doubt

You doubt your experiences with God. I have spent a lot of time here. I always thought doubt kept me sane, especially when I had my first vision and heard my first message, but maybe it just caused my journey to be dragged out. Although, when this all started, I didn't even know I was on a journey. The one benefit of my doubt is that anything I share with you has been subjected to the grueling doubt machine that exists inside my head. It has been rung out and hung out to dry, and if after years of this treatment, God continues to speak to me through visions, words and feelings, then I am confident in passing these things along to you. Of course, there will be those of you who think I am imagining these things, and to you I say, "Doubt away!" It served me well, other than to delay a beautiful and fulfilling relationship with my Self and with God, or whatever you choose to call that force that is bigger than you.

Stage 2: Betrayal

You pray and don't get what you pray for, so you feel betrayed by God. It seems that when people's lives are going well, they take the credit. When things are not going well, many people tend to blame others—sometimes they blame God. At this level of consciousness, people ask "what is God for, if not for making life to my liking?" As I've already admitted, I have had my doubts, but I am not prone to the idea of betrayal. I do, however, know people who are.

In this stage, you pray and God doesn't deliver, so you feel your trust in Him has been betrayed. Alternatively, you pray and get guidance, which you follow, but then you do not get your desired outcome. In this second scenario, it is important to remember not to presume to know the outcome that God has in mind when following His guidance. In either scenario you may perceive that God has betrayed you, but based on my experience, God will never betray you. Once on His path, resistance will only cause you to suffer. If you are truly following guidance, be assured that the outcome will have benefits far beyond your wildest imaginings. Dr. Wayne Dyer says, "When you change the way you look at things, the things you look at change." To put this into the context of our discussion, when you change the way you look at yourself, you too can change from a victim of betrayal to someone who is empowered by his or her relationship with a loving and compassionate God. A God who, once you stop looking for ways in which you are being betrayed, will present you with situations and circumstances to support and nurture your new self-view.

Stage 3: Anger

You are angry with God over not having things your way. Many people are angry with God because their lives are, and the world is, messed up. They feel they should never have been born into that family or those circumstances. They feel they were shortchanged in innumerable ways. These people spend most of their energy on their anger instead of allocating their energies to changing their circumstances. As Eckhart Tolle says, if change is not possible, then we must learn how to accept or remove ourselves from those situations. When everything goes wrong, the only thing to do is to say, "Thank you!" Why? Because you've just received a sign that you need to make changes.

I have prayed and not gotten my way, but I have never felt angry with God. I have gotten angry with people but not with God. The God who has shown Himself to me has never been a vengeful God, so I don't know how to be angry with Him. When, in my opinion, He hadn't pulled through, I didn't have time to spend on anger—I had to get to work on my own solution. I have made poor choices in my life that led to undesirable consequences, which I then had to accept or change. It is not God who made the choices, so why should I be angry with Him? There are those who do not agree with me. I hear time and again, "Why does God allow abuse, war, hunger, shortages of natural resources like water and energy, or natural disasters?"

The answer is that God does not allow this to happen, we do. People make decisions as to how to treat one another, not God. People make decisions to go to war, not God. People make decisions on how to allocate abundant food supplies and natural resources, not God. With regard to natural disasters, I think we know enough about our earth to understand how these conditions come about. Once again, we can take the blame when we choose to build below sea level or in the flood basins of major rivers. Drought is more likely when we build in the desert. Of course, those places will eventually be hit by natural disasters. Is that an act of a damning God? The natural world is actually designed for harmonic existence, but our choices very often cause it to be out of balance. Regardless, when a natural disaster strikes, it is we to whom we can turn to share resources and extend love and caring to each other. And yes, of course we should pray, and miracles can and do happen, but they won't happen without our participation. We are an important part of the Divine plan.

Stage 4: Bargaining

You try a different approach to get God to give to you and do for you what you want. This is the if/then scenario. I've used it. It goes like this, "God, if you get me an "A" on my math test then I'll go to church." If I am honest with myself, God kept up His end of the bargain many more times than I kept up mine. Sometimes I did my half, and sometimes all I did was pray, really, really hard because I screwed up so badly. Still, I thought I was making a bargain with God—that if He bailed me out this one more time I'd never do such and such again. He knew with whom He was dealing. He bailed me out; I failed to live up to my end of the bargain. When it was all over and He pulled through for me, I'd think that maybe I was just lucky, and I didn't really need God anyway, if there really was a God. Then the cycle would start all over again. And God, once again, would come back and hold up His end of the bargain.

Remembering back to those times of praying and bargaining, it occurs to me that I prayed as if the outcome was assured—not in an arrogant sense, but in the sense that I truly had no other choice. More often than not, I didn't have an adult in my life who could help me, so I prayed so intensely that I believed there was no other possible outcome than the one I was praying for. I have often heard Gregg Braden speak about "praying as if it is already done," and I think that must be really hard to do. But looking back I see that is exactly what I did in my teens and beyond. That is what saved me from a life of drugs, early motherhood, crippling injuries, incurable disease and premature death.

Thankfully for me, God is forgiving and unconditionally loving. Otherwise, He'd have left me long ago because of my broken promises. I can tell you, based on personal experience, that He has unlimited patience. Don't ever stop trying because He will wait for you to "get it." He waited a long time for me—why is still a mystery.

Stage 5: Resignation

You give up trying to ask God for help since He doesn't give you what you want anyway. Some people complain that God never, ever helps them. Sometimes those people just give up on God altogether, and perhaps they should. If you are one of them, stop praying and start taking responsibility for your own life. This way you have no one to blame, and you will not be wasting any of your precious energy. Should you get tired of going it alone, God will be waiting for you when you decide to return. He will not judge you or your absence. He will merely begin to offer assistance in accordance with your asking. I have to say that I never gave up asking, even in my deepest stages of doubt because I always figured that I could have been wrong.

Stage 6: Surrender

You start to realize God may not give you what you want, but as the Rolling Stones sing, "If you try sometimes, you just might find, you get what you need." You ask for proof or signs and you get them. Ah, so here is where you begin to find inner peace. You realize that indeed God does answer your prayers, if you are open to all the possible ways He may do so. You may even ask for signs that He is there, and because you have developed a modicum of trust and faith, you receive them.

I had to pay my own college tuition, and so it was that running late for work one rainy Saturday morning, I was driving far above the speed limit on the southbound lanes of the interstate highway. I was in the far left lane when my car started to hydroplane. It lifted off the ground on a thin film of water, and turned 180 degrees, so that I was going backward down the interstate. I had no control over the steering or brakes, so I sat calmly as the car made its next move, turning backward, down into the grassy median and out onto the northbound lanes where it came to rest sitting perpendicular to the oncoming traffic and stalled. The most amazing thing, looking back on the experience, is how calm I was—but I was more than calm. I KNEW WITH CERTAINTY that nothing was going to happen to me. I know now that I was completely surrendered to the experience and to God. Once again, I was in a situation where only God could help. I was beyond bargaining; I knew better and so did He. I had no doubt He would pull through for me, and with the innocence of a child, I trusted Him and He saved me once again. In the pouring rain, cars dashed around me at the last minute and after a few tries, I started the car and drove north to the next exit, looped around onto the southbound lanes and tried again to get to work, albeit a bit more slowly. Oh, and by the way, the car was fine too, except for the really long pieces of grass my father found wedged up somewhere around the engine.

Stage 7: Faith

You learn that the whole Universe is designed to give you both what you want and what you need if only you have eyes to see. Although, paradoxically, at this level, you surrender your wants and desires to those of the Divine. You also

realize that, as much faith as you may have, there are ever deeper levels to attain. I have received so many messages about faith, like this one Linda delivered to me from God while she did Reiki on me in 2006: *Have faith, My child, in My Divine Plan for you. You have nothing to fear as you have much work to do for Me here on Earth. You have never lived your life from a place of fear because, although you did not know it, you had faith in Me. Your "risks" will not always be physical, but will be "leaps" of faith, nonetheless…Fear not the ways of the world. Listen for the guidance. Act on it. Ask for My help, for we are in this together. Practice listening. Your ability to hear Me is strong. Have faith, My child. Speak to Me and know it is I who answers you. Trust in you; trust in Me. You are here until you are not.*

Or like this one that I received from Jesus: *Come children to the hem of my garment. No one who comes unto me will be lost. (Your) faith should come as easily as my breath. Fear not. What comes will come. Always know that I am here to guide you. You will never be lost.* Jesus said I must have faith in his plan. I must take the necessary steps, but in the end I must accept God's will.

The reason we don't surrender is because we don't trust God. We ask, after we fall, why God didn't catch us. He answers: *Because you didn't trust that I would catch you. You had no faith in Me. You put your faith in yourself and blame Me when you fall.* He can only catch us if we allow ourselves to fall back into His arms. *Like a child, you must trust that your Father will meet your every need. You do so exactly as a young child, trusting your Father not only in your mind but also with your whole being. A young child, who has always been unconditionally loved, nurtured, protected and cared for does not know there is another alternative. That is how your relationship with God must be. But you must willingly let go of any notion that He will not take care of you; that He will not provide for you or take away your every burden. He cannot take from you your burdens without your complete willingness to let them go.*

I had to see a lot of proof before getting to this seventh stage, and I can say, it is wonderful, but it was not always a stable state for me. I have to practice walking the fine line between surrendering myself to God and trusting that He will provide what I need. And so it is that after many years of receiving Divine messages and witnessing miracles, I can share with you the link, as I see it, between faith and healing.

I have seen incurable diseases heal firsthand because of faith, and the belief that the diseases could heal, regardless of what the doctors and scientists said. The first step is to think outside the existing paradigm. Don't believe in the limits we place upon ourselves through science. This does not mean that you should not trust what we, thus far, have learned through science. It means to go beyond what we "know" to what we have yet to discover. The boundaries of science can only be pushed via the right questions and hypotheses. Your belief that incurable diseases cannot heal, and may, at best, stay dormant, allows only for that possibility. All I ask is that you allow for the **possibility** of healing. I am not trying to set up false hope, because this is not about hope. This is about FAITH and the miracles that follow.

Our scientific limitations arise from our ignorance of the possibilities as well as the limitations of what our technology can measure. Quantum physicists have discovered that the outcome of an experiment is influenced by the mere presence of, and the expectations of, the observer. As the observer of your own physical, mental, emotional and spiritual life, you must open to the infinite possibilities that exist. You must break through to a higher level of consciousness, one in which healing possibilities exist beyond what the medical community would suggest. This is the starting point for healing. Maybe you or your loved ones are not meant to heal, but maybe you are. How will you know if you don't even believe it is possible?

If you believe in a God with no limits and that He created you in His image, then why should you have limits? *If you are the manifestation of the God consciousness, then you need to set your intention, and know that your intention will manifest. This is why you can manifest—because you are the God consciousness, and as such have all the powers you have historically attributed to God. God wants you to know Him by being Him. Jesus was a son, but so are you a son of God.*

When it comes to healing, doing your part often means going to the doctor. It always means good physical, emotional and spiritual care. But when the illness is "incurable" or the doctor tells you that your chosen health goal is impossible, it is time to set **your own** intention to heal. Set it and ask God if it is in alignment with His will. Your intention, aligned with the will of God, is a very powerful tool. Have faith that whatever is for your greatest good, as deemed by God, will manifest. Align your will with the will of God and have faith. INTEND. ALIGN. HAVE FAITH.

We are not "just channels" of universal or divine energy. We are Divine. Jesus said to me: *I am in you and you are in me.* That gives me the ability to heal. In healing, I am to use my Divinity and, as a co-creator with God, I ask that He decide if the person, myself included, is to be healed. He decides what is for our greatest good. If there is truly **no separation** and that **all is one**, then there is **no** separation between God and us. We can heal by recognizing the Divinity in ourselves first, and then we will inevitably see it in all else. Our job is to recognize the Divinity in others and to let God "create" the outcome.

Miracles are God's medicine. Who lays claim to a miracle is God.

Here are three examples taken from actual client sessions.

The herpes 2 virus is considered incurable. Once it is in your blood, it may stay dormant but it never "heals." In one such case, the client and I decided to put aside the notion that it is incurable. Why should it be? Why can't it heal like any other virus? If we had begun with the notion that it was incurable, then the results may have been very different. In this case, the best possible outcome was attained—a second blood test showed **no trace** of the herpes 2 virus. We did not hope. The client, under a doctor's care, followed a vitamin regimen. Then the client and I opened to a paradigm that doesn't exist: that herpes 2 can heal. We aligned with God by asking that our intention be manifested, only if it was for the greatest good of the client. We held unwavering faith that healing was possible; we did energy work and gave it to God. Mother Mary and St. Thérèse of Lisieux appeared to me and said they would take care of it. I had faith in them, and they healed my client.

In yet another case, a client had polyps on her gallbladder that had shown up on multiple ultrasounds over a long period of time. In a healing session, prior to the surgery being scheduled, she received guidance from my friend and medical intuitive Kim, who was working with me, to have another ultrasound done **before** the surgery. This was so she would see that the polyps were gone as a result of the energy work and her unwavering faith. The doctor refused to do the ultrasound. But sure enough, when the gallbladder was removed, the doctor saw there were no polyps.

In a third instance, I had a Reiki client on whom I "saw" leg braces with the distinct message that he was on a path toward developing multiple sclerosis (MS). St. Thérèse of Lisieux appeared during the healing session, and I watched as she removed the braces, saying that they could go back on as easily as they came off. The vision was a metaphor for her healing the client. I didn't know it when I worked on this client, but he had been to a doctor recently and received a possible diagnosis of MS. St. Thérèse of Lisieux appeared to me again after the session and told me that if I doubted the healing that took place, there would not be a healing. I tried really hard to have faith in the healing I witnessed. A follow-up doctor visit showed no signs of MS in my client.

There will be skeptics who will find reasons not to believe this is possible. I am not trying to convert you, and yes of course, there will be people who don't heal. In some but not all cases, it will be the ego that prevents healing because certain individuals would rather be **right** than heal. However, my background in financial risk management teaches me to look at it this way: opening your mind to the possibilities of healing has no downside potential and miraculous upside potential. You decide if the risk of changing your mind is not worth the potential reward. There are very few decisions we make in any area of our life that have such a risk/reward ratio.

Whether a healing takes place or not, it is important to understand that: *Every person, every situation is there for one reason—to teach you how to love. This is why we have diversity; because without it you could not learn unconditional love. All the multiplicity, all the complexity boils down to this. However, (to learn) the lesson of unconditional love, you must view the situations through your heart or your higher Self.* Some may wonder, as Linda and I did, what the difference is between one's higher Self and God.

The answer came while I was doing Reiki on Linda on February 16, 2011:

Your higher Self is the merging of your perfect Self with God. It's like heaven on earth. It's not purely God; it's you with God. You're meant to be part of the equation. You are here on earth, and you are meant to be integrated (with the Whole). Who you are is meant to merge with God. When you do this, you will always find love as the answer. You will always find **faith** *in a loving God to help you along your path. When you have* **faith**, *you can move forward with inner stillness against all odds.*

A few months after receiving the above message I was reading "Behind the Selma March" in *A Testament of Hope: The Essential Writings of Martin Luther King, Jr.* I stopped to "ask" Dr. King, "How did you do it? How did you have the courage?" I wasn't really expecting an answer, but I heard a response anyway, "I had Love and I had **Faith**." Tears came to my eyes because I knew it was true, and I knew that those are the only things that could guide him so steadfastly through such insurmountable odds. Then I realized how woefully inadequate my own Love and Faith are compared to the likes of Dr. King. I saw mine as a flag wavering in the wind and I saw King's as a flag standing straight out as if blowing in a constant gale force wind, never wavering, never falling. That is the kind of Love and Faith we all need to carry on. I thanked Dr. Martin Luther King for being that example in our lives.

An elderly friend once said to me, "Theresa, you could have such a leisurely life, and instead you choose to do this for all of us." I didn't know what she meant since I loved my Reiki practice, and I loved teaching people how tapping into Divine consciousness could change their lives. It was not until reflecting back on her comments, years later, that I realized she meant I had a choice. At that point in my life, I could have spent my days shopping or lunching with friends while my children were at school. I did not have to share my visions and revelations with people in the suburbs of New York City. These areas are bastions of conservatism, not typically known for embracing people who see visions or hear messages. I was not looking for God when God found me. Yet, once I realized, even partially, that what I saw and heard was true, I couldn't **not** share my experiences with those around me.

In a vision I had in which I saw Moses parting the Red Sea, I was told that **faith** parted the Sea. It is only fear that can keep us from love, from faith, and from marching ahead on that journey where love and faith will inevitably lead. I was told in an early morning meditation on October 24, 2010:

You live in God-time. God-time is nonlinear, nonsequential. It is where miracles take place. God-time exists for everyone at all times. God-time exists within you as a field of ultimate possibilities. Be not afraid to use this—to operate within this field. Take a leap of faith into ultimate and unlimited possibilities. Tarry not for this is the path to your best end.

The problem is people give up too soon. The lesson of faith is intertwined with everything. That is why sometimes things don't happen right away. Faith is not a separate thing. It is intertwined in everything. Visualize what you want, and hold this vision of faith. These things will be reflected back to you in God's hands.

You are being told there are no certainties on this journey except your love for God. Let that guide you…If you want God to catch you, you have to be willing to fall into His hands. The paradox is that when you do that, you hold the earth in your hands.

CHAPTER 5

Unity with God and How Ego Gets In the Way

The absence of the ego allows you to recognize your unity with the Divine and with one another. What you do to others, you do to yourself. In the unified state, you are at peace.

- Holy Spirit, Spring 2011

Unify Yourself with God

Unity with the ineffable Source is a state that already exists and is just waiting for our recognition. Many of us have forgotten this because we nurture feelings of separation from Source energy and from one another. Separation from one's Source leads to a life dominated by the ego, and the ego perpetuates a state of separateness until we have forgotten our unity. I had forgotten enough, or maybe never really knew of my unity with God, to be surprised when Jesus said to me *I am in you and you are in me.* He taught me that there is no separation between him and me, between you and me, between you and God. We are the Unmanifest, manifested for all to see. God said to me: *What is unity but to be one with God. When My children are one with Me, they will be one with each other. For truly if you are one with Me, you cannot be anything but one with each other.* On another occasion, as I did energy work on Linda, God said: *...And it is God's love that flows through you, and it flows through me and makes us one. It's that thread that unifies and joins us with all humanity. It is that thread that has been lost.*

Start by unifying yourself with God; unification with others will follow. Know that you are not arrogant to recognize your unity with God. You must recognize your unity with **humility**. You don't need to live in a shack and shed your designer clothes to be humble. Conversely, a life of asceticism does not guarantee humility. If you truly understand what it means to be unified with God, there will never be a question of your being arrogant because God is humble. If you are not humble, then you must continue to work on your unity with the Divine.

I was doing Reiki on Linda when I heard Spirit say: *Who do you want to be? Do you want to be Linda or do you want to be one with God?* Next, I saw Linda's personal will being aligned with God's will. The only things that can shut down that direct pathway from God to Linda are her mind and her fear. This alignment had to be done in God-time. Any earlier and as Spirit explained, Linda's mind and fear would have chosen not to accept it. Next, I was shown, in a vision, how women in Biblical times would burn an herb, such as sage, above the solar plexus to help people release their fear, allowing it to rise up with the smoke. At the end of this ceremony I heard Spirit say to Linda: *Trust God.* Later that same day, during a healing session with Kim, I heard God say: *First step is thinking. Second step is thinking with your heart. Third step is not thinking at all. Align yourself with God's will and surrender. You only give yourself to Me a little bit, and then you wonder why you fall, but it is because you didn't give yourself fully.*[18]

Many of the messages I share with you in this book, I received by sitting alone in meditation, quieting my mind so that I could hear the Divine clearly. There are others that would not have come had I not been doing energy work with Linda, Kim or a client. Yet others came by following someone's trusted advice to do things I would never have done on my own, like going to sit in an empty church. I can only take the credit for showing up and listening. We are subtly, and sometimes not so subtly, interdependent. Isaac Newton said, "If I have seen further, it is only because I am standing on the shoulders of giants." Our accomplishments and our lessons are bound with those of everyone around us because we are all one. God tells us so, but our egos would have us believe otherwise.

Our ego allows, in fact insists, that we distinguish ourselves from others. It makes us **separate**. It disassociates us from all others and sometimes from ourselves. It is this state of separateness that leads people to act harshly toward themselves and others. While doing Reiki with Linda I heard: *There is no healthy portion of the ego. (The idea that we would) need to call on "ego" in certain situations assumes that divine nature is incapable of handling all situations. This is a false assumption. Intellect does not equal ego.* St. Thérèse of Lisieux and St. Teresa of Avila appeared to me while I meditated and said: *Disburse the seeds of the ego so that they may never rejoin to form the whole (ego) again.* Since our ego seems to be a constant companion, we must at a minimum, turn it from our master into our servant. Then, when we are ready, we can *disburse the seeds*.

Ego as an Obstacle to Inner Peace and Unity

Have you ever berated yourself for not performing in a way you thought you should, either in a meeting, on a test, or—fill in the blanks. We have all done this more times than we care to remember. I am asking that you now take a moment to recall one of these instances. Next recall how that self-recrimination made you **feel**. Did it bring you inner peace? It is difficult to attain peace in our households if we don't have peace within ourselves. If it is so hard to be kind to ourselves, where our ego thoughts are contained within our own body, and if it is so hard to be kind within our families through acts as simple as forgiveness, compassion and love, then it is not hard to imagine how difficult it is for us to have peace globally. Global peace starts with inner peace.

It is the ego that allows one to engage in self-recrimination and non-forgiveness. The ego is causing you to judge yourself against whatever yardstick you choose. Your ego separates you from everyone and everything, making you either less than or greater than the yardstick you happen to be focused on at any given moment. For those who are completely unaware that there exists any other part of them, say their spirit or their unity with God, or have not engaged in a serious meditation practice, the ego-defined self becomes their whole reality. Such people identify so strongly with their ego and all it holds dear that to simply disagree with them in a conversation can lead them to an emotionally or physically violent outburst. It is the ego that allows us to hold so dearly to an opinion that the opinion becomes a part of who we are. It does this so well that anyone who disagrees with us can be seen as threatening our very existence. This is obviously an extreme example, but we have all experienced some level of disagreement that creates inner, as well as outer turmoil. It is our ego that creates the turmoil by allowing us to see ourselves as separate from our Source and from one another. We then use disagreements as further proof that we are separate. This cannot be resolved until we stop judging ourselves.

Recognize the Divine in yourself, and become one with God. Recognize the Divine in the "other" and know that his or her divinity is the same divinity that resides in you and that makes you one with each other. John of Ruysbroeck, a 13th century mystic said, "The image of God is found essentially and personally in all mankind. Each possesses it whole, entire and undivided, and all together not more than one alone. In this way we are all one, intimately united in our eternal image, which is the image of God and the source in us of all our life." Once we have the correct sense of our Self, the ego will have no power over us. Until then, the ego *defines the self because the self doesn't fully recognize the Self.*

Disarming the ego does not mean that you should become a doormat or a victim to abusive people or situations. There will be times when a firm "No!" either verbally or energetically, may be required. It is the energy behind the words that will make the difference. If you are responding with a "no" from the ego, as in "no, how dare you..." then you are likely to generate a negative counterforce. If, on the other hand, your "no" comes from unconditional love of yourself, without judgment of the other person, you are likely to diffuse the situation. It is imperative that, in this process, we recognize the Divine in ourselves and in everyone else.

It is important to listen and act on your intuitive insights, which, in the absence of judgment, I consider to be discernment. Discernment is when you see a person and feel or think he or she is not safe and then act on that feeling. That feeling could be based on something you saw or sensed, which then prompts you to take appropriate action by removing yourself from the situation. Discernment keeps you safe. Discernment turns into judgment when those thoughts go to the next level and you start making, well, judgments about the person. For example, you might start making a generalization about all people of a particular culture, or religion. The list is endless.

Back in the Day

Before I started this inner spiritual work, I never thought much about the concept of unity. I wanted to distinguish myself in every way. The last thing I wanted to think about was that I was one with the average girl or guy next door. In the world I was familiar with, there was no merit in being average. We like to know that we are more creative than, more popular than, more successful than, and smarter than the next person. We fail to recognize the role of the ego in this drama. We don't realize that the ego is at the root of much of our inner turmoil and the resulting lack of inner peace. We conclude that inner peace comes with the next promotion, raise or well-earned vacation. We even have a subset of the travel industry that has emerged around "wellness vacations."

Reading *A Course in Miracles* got me thinking about the relationship between unity, the ego and inner peace. Maybe there was a way to attain an inner peace that endured past my vacation. Maybe there was a way for inner peace to become a part of my life, regardless of what I was doing. I read and meditated on the subject. On one such occasion I closed my eyes and saw myself traveling at warp speed through my own interior castle, to the center of my soul, where Jesus stood and my deceased grandfather said, "See, this is how easy it is to get to the seventh chamber."[19] At that moment, I became one with Jesus, St. Teresa of Avila and St. Thérèse of Lisieux. And there I stayed in the center of my soul. What I saw as "me" then became a swirling ball of plasma, which as it swirled became the swirling cosmos. Back and forth, I transformed between "me" as plasma and "me" as the universe; the microcosm became the macrocosm and visa versa. Next, I was shown a vision of how we, as humans, often see ourselves: we see our "self" as our physical body and mind, and then we see our divine Self as an ethereal outermost layer or, worse yet, we see our divinity as an entity completely detached from our self. Instead, I was shown that we should view what we think of, primarily, as our body and mind as unified with the Divine, making our body and mind sacred. The ego self should then be viewed in the outer layers. This is the first step in releasing the ego.

We have lost the knowledge that our body and mind are sacred. *We have lost our connection between our humanity and our divinity…As you recapture the magic of being Divine and human at the same time, you are recapturing it for many people. It is magic, not in a mysterious way, but in a beautiful marriage of the earthly and spiritual. It is not about heaven on earth; it is about heaven as earth and earth as heaven. Heaven and earth, the material and the Divine Essence are joined in the creation of Love. Earth and the physical (plane) is Love made tangible. Everything that is created when you bring the physical and material aspects of earth and the Divine together is Love. When a person is created it is the material aspect of the earth with the Divine Spark. Humans are the marriage of the material energy of the earth and God's Love. A baby is not just a series of bio-chemical reactions building upon one another. There is something else going on and that is the Divine Spark. You are given a window into this marriage of the Divine with the material world every time a child is born … It is up to humans, married to the Divine at all times…If you don't instill in the child the nature of its Divine Spark it will never be as powerful as it can be. Jesus showed us what the marriage of the Divine Spark and the human looked like…you have to be fully grounded in the human and fully transcendent in the divine magic…*

Our physical form is how God chose to manifest, making us sacred beings. In meditation I heard: *God married His divine nature to our humanity so that we would live in love, peace and joy. We are meant to fully accept both our humanity and our divinity. We are not meant to deny either aspect of ourselves. Allow this marriage within you, and you will experience the love, peace and joy God intends for you.*

John of God Calls

For me, the ego was, and still is, a tough nut to crack. However, once I started down this road of unwinding it and began to benefit from those rare moments of peace that came in its absence, I was hooked. I was determined to release myself from my ego's grasp, and although I was not planning to do so, I went to see John of God for help. It wasn't I who initiated the trip, it was John of God himself—and I wasn't at all pleased. While in meditation on April 23, 2008, John of God's face appeared to me, as clear as day, and he said, "Come work with me."

John of God (JOG) is a healer and medium who has a healing center in Abadiania, Brazil. I knew of JOG through my Reiki Master teacher, Heather Cumming. He has since become more well known through Oprah's television and magazine segments on him. Heather is one of the official translators for JOG and leads trips to see him at the Casa de Dom Inácio de Loyola in Brazil. She is also the co-author of *John of God: The Brazilian Healer Who's Touched the Lives of Millions.* After receiving the message from JOG, I checked Heather's website (www.healingquests.com) only to find that there were no trips scheduled for July, which would have been the only time I could go. I then wrote to Heather asking her to let me know if she happened to add a July trip. Her assistant wrote back saying to call Heather, which I had no intention of doing because, guidance notwithstanding, I really didn't want to go. I get lost easily, so the thought of traveling alone terrifies me. In addition, I am not enamored with travel destinations for which I am required to get vaccinated. But as God would have it, business brought me face-to-face with Heather shortly after that email exchange. She asked about my interest in seeing John of God and mentioned that she would be in Brazil, leading a trip for one other woman on July 14—the only date I was available to go. I guessed that meant John of God was going to get his way.

When I asked Jesus what I should request from John of God, He said: *Tell him you want to be closer to God.* Are you kidding? I have to fly all the way to Brazil to tell a healer that I want to be closer to God? I didn't even know I wanted to be closer to

God. Why did I feel compelled to follow the guidance? What is it that possessed me to follow the words of a disincarnated face that appeared to me in the middle of a meditation, and then to follow the words of Jesus who has not been here for over 2000 years? It made no sense, especially when the instructions pushed me past all my comfort zones. Yet, there is a part of me that no matter how much my rational mind protests, will always do what God asks. And so it was that, once again, I found myself heading into the unknown.

Even though it wasn't in the instructions I'd received from Jesus, I asked the Entities of the Casa[20] to heal my migraines and a few other ailments (which is yet more evidence that I need to rid myself of ego-based thinking). It seems that I couldn't just stick to the plan Jesus designed for me. I had a better one in mind. Knowing this is a problem of mine, I also asked the Entities to replace my ego thoughts with the thoughts of the Holy Spirit. Although I wasn't sure who the Holy Spirit was, I thought it might help since it was a remedy suggested in *A Course in Miracles*. In the span of my first seven days at John of God's Casa, I'd transformed from some-one who could not bear waiting on the two-hour line at the TAM airline terminal (and all the inefficiencies which that implied—a little judgment issue I have) to a person who, after meditating for seven hours, went to sit overlooking the country-side. Now that, in and of itself, is a miracle. It was amazing that, by the seventh day, I had this heretofore unnatural ability to just sit in silence. I had no inclination to read or do anything—not even judge. I was content to sit in complete peace, with an empty mind.

During my visit to JOG, I did get closer to God, first, by ceasing all activity that distracts me from God, and second, by grace. As Jesus knew, and I was to discover, to be closer to God implies releasing your ego thoughts because it is those thoughts that would separate you from Him and from the rest of His children. I was able to hold onto this ego-free state for quite a long time after returning home, but then the ego started to creep back in. It was as if, from an ego perspective, I reverted back to a time many years before any of this ego work was even on my radar. I didn't under-stand why I was unable to regain that ego-free state, so I asked in meditation to go back to the seed point of the most recent ego resurgence. What was revealed to me was that I had re-called my ego self because I equated my ego with my personality. I thought that without an ego I would not have a personality (not that mine is so great, but it seemed at the time that having none would be worse). Linda and I have talked about this, wondering if in the ego-free state one just sits and gazes into the distance. Come to think of it, that is what I did in Brazil, but I don't have that luxury back home, and my guess is, neither do you. If we are to be Everyday Mystics, we need to figure out how to be ego-free and take care of our kids, husbands, wives, relatives, pets and jobs. Life is not going to wait for us while we are gazing at our navels. And no one will want to engage us, nor will we be able to engage another, if we are sitting starry-eyed looking into the distance. We have to engage in and with society.

The meditation helped me to regain my ego-free state. I saw that there was nothing else I had "to do" to keep the ego at bay, except to live in love—to live in the light of Christ consciousness because in that state, the ego cannot exist. I am no longer afraid of losing my personality. I will simply **be**. I will **be**, beyond the definition naturally implied or imposed on me by a personality or ego. I will simply have a new personality, if you will—one of peace and joy. Oh, and by the way, in that state, most of my old friends wouldn't recognize me. I will continue to grow, but I will set my intention for my lessons to come solely through Love. I am done with learning through pain. I see that, in my case, pain arises from my ego because my ego is fearful of annihilation. In Love there is no fear, so therefore in Love, there is no ego. If there is no ego, then there can be no pain. I am choosing LOVE.

In meditation, I was shown that, immersed in the feeling of Love, I am in the metaphorical Garden of Eden. Once I succumb to the ego, I eject myself from the Garden. In the Garden, we have everything we need—Love, Joy and Peace. When we think we need more, and we take the proverbial apple, we take ourselves out of the Garden. The Garden of Eden is always waiting. All we have to do is walk in. And if, right now, you are thinking that you could use more than the Garden has to offer, maybe a fancy car or a vacation, then look a little deeper and know that underneath every acquisition, after your survival needs are met, you are looking to attain Peace, Joy and Love.

Dying to Yourself

I had a situation in which I was working on a client who I'll call Dave, when I felt the presence and power of Jesus within me more strongly than ever before. There were no messages and no visions, except at the very end of the session, when Jesus said: *There are no words. There is only love.* I asked Dave what he felt, and he said he felt absolutely nothing. I felt awful. I told him I'd meditate on the session and ask for enlightenment on why we had such completely different experiences. The first thing Jesus said to me was: *Let go of the need to know why. There was very deep heal-ing done on Dave today. My ways are mysterious. My ways are not your ways.* I guess for the benefit of my client, Jesus then explained why Dave felt nothing: *He set up expectations of what this session would feel like and when he didn't feel what he was expecting, he didn't remain open to another possibility. It would have felt like dying—like losing one's body and joining exclusively with me. It is the loss of self. He wanted to feel the (energy) current in his body as he usually does. He did not want to feel "no body" or the absence of body.* To Dave, Jesus said: *You are dying to the self and being born in me. You must be willing to die to yourself to join me. You could have at any moment given into the experience, instead you waited for what you expected.* I had another client after Dave but before I received the above clarification. She said that during her session, she felt like she died and went to heaven.

For me, it was getting difficult to work in this new way where *there are no words. There is only love.* I had enough of an ego left that I still needed to see evidence of results, whether in my healing work or for the *Global Peace Movement.*[21] It was my ego that needed proof that I was having an impact, especially on my clients. Leave it to my ego to think it had a role in healing, other than to show up and be available for God's grace to flow through me. My need for results was just another way for my ego self to get recognition.

The ego, as St. Thérèse once told me, is insidious. While doing Reiki on Linda, I heard St. Thérèse say: *Ah, the monkey stays on the monkey's back. The monkey is the ego. Get the monkey off your back. The ego is like a drug. Resist every urge to let it engage—complete abstinence is the way. Each time you feel it rise within, fight it back—do not give into temptation. Just like an alcoholic, there is no such thing as "just this once." Just this once starts the whole cycle all over again. Run. Run away. Restrain from all, even the smallest temptation to engage it.*

*The ego creates blocks to unconditional love and blocks complete unity with your Father, Jesus Christ. Doubt me not. Release the ego, and see how quickly you realize complete unity with Christ. With this follows complete unity with one another. If you don't believe me, try it, and see if it is not true. For there is no truth greater than that of unity, and only the **humble** arrive. The choice is yours.*

Do my work, dear ones. Do the work of Christ. The road to egoless living is narrow, but once you cross the dividing line, you will see it is smooth and easy to travel. (In this vision I could see that the road of the ego is wide but full of rocks, difficult to travel, but its breadth deceives us.) *Come off that road you have traveled so long. It is one thin line that divides my road from yours. You are one step, one thought, one breath away. Cross that line, and never look back my dear ones. Unity is the answer. All your questions disappear into the One. Be at **One**.*

I was learning about unity with God through my Reiki practice. I would have times when I could **feel** that unity. More importantly, I felt a shift from realizing my unity with Jesus to doing what Jesus asked me to do. For me, Jesus is a teacher and a role model. Jesus healed and Jesus was who he was because he was the embodiment of Divine consciousness. My shift from Christ consciousness to God consciousness was very powerful. At this point in my work, I was able to see myself as "me," but as completely one with God consciousness. God consciousness is implicit in Christ consciousness because what Christ knew is that he was one with his "Father" in heaven. On August 31, 2010, while I was doing Reiki on a client, I felt that I was "me" but also that I was an empty vessel with no thought of my own. I felt as though all of my boundaries had disappeared and there was indescribable, vast space within me. There was no interference with the flow of God's energy. I was completely unified with the energy I call God. I was told, while sitting in silence, that God is Love. He is the energy of Love. He is the active version of Love that exists everywhere. He is the ineffable. He is not easily definable, and as I have already explained, although I use the masculine form, God is certainly not the white-bearded man on the ceiling of the Sistine Chapel.

God Looks Like You

In meditation on June 14, 2010, I was told: *There is one God, and He or She has many different faces. What He or She looks like is you. You are God made manifest. Close your eyes and invite yourself to recognize your own God essence.*

We needed Jesus to show us what God made manifest looks like, and He looks like us; He is us. As I heard while working on Linda: *…and there is God. He needs no fancy palace. He needs only your heart and an open door to let him in.* Letting God in sets you on a path toward unity. To become one with God and follow His every command, you must surrender your will to the will of God. Doing so makes you God in the **same** way that Jesus is considered God. Jesus was fully surrendered to God's will. He showed us, by example, how a divine being exists in this world. In the un-surrendered state, we are not one with God and therefore we are not God.

We must surrender our own will to be in perfect unity with God. I realize this is easier said than done.

In meditation I heard God speak these words (The "I" refers to God): *Tell them I am God, no matter what they call Me. They can call Me "tree," but I will still be God. It doesn't matter how they reach Me, as long as they reach Me. They can get to Me through a tree.* In meditation several years later, I was shown a vision of a river. I could see individual souls floating down rivers all over the world into the nearest ocean and, although we call them by different names, all of the oceans on the planet are one. Just as a river runs to the ocean, each soul is on its journey back to the ocean that is God. And just like the waters of the earth, The Unmanifest, God, is present in and around each of us, simultaneously. We can activate that Unmanifest energy simply by recognizing it. The Unmanifest is one with us. It is in me and in you, simultaneously.

If you can, visualize each person as a different colored colander floating on the ocean. As colanders, the water is easily visible in us and around us. Each colander may be a different color and shape but what we contain, our essence, is all the same. It is the same in life; but in life, we cannot clearly see that the essence (the water if you will) that flows through each of us, is the same and has the same Source. If we focus only on the container and all of its trappings, we lose our sense of unity. Try not to see only the illusory separation—the outer shell and how we choose to color it. Remember what is **inside** the shell. It is our essence, which is one with the Creator of the essence—and so it is that we are one with each other.

I was told that we are all aspects of God. If that is true then we all need to come together to form the whole so that we can give God back to Himself. We don't need to physically join together, but we do need to come together through love, for it is the glue that binds us.

Being One With Christ

Grandma, who when she was alive was fearful of almost everything, passed away in the spring of 2006. She came to me in a vision shortly after she passed, saying this about heaven:[22] "It is glorious!" She was giddy. There was a sense that what she was experiencing was wonderful and unexpected. "Everything makes sense here. I see now that I never had to suffer—I never had to fear. It was the fear that caused the suffering, but I am free from that now. I want to tell you all to look inside yourselves for peace. Be one with your Divinity, and you will be as free as I am now. There is no need to wait for the change you call death. This death of the body is a new beginning for the soul. A state in which we can remember how grand and perfect our life is. There are no mistakes in the Divine plan. Be patient with yourselves as you walk the earth. You can make no wrong choices.

"You can only **perceive** your choices to be wrong. Every path will lead you to God. I am in the God consciousness now…Oh, it is so glorious! I had nothing to fear. (Again, I saw Grandma downright giddy, beside herself with the joy of discovering what she sees and feels. It is hard to explain, she is like a child who discovers that Santa Claus is real after years of doubt.) Oh, I can't tell you enough to let go of your fears. There is nothing wrong—everything is as it should be—I see it clearly from here. I am much larger than you will remember me. My spirit is enormous, yet I saw myself as small (when I was alive). I did not know the glory that was me while I walked among you. I beg you, please, know the glory that is "you" while you remain on earth—do not wait for the change called death. Manifest your Divinity now—you need not wait. Let it shine. Let God's light shine forth from you. Let it emanate from every cell of your body. Let it sing from your lips. Let it look through your eyes. Let it come through your touch. God means for us to live like this. I'll say it again—we don't have to wait! Recognize that you are not a separate entity from God. You are the Divine made manifest. Walk your journey with this knowledge. Perceive everyone in your life as a teacher; perceive every experience as part of a Divine plan and be at peace."

When Grandma finished, Jesus spoke: *And in me they will dwell. Know that they (my grandparents) are well taken care of in heaven. They are one with the God consciousness. Amen.*

On another occasion, I heard these words from Spirit for the benefit of my Reiki client: *Christ is alive in you; you need to remember that. He's alive in you in all his glory. You must walk with that confidence. That's the kind of confidence … it's like confidence and humility at the same time. It's a natural combination when it comes from Christ—when that confidence comes from Christ. And it's in that knowing that he's in you, that gives you that co-creative power…Because God can create, and so can you because you are one with God.*

That is the travesty of religion. It is that it has hidden that truth not only from you but from all of God's children. What God can do, you can do— just do it with love. When you know your unity with God, the love comes naturally. There is never any danger in what you create when you create with God.

Priests were the first ones to abuse the creative power, which is why they recognized the danger. They saw the danger in themselves—that is what has scared priests through the centuries. Throughout history priests were so hungry for power, they thought everybody would be hungry for power; and they didn't want to give up theirs—so they hid the truth. They hid the co-creative power for so long that they lost the knowledge of it. It's time to reclaim the truth for yourself. Just live it in your own life. Start living it. The best you can do is start living that truth of your co-creative power with God in the knowledge that not everybody is hungry for power. You are hungry to know your union with God and to know all that's rightfully yours that comes from that union. And what's rightfully yours is the ability to create…Go in the knowledge of your unity with God, and there will be nothing you cannot do. Always ask for the humility to carry it out.

…Don't regret time lost because the grounding of the humility is very important as the foundation for that power to come. For that power can only rest on a very solid foundation of humility. Without that foundation of humility … you become afraid to use it like the priests of the past. They worked in fear. Only the humble can survive this power. Only the humble become co-creative forces with God and are not afraid to share that. So don't be afraid to let your light shine, and don't be afraid of the power that's yours…of being unified with God…

…that is what is meant by "the meek shall inherit the earth." Because it's the meek… or humble—it's the humble who will inherit the earth because it's the humble people that will finally recognize their co-creative power with God. Don't forget this … This is a very important lesson for you and for everybody. Don't say no to God. Accept His invitation to be His co-creator.

Tell Him now what you want … in doing so you are going to be co-creating what you say. The difference is that now not only are you asking, but you are allowing it to come in. It's like making a cake. It's like you do your part, and then you put it in the oven, and you allow it to bake—you allow it rise. That's God's part. You've set your inten- tion as the co-creator with God, and then you have to give it to Him so that you allow your creation to bake. If you keep opening the oven door, it is not going to bake. You just have to trust God, just like you trust the oven to bake your cake. Trust that God is doing his part.

Judgment: The Great Separator

Back in 2005, I sat through a service at a Spiritualist Church and all I could think as I listened to the minister was, "Why do they let crackpots (and yes, I understand that you may think I am a crackpot) like this preach?" I definitely wanted to feel separate and superior to this guy. At the end of the service, he channeled messages for the attendees. He zeroed in on me saying he saw a female figure standing behind me with this message: "I never looked at what was right. I only looked at what was wrong. Even when you were a child, I could only see that you were getting dirty; but it was all right. You are looking at what is wrong around you. Change that." Alrighty then. Either the minister could read the look of incredulity on my face or my deceased grandmother, the other one, who was prone to condemnation, was there passing on a valuable lesson. I am now grateful to my friend for taking me to the service and to the anonymous woman who wrote down the message the minister delivered to me. Who writes down messages for people they don't know? I guess that was the Universe shouting at me to stop judging because, as I now know, when I judge, I separate myself not only from God but also from His other children.

I heard this message from Spirit while working on a client: *What you say or do is not the cause of the reaction in another. Reaction is completely the domain of the person reacting.* What I like about this message is that, in addition to the obvious, it teaches us to take responsibility for our own reactions. My reaction to the minister was not because of his inadequacies as a preacher. His style or words stirred something in me. I am responsible for my reaction, not him. I am sure he stirred some sense of inferiority in me. Diane Berke of One Spirit Learning Alliance gave me an effective exercise for such cases. When you come across someone whose behavior irritates you say, "I am also that." I have found that using that phrase in situations like this can bring me peace. It helps me to see myself in the other person. It helps me to see our unity, even when I don't want to. I usually find that, once admitted, I can laugh at myself, and then work to change those behaviors that no longer serve me.

Unfortunately, messages on judgment never seem to be out of style. Many years later, I was still receiving such messages on behalf of clients and, by proxy, myself.

The most powerful message I received on the topic was when Spirit said: *When you judge you are so condemned. You are not made to carry the weight of that judgment.* Since hearing it, I have spent many days and nights repeating the message to myself until I **felt** it in my very bones. The first test was at a family gathering where, because I did not carry the energy of judgment, no judging words were heard from any of my family members. If your family is like the families I know, you will have plenty of opportunities to test this for yourself and realize what a miracle it is.

On another occasion Spirit asked me to deliver this message to my client: *Not judging yourself is the same as loving yourself unconditionally. That is what unconditional love means—no matter what, you love yourself and that is how God loves you...There is no judgment that resides in your heart. Judgment comes from your ego. Your mind has become a slave to the ego. Let your mind work for your heart; let it be entrained with the vibration of your heart. The heart only knows love for yourself and love for others. You want your mind to walk, to march, in lockstep behind your heart, and in that way you will see the world the way God sees the world. When you are looking at the world through your ego, you are looking at the world through the lenses that have been defined by others...Your heart is so powerful that it knows only love. Your heart knows not of judgment or condemnation. Let your heart lead the way...Until you have compassion for yourself, no one can have compassion for you...Have mercy on yourself. As you judge yourself, you judge others. As you judge others, you judge yourself. These are universal truths...Don't put limits on your Love; God has put no limits on his Love for you.*

Aligned With God's Will, the Ego Becomes Obsolete

If you are in complete alignment with the Divine, do you really think that there will ever be a situation in which you say, "Stand back God, this situation is too big for You. My ego and I will take it from here." When looked at from that perspective, it is absurd to think that there is a situation that God can't handle. When you are in alignment with God's will, 24/7, you do not need to depend on your ego. You must let go of your ego and allow God's grace to flow through you to handle every situation that arises. It is up to you to trust God as much as you now trust your ego. And know that it is only through practice that you will begin to learn what is God-aligned action and what is your own. This is the hard part. It is just like learning to ride a bike—you won't learn by reading about it. You learn by getting on the bike and falling off, as you try time and again to find your balance, that one point at which you can stay upright, pedal and move forward without falling. It is the same with taking action aligned with God's will. You have to work on finding your balance point, which is your alignment with God. No one can do it for you. Develop a spiritual practice and practice, practice, practice and then practice some more.

Some people will tell you that they know what God's will looks like. Is it to accept everything that comes your way without standing up for what is right? Is it to say, "Is that so?" to all forms of injustice and then walk away? Your views will be formed by your own spiritual beliefs. There are many great people that can guide you including Jesus, Buddha, the Dalai Lama, Gandhi, Mother Teresa, Dr. Martin Luther King, as well as great books like and *The Bhagavad Gita*. In my own experience, God oftentimes guides me to take action, but characteristic of all of His guidance, it has love at its core. It always stems from love for myself and love for the other. It sometimes involves standing firm in my position but never involves demeaning another and has never involved harming another. The greatest gift you can give to yourself in working with God is to let go of your expectation as to what His solution will look like.

Here is an example of how God intervened in a situation in my home. It may seem mundane, but quite frankly, that is the point of this book. We need to find God in the every day because that is how we live, day by day. Eight years ago, I had a drainage system installed along the interior perimeter of my basement to catch water and funnel it to a sump pump. Subsequent to that installation, water would accumulate on a portion of the basement floor every time we had a heavy rain. I assumed that the company (let's call them Company A) who'd installed the drainage system did the best they could, given the age of my house. More recently, after hurricane Irene, we had work done by another drainage company (Company B) on what I thought was an unrelated issue. Company B discovered the cause of the water problem I'd been experiencing over the past eight years. As it turns out Company A, to install their perimeter drains, had jack hammered through an existing underground drainage pipe that carried water from an outdoor drain, under my basement floor, to a dry well on the opposite side of my house. They then laid their perimeter drain right inside the cast iron pipe they'd jack hammered open; so it would have been very obvious to them that they cut open an existing drain pipe.

Thankfully, Company B photographed what they'd found before they pulled out Company A's perimeter drain and repaired the broken cast iron pipe. We would no longer have water accumulating in our basement during a heavy rain, but the removal of the perimeter drain caused Company A's system to be completely ineffective. It needed to be reinstalled without cutting through the newly repaired cast iron pipe, so I called Company A to explain the situation.

After putting me on hold for an interminable amount of time, Company A wanted to schedule me for sometime in the next three weeks, at which time they would send out a "technician" whom I am sure would have had no authority to do anything. For eight years I'd assumed they'd done their job well; therefore, I had lived with a water problem that was actually caused by their installation. I listened to a prerecorded loop, while on hold, which told me that the company was number one in customer service. Given that reputation, I asked for the president's email address who, I reasoned, would want to see what his company's installers had done. I was told he didn't have an email address. Really? The head of a company in 2012, ranked number one in customer service, in one of the wealthiest suburbs in the United States of America, didn't have an email address? I lost my calm. I would not let the attendant off the phone until he put me in touch with someone who could actually understand the enormity of the company's negligence, and then rectify it. I stayed on the phone until I was directed to the customer service manager and the president's secretary. After seeing the photo, the customer service manager admitted to the mistake and arranged for the entire drainage system to be replaced at no cost to me.

I am sure they thought I was a bit extreme not letting them off the phone and, at the time, I thought it was my ego that had saved the day. Reflecting back on the incident a few months later, I realized that this had been an outrage I could feel in my heart. My heart actually hurt as I spoke to these people, and at points in the conversation, I had to hold back tears; whereas, the outrage of old, the ego sort, would have been seething with anger saying, "How dare you do this to me..." Instead, I felt that God had been guiding the whole process. He had provided me with the evidence I needed via the photograph, and then it was up to me to take action. The next step I took needed to be in alignment with His will. Was it to sit back and say, "Is that so?" and live with a very expensive but now, completely ineffective perimeter drain for another eight years? Was it for me to call Company A and wait three weeks for a technician, with no authority, to come and look at the problem? Or was it to do what I did with love in my heart for myself, stay firm in my belief that it was a miracle that I had a photo of Company A's misdeed, prior to the pipe being fixed by Company B, and hold to the belief that Company A would want to do what was right and rectify this gross negligence.

It is hard to know the mind of God, and so it is hard to know God's will. Nonetheless, we all have to try our best to align ourselves with it because what we do know is that our egos have gotten us into nothing but trouble. To align ourselves, we must be in constant contact with the Divine. At first this will feel awkward, but it will become so natural that you will not even realize you are doing it. It will be like getting on a bicycle after you've been riding it for years. You won't even need to think about it. In the interim, constantly ask yourself if your actions are aligned with love.

I asked myself why I didn't question Company A about the water coming into my house, following their installation eight years ago. I did assume it was due to some quirkiness of my 100-year old house, but in the final analysis, there was no good reason not to have questioned what was happening—and it didn't have to be my ego that questioned it. In fact, maybe it was my ego that decided not to question it. Maybe I should have meditated on this eight years ago instead of just assuming (a clear ego move) that Company A did all they could and that I had to live with the water.

Overcoming the Ego with Love

As the Universe would have it, lessons in the ego and how it continues to separate one from inner peace abound; but airports are not places I am usually looking to test my ability to overcome separateness. However, I am also not one to miss an opportunity to test a concept that resonates with me. And so it was that on a flight to Miami I came to test the theories put forth by Marci Shimoff in *Love for No Reason*. I put the book down and decided to love everyone on the airplane for no reason—not something I am inclined to do when focusing solely on their outer shell, so I closed my eyes. What I saw and felt was overwhelming. In my mind's eye, I was able to see the energy of everyone on the plane, and it was the energy of love. The overwhelming beauty caused me to weep. This is the state that brings me inner peace. It is a state where my ego is not in charge of my thoughts, feelings, actions or words. When my ego gets out of control, I remind myself that I am not those **things** that the ego identifies with; I am merely an observer and peace reigns within me. When peace is within me, I am in a position to offer peace to the world. In a state of inner peace, I realize that I am happy to be just another person who embodies unconditional love at all times and in all situations. I don't need to do anything with it.

While Kim and I did energy work on Linda, I heard: *Christ consciousness is a step most must go through on their way to recognizing God consciousness. Jesus pointed us in this direction. He tried to explain and show us our divine unity, but we refused to listen. And now you must know that the consciousness that makes you Divine is so much more powerful than you ever imagined…You can co-create. He is pointing the way to God consciousness. You too reside within the Consciousness. Never doubt your place in this eternal landscape. You must know that you are wrapped in the arms of Love. So where you go, Love goes.*

Find Heaven In a Rose

On August 7, 2012, God gave this message to me to deliver to my client: *Heaven is in a rose* (I was shown a vision of a red rose). *Look upon the rose until you see heaven. I am in the shadow and in the light. Look upon **everything*** (rocks, animals, people, etc.) *and say, "God what do you see here?" Do that with everything until you can look upon any person and say, "God what do you see here" and He will say, "I see Me."* (And when you look upon that person, you will see yourself, and in so doing you will see your unity with God). *Go in peace and the knowledge that I am in you, with you and around you; and that you are in Me, with Me and around Me. It can be no other way.*

The day this message came, I went out and bought a rose for myself with the intention of doing this exercise twice a day until I saw heaven in the rose. I meditated on it morning and night. I began the meditation with, "God, what do you see here?" and He replied: *I see everything I have asked it to be. The rose does not resist Me. It contains its beginning* (the center was still unfolding) *and its end* (the outer leaves were beginning to age and shrivel at the edges) *at the same time. There is beauty you can only see by beholding the rose, but not by being the rose. Climb from the dark crevasse where the petals cling to each other. Climb up and out, and look upon it as I do, and you will see the beauty that comes from the light and the dark. As you gaze upon the rose, I gaze upon all of you. I see the living and the dying, the old and the young, the light and the dark. I look and I see Me. I am all of those things. I see the galaxies swirling. I see the microcosm of the macrocosm.*

My intent is to do as God instructed with the rose, then with each and every object I come across until I am ready to do it with people. I will do it first with people I love, and then I will look at myself in the mirror until I can see God in me. Then I will look upon those who annoy me, then those who annoy me even more until I can look upon even the worst offenders of society and see God in them too. I am under no delusions that this will be easy. I realize it could take the rest of my life.

CHAPTER 6

Ten Steps to Inner Peace

You do not have to reach for the "ring" of inner peace. It is already there inside you, and with it comes global peace. With inner peace comes peace on earth. Do not shut yourself off from this possibility. Only through you can God's Garden be re-cognized on earth. It is waiting to be rediscovered.

- Mother Mary 2-1-11

This book is for the 99.99 percent of us who are forced to find inner peace while living in the chaos of our daily lives. So if you are looking for a shortcut, I am sorry to say, you will not find it here. Inner peace does not come about simply by sitting cross-legged and "Om-ing." That is good news for those of us without the luxury of jetting off to an ashram for a year or trekking to a mountaintop in Ladakh. In fact, even for those who do trek halfway around the world looking for it, inner peace only comes about with some effort.

It is not that God can't miraculously grace you with deep, inner peace. He can and does. There are those people who one day awaken to see the world through God's eyes. We are told of the profound beauty and peace that they see and feel, but what we often miss is the story of how much work it took to get to that point or how much work it sometimes takes to stay in that state of bliss. They don't tell you that the state of ecstasy or ecstatic union that brings profound inner peace doesn't always last. Don't get me wrong, it can last and change one forever, but in most cases, the enlightenment, that moment of ecstasy, is just the beginning. If we are going the route of inner peace through God, it requires us in no small way to be available to God 24/7 in order to **allow** God's will to be done through us. It requires us to **align** ourselves with His will, to **surrender** the outcome of our actions and to have **faith** in a divine plan.

Allowing God to work through you is a scary thought; to accomplish it, you must realize that it is the divine feminine in each of us that **allows.** In a channeled message, I was told that men and women need to take back the co-creative force of the divine feminine—to embrace the divine feminine and the divine masculine within each of us. It is through the divine feminine that we gain cooperation and veneration for all living things. Later in that meditation, Mother Mary appeared and said: *You do not have to reach for the "ring" of inner peace. It is already there inside you, and with it comes global peace. With inner peace comes peace on earth. Do not shut yourself off from this possibility. Only through you can God's Garden be re-cognized on earth. It is waiting to be rediscovered.*

The words to the *Meditation for World Peace*[23] tell us: *The power of peace lies within. It is a state of being that already exists. It is up to you to see it…*

So the practical question is HOW? How are we to attain that state of inner peace that Mother Mary and God say exists inside each of us? The answer came in the form of ten simple steps, which were channeled to me early one morning. But first I need to explain the concept of being on Team God.

Team God

While doing Reiki on a client, I saw Jesus talking to my client's three sons. It was as if he was giving them advice, pointers or guidance. What followed was an image of them playing a team sport, like soccer. In this metaphor Jesus, if you will, is the coach giving us guidance in the huddle, but when we are on the field, **we** must perform to the best of our ability. We can't stop at each moment and ask what to do next. If the ball comes to us, we are expected to take action.

This image was the perfect metaphor in answer to my own question of how to get clients to understand the balance between **living** their lives and following guidance. It seems that some people get spiritual guidance, and then they spend all of their time mulling over the message and forget to take action. Or they sit back and do nothing because Jesus said such and such was going to happen. As Jesus showed me in the vision, he is there to guide and advise, but once we leave the coach's huddle, we must take action; we must play the game we are in. We must deal with all the unexpected plays from the other team, the fouls, the injuries and whatever else arises.

Certainly, if we have faith and we play the game with a coach like Jesus, anything is possible. However, all the coaching and faith will not get us anything if we are not in the game. Sitting on the sidelines **listening** only gets us so far. Similarly, one does not become a good soccer player just because he has faith in the coach. One becomes a good player by listening to the coach, having faith in him **and putting the guidance into action**. And, most importantly, when the play doesn't go exactly as planned, you are expected to do the best you know how. That's the part some people tend to forget when they start down the "spiritual path." As E. M. Forster says in *A Room With a View*, getting through life is like "a public performance on the violin, in which you must learn the instrument as you go along."

Finding God, or living a spiritual life, means LIVING **and** PLAYING. God gave you LIFE—LIVE IT! God gave you a coach and teammates—count on them! In this vision God said we need our teammates; it is the only way for us to win the game. If we didn't need teammates, then God would have created just one person—but He didn't. He created 7 billion and counting. We are all each other's teammates. We are part of many different teams at the same time. We are members of Team Family, Team Community, Team Country and Team God, which includes everyone. Until we realize that all 7 billion of us are on Team God, we cannot win the game. We are all one. We are all on the same team and we have the greatest coach ever.

As hockey great Wayne Gretzky said, "You miss 100 percent of the shots you don't take." So start playing and taking shots at the goal. You won't make every one, and you are sure to make mistakes, but you will certainly not make a goal sitting on the sidelines, no matter how much you listen to your coach and no matter how much faith you have in Him or him or her.

I then wondered if we can ever be in the game and simultaneously be receiving constant guidance. The answer, of course, is "yes." The next step after learning how to play the game with Jesus (or another enlightened being) as your coach is to learn to access the same guidance that Jesus accesses: God. Once you have found your unity with God, you can have access to a constant stream of Divine intelligence. Some of you may not even need to go through the step of having Jesus as your coach and may already be hooked up to God streaming live. Whatever your method, the goal is to get to God streaming live so that your every thought, word and action is in alignment with God's will. To attain this we must surrender our will to the will of

God and follow the ten steps. Living life in alignment with these principles will help to bring you inner peace.

The Ten Steps to Inner Peace[24]

Step 1: Apply What You Learn

You must incorporate into your life new principles that resonate with you. If the ego work in *A Course in Miracles* speaks to you, start doing it. If principles about living in the present moment speak to you, try them out in your own life—just as you practice riding a bicycle until you are able to do it without thinking. There is an extraordinary life waiting for you right here, right now, in between trips to Walmart or Neiman Marcus. Some people go through a dramatic awakening and consequently leave ordinary life behind. For most of us, however, the awakening is subtler and ongoing in the midst of ordinary life. Tell God you are signing up and then attend the meetings with Him, which are completely up to you to arrange. He is available 24/7. Then **do** what you are told.

Step 2: Remember That A Poor Craftsman Blames His Tools

I received a call from an angry person whom I'll call Carla. Carla was angry because she had been trying to utilize tools, like the ones I describe here, to bring inner peace, a new job and a few other things into her life that were not forthcoming. She had glimpses of inner peace but the states were not long lasting. She asked God to speak to her in very specific ways and she was disappointed when she thought God did not answer. As a result, she was angry with God and angry with everyone who teaches this nonsense. I suspect there are many people who feel the same way.

So, if you are like Carla, you have two choices. First, take God out of the equation. If He is not helping you, forget about Him and help yourself. Second, if you prefer to continue to work with God, examine the following analogy. Pretend I give you a bike and share with you all I know about it. Pretend I even show you how I ride a bike, and then I hold it while you get on. If I let go, and you fall off, is it my fault? Is it the bicycle's fault? Of course not. So why, when you ask God for help, and you don't see the change you are looking for, is it God's fault? Maybe, in answer to your prayer, God gave you the proverbial bike. Maybe, He even gave you some teachers to share what they know about the bikes, which may not be everything, but just enough. Maybe, it is not the fault of the teacher or of the bike but of Carla who hasn't yet learned how to master the bicycle.

The frustrating piece for many people is that unlike learning to ride a bike, learning life lessons can sometimes take years. There will be times when you think you have learned the lesson then you crash. This happens at every level of proficiency. Even professional cyclists crash. When you crash, you must get back up and try again. You don't get angry with the person who introduced you to cycling, and you don't get angry at the bike. Of course, you can choose to do that, but if you do, you will be expending a lot of energy on the anger instead of funneling your energy into rebuilding and practicing, and you will not attain even the slightest degree of inner peace.

Step 3: Listen for God Streaming Live and Jump on His Jet Stream

First, look back at your life and see if you haven't already had God streaming live and that perhaps, like me, you chalked it up to one too many parties in your teens. Write down these experiences. The whole point of the mystical experience is to get you on God's jet stream. Start by listening to, as opposed to talking to God. Ask Him a question while you are waiting to pick up a child from school. Take a few minutes, either at the end or at the beginning of your day, to listen. The difference between you and the mystics is that they **listened** and **acted on** what they heard or saw. This is where you get to stop struggling, resisting and judging, and align yourself with God's will (or if you prefer, the will of your own higher Self). Take a class, read a book, take a walk, set aside a few minutes each day to **listen,** and don't get discouraged. Open your heart and your mind, and when you are ready, increase the time you spend in silence. The coach is there for you.

Sometimes, we need someone else to confirm what we are hearing on God's "live feed." In 2003, while in the midst of one of my many struggles with being able to surrender my will to God's will, in this case, regarding my role as a "healer," I received the following channeled message from internationally acclaimed channel and author of *And Then There was Heaven*, Roland Comtois: *You are meant to be a healer. You have such incredible, intuitive sacred energy that you are going to be using as a tool…as a channel for those who are in need. You will bring peace.* I intuitively knew this to be true and that this was God's will for me, but I was not sure if it was what I wanted for me. In spite of my doubts, I decided to give this "healer" business a try and put the gears into motion.

After acknowledging the healer within me, I decided to see Reiki clients full-time and put what I had learned about energy into practice. I cleared my calendar of non-essential obligations—volunteering was eliminated. Child-care, cooking, homework help, laundry and grocery shopping stayed. I wrote a business plan stating how many clients I would see a week, how much I would charge and how I would give back to the community through Reiki. I even had a marketing plan, timeline included, which I never got to implement. I gave the written plan to God by setting my intention, from deep within my heart, that this would be my path. Before I had a chance to execute my marketing plan, the telephone started ringing with client appointments. I was new to this at the time, so I was still sufficiently surprised to know that this spiritual/surrender stuff really worked! Giving my business plan to God was a momentous act of surrender. I let it go and had faith that if my plan was in alignment with His will, my Reiki practice would be established—and it was. This was a big test and one of my first conscious rides on God's jet stream.

Step 4: Come Out of The Closet

Come out of the closet and tell everyone that you hear, see and feel God. This is not just the realm of saints and mystics who lived thousands of years ago. God is just as available to you now as He was then. And, although emotional, physical or existential breakdowns can lead to a mystical experience, they are not a prerequisite.

God means different things to different people. Call on the spirit or energy with which you are most comfortable. Early in my own journey, I shared with a local priest with whom I did not have a relationship (since I didn't, and still don't, go to church) that I was receiving messages and visions from angels, Jesus and Mother Mary. His only response was to tell me to notice that the messages were coming from those with whom I had some, albeit little, knowledge. I wasn't hearing from Moses or Quan Yin or Buddha or Krishna (although they too would eventually come to me). People ask me what Jesus or Mother Mary look like when they appear to me. They look like what you'd expect, if you were someone raised in a white, middle-class suburb of New York City; they are white with brown hair. The fallacy would be to think that this is how they always appear. Do we think the image of Our Lady of Guadeloupe is not really Mother Mary because she is not white? Of course not. The vastness of the Divine Essence is such that It can show Itself to every culture in a form that will be understood. God has no ego. He will show up in a way you too can understand.

Open the door in your heart to the infinite possibilities that are born of faith in an All Loving Being. Open your mind and your heart to the infinite ways the Divine may be communicating with you. Are you receiving messages through songs on the radio, from serendipitous coincidences, when you are in nature, in a phone call resolving a problem that you receive minutes or seconds after you just finished complaining about something? Start to pay attention to these "coincidences" and don't be afraid to share them with others. If we don't make this commonplace, it never will be. Everyone will continue to think they are the only ones who hear the voice of the Divine or see angels. To hasten humanity's evolution to a higher level of consciousness, you must come out of the closet.

How do you know if you are hearing God's voice? God's voice is always unconditionally loving, compassionate and non-judgmental. It will never be the voice telling you to harm another in any way, shape or form. You will never hear the voice of the Divine, in any of its many forms, telling you someone is a jerk. If you do, you can pretty much assume you are hearing your own thoughts. (More on this under Step 9.)

Step 5: Operate in God-Time

I have learned from Spirit that nothing can be born before its time, and often, we don't know that time until it is upon us, and in some cases, we don't know that time until we are beyond it, looking back. We truly operate in God-time whether we think so or not. The point is you must live your life, but remain open to the miraculous. Remain open to the extraordinary. Remain open to what God, or your higher Self, has to say. Listen as often as you can, and **practice** listening if you can't already do it. You cannot learn from God if you are the one doing the talking. And when you get guidance, you must **act** on it or **be** it in order to effect a change (even if that change — and in fact, most importantly—if that change involves raising your own level of consciousness). According to David Hawkins, M.D., Ph.D. author of *Power vs. Force*, that is the greatest gift you can give to humanity and I will add, to yourself. Listening and acting on God's wishes puts you into God-time because He will tell you what He wants, when He wants to. It will be up to you to act or not act. It will be your choice to step into God-time or to stay on your own schedule.

We are all on different paths but ultimately **we all have the same job: to be love, to extend love and to forgive.** And then, once you get to a level of loving unconditionally, you will see that forgiveness is no longer necessary because it becomes implicit in the act of loving unconditionally. Act now, start your journey or simply recognize that you are already on one. We're all headed in the same direction back to LOVE. As rivers flow to the sea, we are all flowing to Love. You can resist or you can allow your boat to be carried on Love's current. St. John of the Cross said it best:

> And I saw the river
> Over which every soul must pass
> To reach the kingdom of heaven
> And the name of the river was suffering—
> And I saw the boat
> Which carries the souls across the river
> And the name of the boat was love.

Set sail on this river and let the current carry you to the kingdom of heaven, which is Love. You need not suffer if you do not resist the current. Jesus told me: *People suffer because they think they have to suffer.* Jesus taught me that acceptance alleviates all suffering. Once you step foot in the boat of Love, you will be operating in God-time. Be patient as the boat navigates the river of life carrying you through each event at just the right moment. It's all about participating in the process so that the grace of God may help you in His time. You will have the rudder, so it is still incumbent upon you to listen and act on your divine guidance to stay in God-time. God-time is truly miraculous.

Step 6: Recognize That There Has Never Been So Much Love

I heard God and Mother Mary together say: *Give your pain and suffering to God by accepting His will. Never, ever believe that you are alone, because you are not.* God continued saying, *Ask that God's Love infuse all of you and give you the strength and power you need to persevere because what is true is that there has never been so much love on the planet at one time, and that makes all of us stronger. We are able to cope with the lessons that this life brings us. This is now a time that humanity truly has the ability to transcend to higher levels of consciousness, to higher levels of love, and you are an important part of that—everybody has a part. But know that your own healing is entangled with the accomplishment of those goals. You are not alone, nor is your journey for the benefit of only you. None of us are on a journey that is solely for our own benefit. You are all tied to My universal plan, the achievement of which will be a life of unconditional love above all, for all, by all of us. Go now and hope and pray for the salvation of everyone because never has there been such an opportunity for Divine Love to prevail.*

Step 7: Love and Forgive

When I was in high school, I wanted to be an architect. Frank Lloyd Wright was my idol, but he was an engineer as well as an architect. And, even before I got started on my path, I reasoned that I could never be a good engineer, so I could never be a good architect. Talk about my inner saboteur archetype—there it was derailing me at the age of 16. My inner saboteur worked overtime most of my life. However, when I read *A Course in Miracles* my inner saboteur must have been sleeping.

I learned much from *A Course in Miracles* but the two things that stuck with me were the principles of **Unconditional Love** and **Forgiveness**. At least from the author's point of view, it seemed that if we could love unconditionally and forgive all those who trespass against us then we would be doing what Jesus asked of us. I couldn't be a great engineer and architect like Wright, but I could try to live by these guidelines. I have no idea why I thought this would be easier than becoming an engineer. I don't know why my inner saboteur didn't show up here—maybe because the goal was too esoteric—and maybe because there was no predefined path that my saboteur could attack.

The guidelines made sense to me, at first, only on a personal level but then much later in my life, on a global level. I reasoned that if I could learn to love unconditionally and forgive, that my life would be more peaceful and satisfying. I later realized that if I could be more peaceful, I could bring more peace to those around me. I was being exposed to this idea of unconditional love and forgiveness for the first time, and like all things I learn that I think can benefit me, I had to give them a try. They are of no use to me if they just become talking points in conversation. I needed to get on the bike and see if I could ride. Well, I fell off a lot and I continue to fall off. I have found that loving unconditionally and forgiving are life-long pursuits. But God in His infinite wisdom continues to give me opportunities to learn how to ride that bicycle of unconditional love and forgiveness. He continues to give me opportunities in my personal life, and as with all of us, opportunities in the global arena.

Never has there been so much love on the planet, and never has there been a need for even more unconditional love and forgiveness. We have nothing to lose and everything to gain by trying to live by these principles. If even one ounce of you resonates with these two principles, then you have to put them to the test—start practicing them now and be prepared to fall off the bicycle and to get bruised a few times. Judging by my own experience, I can tell you it is worth the bruises, the hurts and the embarrassment. Eventually, you will learn to fall less and one day you will be able to ride for miles, days, weeks and even years without incident. I haven't personally gotten up to "years," but I am optimistic.

If we could each get to the point where we could love **ourselves** unconditionally, then we would love each other unconditionally. This would make forgiveness implicit.

Step 8: Learn to Love Yourself

In meditation I saw that I was locking a piece of myself in a closet that we use to hold dirty laundry (you don't need to be Freud to figure this one out). I saw that God wanted me to love every part of myself as He loves me, so I reluctantly unlocked the closet and took that part of myself into my heart. I was surprised to see and feel that there was an inordinate amount of room in my heart for that part of myself. I took her in without an agenda. I took her in simply to love her. With all that "room" in my heart, I realized I had plenty of space to love even society's worst offenders, so I took them into my heart as well and surrounded them with unconditional love. I have read about unconditional love, and I especially like Paul Ferrini's *Love Without Conditions*. However, reading about unconditional love and experiencing it are two different things. I saw after that meditation that until I loved every piece of myself, even that piece I had unknowingly locked away, I couldn't love others unconditionally. Once I loved even the less desirable aspects of myself unconditionally, I had so much room in my heart to love those aspects of others.

I learned late in my journey to love myself as I am. Loving myself doesn't mean I won't continue to work on improving myself, but what it does mean is that I accept the starting point as being who I am now, the good and the bad. Until this time, I had wasted energy resisting the aspects of me that I thought needed improvement. By loving myself as I am, I have more energy left to propel myself further along the path of love and healing. When we don't love ourselves, it is because we are falling prey to our ego-minds. Our ego-minds will ruthlessly judge ourselves, and when that happens we are bound to fall short. In a message I received from Jesus, he said: *When you judge, you are so condemned. You are not made to carry the weight of that judgment.* I see now that the changes I make must start with me. As Jesus said to me: *The new world order starts from within. It is an internal revolution.* My inability to love another unconditionally came from my inability to love myself unconditionally.

Since the macrocosm reflects the microcosm, we must heal ourselves before we can heal our family relationships and before we can heal the world.

Step 9: Listen and Act When God Speaks

I was on the phone with someone, whom I'll call Ernest, who was complaining about how miserable he was at work and how he never has enough money to pay the rent. Not seconds after he hung up, a friend of mine called saying that her elderly father-in-law, a darling man whom I knew, needed a live-in companion. He required someone to be with him just in case he fell, but he was otherwise healthy and self-supporting. The companion would get free room and get paid for his time. Furthermore, the job and home were in the same town in which Ernest lived. This is how God works. He answered all of Ernest's concerns: he could quit his job, eliminate the rent payment, move to a better part of town, and move into a private home thereby getting rid of the hassles of apartment living. Oh, and he could bring his pets, since the elderly man loved them and had a few of his own. Needless to say, I called Ernest back in a hurry saying that the perfect solution had presented itself. He declined.

Don't be like Ernest who, when God answered, said, "No thank you. I've got problems, and that is not the solution I am looking for." It's like the joke about the man stranded in the ocean who turns away three lifeboats saying, "No thanks, God will save me." When he arrives in heaven, incredulous at his own death, he asks God why He didn't save him. God responds that He sent three lifeboats, all of which the man turned away. Pay attention! As was the case with Ernest, and the man in the joke, you too are receiving Divine solutions. Set aside your ego, along with the notion that you know how the problem needs to be solved. We would find God sending help if only we would open to the infinite possibilities of how and when. We must stop asking for guidance or help by telling God, or the Universe, what the answer should look like. Do what you can, and at the same time, allow for the helping hand of the Divine. Whoever said the solution was either up to us **or** up to God? Why can't it be both the Divine and us **together?**

At one time in our history, we thought that everything was outside of our control and that our fate was in the hands of the gods. Then came the Age of Reason, when we learned about our own power to alter our circumstances. Now it is time for the pendulum to swing back to center so that we can partner our body and mind with Spiritual intelligence. It does not need to be, and it shouldn't be either our mind **or** God. This is a time in our history of integration. *Spiritual intelligence is what links... intellectual intelligence to the Divine. When your intellect is open to the Divine, there is more compassion in everything you do—compassion for yourself and more compassion for others. It is the rebranding of "no child left behind." No child left behind is really NO ONE left behind. When you have spiritual intelligence, you have **no one** left behind.*

Quantum science points back at us, telling us that **we** have the power to create and to alter an event based solely on our observation or participation in it. It's a dance we do together with the Divine, not alone. It is time to reunite with a higher source. Jesus said to me: *This is the Age of Light. This is the Age where the Light of the heart and the Light of the soul shine brighter than the Light of the mind.*

After writing the above entry, I came across this passage in *The Bhagavad Gita*. "*The Lord Spoke*: O sinless one, twofold is the path which I have declared of old. The path of Understanding is for the meditative; the path of Action is for the active. No man can attain freedom from action by abstaining from actions, nor can he become adept in understanding by mere casting-off of actions. For no man ever, even for a moment, rests without action; everyone is compelled to do work by the Moods born of Nature."

So, how do we know when we are being presented with Divine guidance? Simple. As the example of Ernest illustrates, it will be a win-win solution. This does not mean that everyone gets what he or she wants. It does, however, mean that everyone will get what is for his or her greatest good. And, as I've said, in my experience, God doesn't ever seem to guide people to yell at someone or physically harm another person, or worse. Another test to distinguish between your thoughts and Divine guidance is this: a thought forms in your brain; Divine guidance is something your brain becomes aware of; it is very clearly from a Source outside of you. You will learn how to distinguish between the two with practice, but in the meantime, know that **Divine guidance always boils down to one thing...LOVE**. As Jesus told me: *(life) is so simple. It is all about love.*

How do you know you are hearing Divine guidance, and you are not simply crazy? Here are some clues: You will struggle less and laugh more. You will fear less and love more. The world will become a friendlier and less threatening place to you. It will ultimately reflect back to you who you have become. The world around you will be filled with love, peace and joy. What do you have to lose by trying?

You are not crazy to feel God's presence, and you are not crazy to feel your unity with others and with the earth. You are simply recognizing your divinity and recognizing the power of Love. We may never become as holy or have the same number of divine experiences as someone who devotes his or her life to God, but we can indeed experience the extraordinary in our quite ordinary lives. We too can hear, see and feel the Divine. We will just do it while meditating a few minutes in our cars while we wait to pick up a child at school, or when we watch a sunset, or in between loads of laundry, or in the time we set aside after a long day at work. Why do you think it is okay for a monk in a monastery, a nun in a convent, or a guru in an ashram to have a mystical experience, but not you? Do you think they are more worthy or special than you are in some way? They are not. They are you and me but on a different career path.

Step 10: Practice, Practice, Practice

Much later in my career, after my Reiki Master training ended, I invited the other three women in my class to exchange Reiki with me on a weekly basis to practice what we had learned. This rather self-serving beginning ended up yielding one of the most important friendships in my life, along with the development of, what has now become, a consistent weekly Reiki exchange since 2003. The point is that if we want spiritual teachings to change our lives, we must **practice** what we are taught. Our lives are not going to change by listening to someone else's story, or even by learning what they practice, unless we take the pieces that resonate with us and put them into **practice**. My spiritual life, and Linda's, grew tremendously as a result of practicing our energy work every week.

Practice is hard work and takes commitment, but, then again, so does anything you want to get good at. Read the books, go to seminars, but when your life doesn't improve, ask yourself what you have done with the knowledge. How many hours have you spent honing your spiritual muscles? Knowledge, whether from books or seminars, doesn't change you. **You** change you. If you want inner peace, you must practice those things that bring you peace. Spirit said to me: *Look inside yourselves for peace. Be one with your Divinity, and you will be free. Recognize that you are not a separate entity from God. You are the Divine made manifest. Walk your journey with this knowledge.*

PART II:
BIRTHING A NEW WORLD

The new world order starts from within. It is an internal revolution.In the new world order you are ruled by your soul not by your mind.

- Jesus 12-30-06

CHAPTER 7

The Reluctant Activist

Touch the world—because it needs it, and you can.

- Roland Comtois 1-28-10

I received a message from Jesus to create a newsletter called "Birthing a New World Order." I asked if a newsletter was the right vehicle for delivering his messages and Jesus answered: *The newsletter is one vehicle but not the only one. You need practice getting your ideas out there.* The first topic for the newsletter had already come to me, but I was hesitant to release it. As someone who thinks the mail is an invasion of her privacy, I was concerned that I'd be bothering the Reiki students who were on my mailing list with unsolicited information. What if they didn't like it? What if they thought I was crazy? OMG, what a nitwit God had chosen to do His work. When Jesus said I needed practice getting my ideas out there, he was right. It was not only my ideas I was afraid of putting out there, but also, to the extent that my ideas could be identified with me, I was afraid of putting myself out there. Many years later I read *The Boy Who Met Jesus: Segatashya of Kibeho* by Immaculee Ilibagiza. In it, Segatashya travels across Africa to deliver Jesus' messages. I couldn't even distribute his messages in a newsletter.

I eventually obeyed Jesus' request and from that was born my first duty as a reluctant activist. I gave birth to a newsletter not so aptly named, "Birthing a New World Order." I say not so aptly named because I wasn't aware, until nearly five years after its release that New World Order (NWO) more commonly refers to the emergence of a totalitarian, one-world government. The new world order Jesus referred to has nothing to do with NWO. Jesus explained his version of a New World Order this way: *The new world order starts from within. It is an internal revolution. In the new world order, you are ruled by your soul not by your mind.*

With all due respect to Jesus, I dropped "Order" from the end of his message because I am certain that Jesus has nothing to do with the conspiracy theory of world domination as it is used by NWO. The message I received, which became the basis for my first newsletter, had to do with our endless conflicts over non-renewable sources of energy, especially oil: *...we have an unlimited supply (of energy) within ourselves. What if instead (of searching for oil) we spent more time developing the use of our divine potential? We could move mountains without bulldozers. We could keep ourselves warm without heat. We could keep ourselves cool without refrigeration. We have unlimited potential—we should not be chasing a limited resource. Although oil can be converted into energy, it is not the ultimate source. We are. We contain all we need within ourselves. Instead of drilling for oil, we should drill down deep to tap our own reservoir, which is bottomless. Power comes from love not dominance. The energy to create that power comes from within. It is our gift.*

God knows that, in spite of hearing Jesus' voice so clearly, I needed proof that the above message was, in fact, correct. Through His grace, that proof came one summer day while I was waiting for my daughter to finish work. Being early, I decided to meditate. I sat in my parked, standard transmission car, in the sun, with the windows open, the gearshift in neutral and the ignition off. Deep into the meditation the car jolted forward, held back only by the emergency brake. I turned around to see if anyone had backed into me, but there was no one in sight. I am convinced that the higher vibration of my meditation generated the energy that caused the car to lunge forward. Trust, as I now do, that you have all the energy you need within. Your own energy is very powerful and can likely propel you to wherever you need to go.

The Power of Intention

It is our **intention** that helps us to create the world around us. We alone have the ability to create from the inexhaustible source of our Divine energy. We have the ability to bring peace and joy to a suffering planet. Set your intention every day and trust that you will create what you intend. Since we create both good and bad, it is critical to be of pure heart and mind.

If you are dubious that one person can make a difference in the world, consider the results of the International Peace Project in the Middle East, as presented in *The Divine Matrix* by Gregg Braden. "During the Israeli-Lebanese war of the early 1980's, practitioners were trained in precise techniques of Transcendental

Meditation to create peace in their bodies, rather than simply thinking about it in their minds or praying for it to occur." On specific days and at specific times, these people were stationed in and amongst the high-tension areas of the Middle East to meditate on peace. During these periods, "…terrorist incidents, crimes against people, emergency room visits, and traffic accidents all declined…" From this study, scientists were able to calculate that "the minimum number of people required to jump-start a change in consciousness is the square root of 1 percent of the population." This means that in a world of 7 billion people we need approximately 8,367 to make a shift. This may be why "…so many wisdom traditions emphasize the importance of the individual to the whole." Our actions play an integral part in the manifestation of both inner peace and, by extension, world peace.[25]

After reading about the above experiment, I felt I needed to do something to help people to participate in this movement to embody peace and love. The problem, as I saw it, was that most people are intimidated by the thought of meditation. Who can blame them, given all the different techniques and training required. One solution that came to me was to produce a guided meditation that was accessible to beginners and experts alike. I quieted my mind and listened to what God had to say. The words to the meditation came streaming in almost faster than I could capture them. I was hearing the words and seeing the visions at the same time. It was all so clear and so simple. If a few people could make a difference in the Middle East, then imagine the impact of tens of thousands of people in a stadium, simultaneously practicing the *Meditation for World Peace* before a concert or a sporting event.

Birthing a new world is not the provenance of a few special or chosen people, and fortunately, it does not always require activism or marching on Washington, D.C. It requires that each of us set our intention, every day, to live in a world that is filled with Love, Peace and Joy. Try it. Every morning upon awakening or in the evening before going to sleep say, "I choose to live in a world that is filled with Love, Peace and Joy," adding or modifying as you see fit. Phrase all statements in the affirmative. Try not to tell the Universe how it should be done because it is likely that the Universe has ways to do this about which you cannot even conceive. Trust that the Universe's wisdom is infinite and Divine. After setting your intention, trust that your intention will manifest in Divine right order. Ask your friends and family to participate—there is power in numbers. There is no downside potential to this, and there are no losers. *In the new world everyone wins—it is no longer a zero-sum game.*

We have the power to reduce violence and to tip the world toward love; that power is locked in our hearts until we decide to unleash it. *The Meditation for World Peace* is one simple way to participate in creating a more peaceful world.[26] Its power lies in the words, which were given to me by the Divine, and the music, which was divinely inspired.

Channeled Text to *Meditation for World Peace* (I, My and Me refer to the Divine)

The power of peace lies within. It is a state of being that already exists. It is up to you to see it and as you see it, you project it into or onto the world. The current world is the projection of the global hologram—it is the world that people think it must be, even though they'd like to have it otherwise. It is up to you to see it anew. Envision the world as it can be—as it is under the blanket of scarcity and fear that you have lain upon it. The state of peace and unconditional love of all, for all, is already there. Pull back the blanket. Uncover the world as I know it—as I see it. See with My eyes. See the beauty—the love—the peace and the joy. Live in this world. Project your perception out into this room—into this city, state, country and world. You alone have the power to create the world you are now seeing.

Do you see people shaking hands, enemies embracing, lovers hand in hand? Do you see races, religions, ethnicities coming together in love and peace? Do you feel the joy? Do you see a world without borders where there are resources aplenty? Walk with Me in this world. You are not limited by space or time, so walk freely around the earth. Look in every corner, and see what you have manifested. See this new earth. You are the givers of birth to a new world order. You are manifesting the world anew, in My image.

The world doesn't reach this point on its own. It gets there through you. You are what makes the world complete. Your projection of love makes it whole in love. You have come back to a time before time, where there is harmony, peace and joy, where no one is better or worse than the next, where we exist as one. And so as one heals, we all heal. As one loves, we all love. As one experiences joy we all experience joy. Peace happens for us all, or for no one; but it must start with you—with your vision, which cannot leave anyone out. It comes from the deepest recesses of your heart and soul. It is the dream of the creation that you live anew. Embrace your power to create the world in My image, for it is through you that My world comes to fruition.

See the spinning earth and the love vibrations that emanate into the cosmos. For as you see peace on earth, you also bring peace to the entire universe. May you be blessed to live the life you are now manifesting, in a world that reflects back to you unconditional love, peace and joy.

May peace reign upon you. Namaste.

Going Global

I managed to get over my fear of invading my clients' privacy and published my first newsletter. I also managed to produce, by the grace of God and the generous help of my cousin and his band members, the *Meditation for World Peace*. I say by the grace of God because it just so happened that after I set my intention to create the Meditation CD, I ran into my cousin Rich who casually mentioned that he had a recording studio. Bingo—God's grace in action. I was thrilled to have the CD and to offer the Meditations at my home, inviting our Reiki clients and friends.

Several months later, sitting in deep meditation in a private session guided by Dr. Jude Currivan, I heard the following message from Spirit: *This is what you are meant to do.* The words came along with a vision in which I was with many people. I saw them as me, and all of us as Divine. This is how people heal, through the recognition of their divinity, and the time is now.

After receiving this message, I felt it was time for me to give Martha Hamilton-Snyder a call to do a reading for me. Linda had told me about Martha, a spiritual intuitive and channel, whose reading for Linda, years earlier, had proved to be highly accurate. In her readings, Martha's spirit guides connect with her client's spirit guides to deliver messages and answer questions. I had a lot of questions.

Here is an excerpt from Martha's reading regarding my purpose in this lifetime:

For you dear one, the path ahead is indeed one of being the light and allowing the Light of Christ to Flow through you. Being at one with the Light of Pure Love within you is central and is all that matters in your life.

There will come a time, when millions around the earth desire to be fully attuned to the Christ energy, and at that time you will participate, as will others, in serving as a living channel for this energy to transmit to large numbers of people. It is important that those such as you remain willing to be the beacons of light because the world can only be transformed when this light is strong enough to illuminate all that is not true that people have been given to believe. It is only through this light that the transformation from a world of dark and fear, into a world of illumination and peace, can be accomplished. What greater mission would you desire?

Prior to contacting Martha, I had gone to see Roland Comtois. I would typically see Roland once a year, asking what the divine realm had to say to me. In one of those sessions, he had provided specific direction about the more public path that it seemed I was being guided toward. Roland told me that my Reiki practice was slowing down to give me more time to reflect. He said that it was time to take the *Meditation for World Peace* to the global community to touch the people of the world. Being quite practical, I asked how I was to do this as a suburban mom. Roland explained that I was to build a website so that people could listen to the *Meditation* from all over the world. I was also instructed to conduct monthly *Meditations for World Peace* that extended beyond my circle of friends and Reiki students. Apparently I was at a crossroads.

Maybe Roland was on to something. I had an experience during a pedicure (nail salons are yet another venue for the in the life of an Everyday Mystic) that confirmed the power contained in channeled words and, therefore, the potential impact of the *Meditation for World Peace*. I had nothing to read, or more accurately, to distract me during my pedicure, so I closed my eyes to meditate. Andrew Harvey in his book, *Son of Man*, talks about imagining Jesus with you as you say The Lord's Prayer. So I chose to do that as the pedicurist began her work. I immediately saw Jesus and then tried to inconspicuously lay my hands on the chair's armrests. Jesus told me to put my hands in prayer position, so I folded them on my lap. He said, *No!* And I saw, in the vision he shared with me, that he wanted my fingers extended with the tips touching—so I did that. I kept my hands down low, still not wanting to be seen. Jesus asked me if I was embarrassed—of course I was. There were four women sitting to my left along with a pedicurist working on each of them, but Jesus insisted that I raise my hands to my chin in prayer position, and I relented. I closed my eyes before I could see if anyone was watching. So positioned, Jesus began to silently say the Our Father with me. When we got to the third sentence, "Hallowed be thy name," Jesus explained to me that it meant: *God's name has a powerful energy. It has the power to transform us when said with reverence.* I had never understood what that meant, and I have been saying this prayer since I was five years old. And at age 53, I was finally taught the meaning of those four little words. I never got to finish the prayer as, after the lesson, Jesus told me that I was done. I guess he figured that was a large enough lesson for a nail salon and that I had had enough humiliation for one day.

Humiliation aside, once it was over, I found no one was looking anyway. Everyone was absorbed either in a magazine or the television. Could you imagine if everyone, instead of flipping through a magazine or watching television, was meditating, praying or having a mystical experience, even one as simple as the one I'd just had? I had 20 minutes in a nail salon. I didn't have a mountaintop in Bhutan or Nepal. You would be surprised at how many five, ten or 20-minute slots we have available to us during the day if we choose to use them to connect with our higher Selves or with the Divine. Can you imagine the energy that would be created by a row of five of us meditating during our pedicures? How about a train full of meditating commuters? Start to imagine these things. As Einstein said, "Imagination is everything, it is a preview of life's coming attractions."

God doesn't ask that each of us sit on a mountaintop and chant. Some will be asked to devote their lives to silence or to God, but most of us are asked to live life. We have children, husbands, wives, friends, lovers, pets, ex-husbands, ex-wives and ex-lovers. It gets complicated out here. We are asked to love God and to love life. We are not meant to just be ordinary and to leave the mystical to those with a special calling. Abandon all your senses at the nail salon, and go to a place where you meet with God alone and listen to Him. When you are there, it doesn't matter what is going on around you. You do not need candles and incense burning. You don't need music playing. It is nice to have those things, and if you need them to get started, use them. But once you get the hang of it, know that you can connect with God anywhere, anytime. He is never too busy. He is always ready for you. And please note that the mystical experience doesn't have to be something profound for the benefit of the world. It could be something that is just for you, like what Jesus taught me. Oh, and if you are not familiar with meditating or it sounds or feels too foreign for your taste, then use contemplative prayer, where you say a line of a prayer that you know and then become silent.

And, lest you start jumping to conclusions here, let me explain that I get maybe three pedicures a year—it is not something I spend a lot of time on. However, if you happen to be someone who gets weekly manicures or pedicures, even better—start a trend at your nail salon!

Roland and I had a follow-up meeting during which he laid out a plan for me. He received a message that I am one of the global practitioners. He said: *This is big—very big. Do you understand what I am saying?...This is going to make a HUGE mark on the world.* It was partly about peace and partly about me understanding my role and the truth of who I am. Through this process, I am supposed to find out how the rest of the world sees me and what my role is in the greater plan.

My instructions from Roland were to create a website and that the word GLOBAL was important. He said I should also have a logo and letterhead. I was to start offering the *Meditation for World Peace* at local venues and not to get too caught up in the number of attendees, which turned out to be a good warning since sometimes there were only three people, and other times they were cancelled for lack of interest. I was to go slow but to get going.

A year later, in a channeled message, Roland said to me, *You have a purpose that overwhelms you, but you can do it. The angels are glad you are finally "with the program."* Then, at a group event, Roland gave each person the opportunity to ask a question to which he would respond with an answer from his guides. I asked if I was on the right path and his guides responded, *You're kidding, right?...You need someone to tell you. You need the stamp of approval...It will take you to places... Believe in the power of the words (of the Meditation for World Peace)...Your work is sacred work.* Roland confirmed that I was still holding myself back. I still needed to let go of my resistance to doing this work.

Fools Rush In

Although I was grateful that Roland wanted to help me spread the *Meditation for World Peace* in the local community, I was not so thrilled about the website idea. He said it was an integral part of the process and because I trust his guidance, I pushed past my comfort zone and wrote the text for my website. I then interviewed a number of website designers before finding David Greenberg, at *Success By Design,* who brilliantly designed my site. (When you have time, take a peek at the site by going to http://www.globalpeacemovementnow.com.) David made an otherwise odious process palatable and was very patient with a neophyte like me. He didn't know it, but behind all of my many questions lay my persistent fear of having a presence on the web. I would wake up in the middle of the night, in a sweat at the thought of my photo and my name on the Internet. Maybe it's generational. Maybe it's that I was afraid of the unknown. Who knows, but all I can say is that setting up a Facebook page for my *Global Peace Movement* was even worse. Once again, I was in good hands. Deirdre Corcoran Foote of *Super Dog Social* was wonderful; she held my hand each day, but fear of being "out there" would consume me each night. Again, I worked at pushing past my fear. By now I had learned enough to know I should make decisions from a place of love. If in a state of love I received guidance not to proceed, I would have stopped. But it seemed the only time I wanted to stop was when fear of the unknown kicked in, and I wasn't about to let that be the basis for my decisions.

Privacy is a big issue for me. And just as I was becoming more comfortable with the idea of being on the Internet, Linda received guidance that I should write a book in which I was to share my personal journey and the messages I had received. Of course! This is exactly how God works when He wants me to resolve an "issue." He kept giving me opportunities to learn, and at each juncture, I had the choice to cower in a corner or face my fears. I chose the latter. Roland, as if to confirm the book idea and knowing nothing of Linda's guidance, said in another channeled message: *Record your words...write the book.* Once again I tried to push past the fear. I did everything I could from just plugging away each day, writing one entry at a time, to seeking outside help whenever it appeared.

One such instance occurred after we met Steven Gottlieb of *Energy Empowerment.* Linda and I had invited Steve to speak at a Reiki Master class we were teaching. After hearing him describe The Emotional Freedom Technique (EFT) and how he used it in his practice, I decided to make an appointment for a session. It turned out that Steve was also an intuitive healer. Without any input from me, he identified doubt and loss of privacy as two key issues that were preventing me from moving forward. He "reversed" them using EFT. Today, although I still have doubt, it is significantly less tangible than it was, and the fear over my loss of privacy is much more subtle.

In the midst of grappling with my terror about "going global," I came across this quote: "Fools rush in, the rest of us tremble." I've learned that if I am to overcome my fears, I sometimes have to be the fool. So I created my website, and I wrote the book, which you are now holding in your hands. All I can do is take one step at a time and do what I am asked to do by Jesus—or do what I feel is the right thing at any given time. When I feel stuck, or in need of additional divine guidance, I seek help from the trusted sources I have mentioned.

At some point after creating the *Meditation for World Peace*, the *Global Peace Movement* website and accompanying Facebook page, I read *The Hope: A Guide to Sacred Activism* by Andrew Harvey. Apparently, there was a term for what I was doing. Andrew Harvey called it Sacred Activism and he had a website where he posted links to other Sacred Activists. I thought maybe my *Global Peace Movement* would qualify, so I contacted his office. Sure enough the *Global Peace Movement* was added to Andrew's website under "Sacred Activism, Networks of Grace," which you can access at http://www.instituteforsacredactivism.org/. Who would have figured that someone like me, who walked reluctantly through every step, would turn out to be an activist—sacred or otherwise?

CHAPTER 8

Sacred Activism

...You must be the doer of the deeds but always remember the Source; it is your Lord, God, the Holy Spirit—It is the Holy Spirit that resides in you and gives you guidance...

- St. Thérèse of Lisieux and St. Teresa of Avila 11-26-05

With my youngest child off at college, I treated myself to a weeklong initiation into Sacred Activism with Andrew Harvey: mystic, scholar and author of many acclaimed books. At the end of the workshop, Andrew asked each of us the following question, "If you had three minutes to tell the class about sacred activism, what would it be?" I am sharing my presentation with you here because after I finished it, Andrew asked that I include it in this book. Before I do, however, there are two concepts that were presented in the workshop that will help you to understand the full meaning of my presentation.

The first is the symbolic meaning of the lion. According to Linda Tucker, author of *Mystery of the White Lions: Children of the Sun God,* "The lion is the symbol of the soul essence of humankind." She points to the many references in *The Bible* "equating Christ with the lion...*The Bible* tells us that Christ is of the tribe of Judah. In Genesis, it is explained that the tribe of Judah are the lion people."[27] The second is the concept of the shadow. At the workshop, Diane Berke of One Spirit Leaning Alliance discussed, what she called, the "shadow of humanity." She explained that the shadow is that part of us that we don't know about, that has been hidden from our sight, or that we have banished. In the *Gospel of Thomas,* Jesus says, "If you bring forth what is in you, it will save you. If you do not bring it forward, it will kill you." Berke explained that in order to heal and to see without fear or judgment, we must lose all of our illusions about the world and ourselves.

You will see how this information clarifies the metaphors in the following message, which I received from St. Thérèse of Lisieux well before I knew anything about lions being equated with Christ, or about the shadow. I believe that St. Thérèse uses the panther to represent the shadow of humanity. But as with all sacred texts, which I consider St. Thérèse's words to be, the meaning changes as the reader changes. It is with this foundation in place that I introduced to the class, and re-introduced to myself, the very first message I had ever received from St. Thérèse of Lisieux. She meant it to be shared with all who would listen, and she told me that the symbolism would become clear. She was right—it became clear in Andrew's workshop, almost six years to the day after the original message was received. When you read her message, you will see that St. Thérèse of Lisieux is saying that the shadow and the light, represented by the panther and the lion, will join together for the rebirth of humanity. Life will be *at its beginning and its end at the same time.*

What Is Sacred Activism?

The first time St. Thérèse of Lisieux appeared to me, she said:

Come, little children, into the folds of my garment, and I will protect and nurture you. Peace to all I see, even for an instant.

Peace to the planet, the ants and anthills, the achievers. Peace to all who seek it and to those who don't yet realize they need it. Peace to my brothers and sisters. Let the light of creation rain down upon the hills and valleys, upon the huts of mud and straw, and upon the castles. Men and women rejoice in the second coming for it is already here. Open your eyes and hearts, and you will see. It is through your sight that you manifest its (second coming) brilliance and healing power. Follow the path I have set before you. Lay down your guns and your anger. Oh, beautiful children of God, drink up the rains of peace as they fall upon you from the heavens. Heed My call.

... I drop to my knees and beg of you to follow me. We can't live without it (peace). Leave not this earth without sowing peace in your own backyard. In the second coming, the panther lies with the lion, who lies with the rabbit, and we feed on love. There is no more. Life is at its beginning and its end at the same time. It just is. It is the present moment manifest in all its glory.

I asked, "How does it happen?" and she replied,

Lay down your swords and pick up a broom to sweep away the obstacles to peace— misunderstanding, judgment, and a sense of lacking. You lack nothing. I have provided for you everything you could possibly need. You misallocate and mismanage. There is no lack of anything but understanding and trust in me. My knees bleed I've been on them so long. Please waste time not and spread my word. Amen

She appeared again several months later and said:

There is much work to do. Rest. The lion, the sheep and the rabbit await your call. They are your "army;" you will see how when the time comes. Remember their symbolism. Fear not the lion for his mane deceives you. Take not the rabbit for granted for he is a gentle symbol of rebirth. And the lamb, ah—the lamb, he is but all of you (humanity). Power used wisely will be the rebirth of humanity. Stir them with love (the key ingredient,) and we have "as above, so below." What is "above" is already "below"…my work is done in pairs. You will each have a role, and judge not the roles I assign. One is not lesser nor greater than the other. Do not assign order of importance to what I do, what comes from the heavens. There is no order; there is only the glory of all. We are all one with the Almighty creator of all that is. Jesus was and is a tool for all to see that. You…are also tools in the workshop of the Almighty creator of all that is. He will use you as he sees fit. He does not have one task that is more or less important than another. Jesus' job on earth was no more important than that of every mother taking care of just one child; of every child who manifests himself as just what he is, a child; or every grandparent that pats the head of a grandchild; and on and on. There is no end to the magnificence of each and every person or action. Think not that one is "above" and one is "below." We are all on the same level, of the same importance and glory in the eyes of God, the Almighty creator of all that is. Walk not in darkness—the darkness of ignorance of assigning importance or status to anything in life. It is an illusion. Let go of that tendency, and you will release ego and judgment. It is the way I have chosen for you…Go in the name of the Father, the Son and the Holy Spirit who resides within. Amen

Many Christians and Jews say The Lord's Prayer. In it are the words, "Thy will be done on earth as it is in heaven." I used to think that this was a plea to God for Him to take over things down here and bring heaven to earth. Then it dawned on me that God's will is done **through each of us**. In a story typifying the life of an everyday mystic, I was sitting in my parked car, watching people from all walks of life going in and out of CVS, while my husband was inside at the Minute Clinic getting tested for strep throat. After a half-hour of waiting, I closed my eyes. Something about watching the people coming and going prompted me to ask God to help those in need. I told Him (as if He didn't know) that sometimes it's really hard down here for those without money—and then I dropped into a deep meditation. A loud noise jolted my attention back to the parking lot. All the cars that had been coming and going had disappeared. The parking lot was empty, except for a young man wearing a leather vest, with arms covered in tattoos, walking toward my open car window.

He asked if I could give him some money, followed by a story about running out of gas. I got out of my car to get my handbag, which was in the backseat. As I opened the backdoor, my handbag toppled out, splaying its contents onto the pavement. I bent down to pick up everything and gave him money, naively asking if it was enough. He explained that he needed to buy a gas can too. So I gave him more money, all the while being keenly aware of the possibility that I was being duped, but also aware of the prayer I'd just said.

The young man left and I laughed to myself—I never know how God's "will be done." I easily could have judged this person and turned him away, perhaps interfering with God's will, or perhaps turning away God himself. I realize I didn't solve the nation's poverty problems that day, but maybe God was showing up through this young man and through me to illustrate how His will is done through each of us. I had a choice—to do His will or not. To do it, I had to put aside all my judgments and preconceived notions and not assume that God was going to give this man gas and a gas can so that I could just go back to sunning myself and praying. We have the ability to create heaven on earth by **allowing** God's will to flow through us. We truly are the ones we have been waiting for.

To allow God's will to be done through us, we must first, and most importantly, **align** ourselves with God's will. As we all know too well, many of the worst atrocities have been committed in the name of God. In my experience with God, there is only unconditional love, forgiveness and non-violence. So, when people exclaim that the atrocities they commit are guided by God, know that this statement is a contradiction.

Furthermore, when you ask how God can let these atrocities happen, you are asking the wrong question. The question is, "why is that person not allowing God's will to be done through him or her?" And, by the way, we are all guilty of this at some level. We may not be guilty of atrocities, but there is likely not one of us that can say we have allowed God's will to be done through us 100 percent of the time in our thoughts, words and actions. "God's will be done" starts with you and me. The more frequently we allow God's will to be done through us, the less conflict we will have in the world because God's will is Unconditional Love. When you are feeling and acting in accordance with unconditional love, you are allowing God's will to be done. When all 7 billion of us can do that, we will open up the morning newspaper and find nothing but good news. How fast this happens is up to each of us. And if you don't believe in God, then just let yourself be guided by principles of unconditional love. It is really quite simple.

The simplicity, however, belies the fact that this takes a **committed spiritual practice**. At one extreme is the Dali Lama who commits six hours per day. But this is something you might expect from someone whose job it is to be a spiritual leader. I, on the other hand, have to fit in my spirituality during the course of my ordinary life, which means I try to meditate at least one to two hours a day. If I am seeing clients, several hours more are spent in communion with the Divine. However, life happens and my schedule changes. Sometimes I go for months or years where this works and other times, like now, with my recent move and my hot flashes waking me up seven to eight times a night, I am finding it difficult to meditate more than an hour a day, and sometimes even that is difficult. Whatever your personal threshold, I assure you that to find that alignment with God's will, it will take more than one hour a week attending religious services.

Once you have aligned yourself with God's will, and you know that your activism is what God has chosen for you, you must **surrender** yourself and the outcome to God. God asks you to own the deeds, but you do not own the outcome—that is up to Him. Surrender is the only hope you have of attaining inner peace on your journey as a sacred activist. In fact, it is the only hope you have of attaining inner peace in your life. St. Thérèse of Lisieux and St. Teresa of Avila appeared to me simultaneously while I meditated and had this to say: *Yes, we are talking to you as we have spoken to hundreds and thousands of people already. God chooses who we speak to. The messages belong not to you but to the world. You must share them in all humility for you cannot do our work with an ego intact. Disburse the seeds of the ego so that they may never rejoin to form the whole (ego) again. We own not the words, nor do you. But God does ask you to own the **deeds**. You must be the doer of the deeds, but always remember the Source; it is your Lord, God, the Holy Spirit—It is the Holy Spirit that resides in you and gives you guidance as do we (give you guidance). Fail* *not my child for it would be impossible when you follow our words. Look for our signs everywhere. Amen.*

Lastly, you must have **faith** in a divine plan. Set your intention to accomplish what God has guided you to do, and then have faith that He is working with you. The obstacles may seem insurmountable, but nothing is impossible with God. You will be working in God-time, which is nonlinear, nonsequential and includes the realm of all possibilities. You alone can't turn the world around, but you, together with God, can.

In a heart yoga session led by Karuna Erickson during the Sacred Activism workshop, Jesus said to me, *I am the living God. I am in you. And when my children learn their unity with me, there will be no more darkness.*

Thus, the steps for the sacred activist are to:

- Allow
- Align
- Practice
- Surrender
- Have Faith

Allowing God's will to be done **through** you is the way in which you put the sacred into your activism.

Sacred Activists: Soldiers of Love

One of my concerns with suggesting that everyone can hear God's voice or align with His will is what happens if all 7 billion of us are hearing God and we all hear a different message. Anyone can say he or she hears THE truth; and we have enough of that going around already without me writing a book telling those not yet hearing His voice to join the party. In case we all start hearing different messages, I thought I should ask God whose message(s) will prevail. He answered: *There is only one message and it is LOVE.* This message can be delivered in 7 billion ways, but if it is from God or Jesus, it will always have LOVE at its core—unconditional love of all, for all. I am begging you to give unconditional love a chance. It is all we have left in our arsenal that can work in the short time we have left to elevate the human condition. As St. Thérèse of Lisieux said about love: *There are many ways to save the world, but only one is through God, and it is guided by love—it is love.*

St. Thérèse of Lisieux delivered a message through me that, unbeknownst to me at the time, provided guidance on how to be a sacred activist:

May the peace of God be with you…as you travel the path I set before you. My path is not lined with gold, but it is as surely lined with love and will lead to love. It leads you straight into the arms of my Savior and yours Jesus Christ, where you will reunite with him and the kingdom of his Father. Ah yes, that (He) is a Father! For in His house, you are safe. There is balance. There is peace. There is unconditional love and kindness. When you reside in that house, these qualities become a part of you, and you bring these qualities to the world by being the embodiment of them. That's it. There is no grand plan. There is only a "grand being"—a state of being that is so "grand" it is capable of bringing peace and harmony to the planet. That is what I mean by being a "soldier of love." It is a state of being so elevated that it heals not only in your Reiki room, but it heals everyone in your path, whether you recognize it or not. This is what you are called to do. My soldiers carry no weapons. My soldiers embody love. They know they are one with the Father. They know they reside in the Father's House, which is the source of all that is good. Abide with Him, my dear ones, and know His ways as your own. Become one. Unite, not as men unite with one another to form an army, but unite your spirit with the spirit of my Father, your God, and you will be part of the greatest "army" on earth.

Roland, in yet another vision, saw me *getting ready to expand (my) work…* He said to me in a group session, *…the numbers of people that you will reach are millions! Don't let that overwhelm you. There isn't a doubt in my mind that you have walked the holy grounds. And the reason you walked them was so you could bring the energy back here. And your mission is going to be to tell the story…you're going to help people find the holiness within themselves. You've been summoned to recreate this energy for people to find their way… You have no idea that you are going to reach millions of people exactly at the same moment of time. And the worst thing that could happen now is that you go into a place of fear about that. You're being summoned. You're being asked, and you're being provided for—and you're going to be given everything that you need…You have one purpose and that is to help everyone find their holiness. You have one purpose and that is to (help them) find that something inside themselves. I hear now that they say you're worried because sometimes it is not easy for you* *to get there because of life. But they are making room in your life for this experience to evolve. They are freeing you somehow to get to this place. Hold on. …oh, wow you are so loved. Your voice will be heard by millions…and your heart will be felt by many more…When I saw you here, you were the only person I saw with a white aura.[28]You want to ask me how many times I've seen a white aura? Not many. Not many. It's not a judgment! It's a state of evolution. It's a state of ascension. We're all here to ascend in the physical plane, to grow spiritually, to learn from our life experiences, and take those life experiences and understand the spiritual message behind them and teaching behind them and grow. You have done that and you're doing it … You shouldn't move ANYTHING. You should sit in front of your altar. Do you have an altar? It's time to create one somewhere; a place where you can sit, a place where you can pray, a place where you can be. Don't ask any questions yet because here is the answer to the question…they say that you'll just keep the pace as it is. They say you're already thinking, "How am I going to do this?" You're trying to construct this already, but there is no construction needed…*

Birthing a New World: Sowing the Seeds of Love

In meditation one morning, God told me to write. I hadn't written anything in over a week and didn't have anything to write about, so I made tea and started reading the newspaper. I read about the Arab Spring and that Qaddafi was killed. Bizarrely, I started sobbing. I found Qaddafi deplorable, and even though I find most of the news to be awful, I am not prone to crying as I read it. I was completely broken open and unexpectedly brought to a state of unity with God, during which time I clearly heard His voice, and we had the following conversation:

Me: God, why am I crying?

God: *Because you see what I see.*

Me: What is that?

God: *They are going about it all wrong. The transformation they are looking for will not come about by tearing things down but by building things up—by building bridges of love between all people. This is so easy. All people must do is extend a hand to another, and say "how can I help?" But then they must act. They cannot just ask how they can help. They must help the best they can. The bridges will be built in this way. Theresa, you know that the only thing that will heal is **love**. It is not democracy or autocracy. It is* *anything done with **love**. It is not the form of government. It is what is in the hearts of the people, both in and out of government. Don't cry. Be the Light.*

Me: I don't know **how** to be the Light.

God: *Yes you do.*

So, there I was, starting a very ordinary day and having the extraordinary experience of God at my kitchen table. The tears stopped as I felt a sense of calm wash over me, along with a feeling of complete surrender. I was depleted by what I had just experienced. I don't know how to be the Light, yet God tells me otherwise. I sensed that there was no more to be said. There is no instruction manual. All I can do is take one step at a time as I did today. I had nothing to write when God told me to write that morning, yet this is what He must have intended for me to share. And so it will be with the Light—I will be available and listening so that when He shows me how to be the Light, I will do it. As I write this Bob Marley is singing "... every little thing gonna be all right..."

Months before Qaddafi was killed, I was asked if I felt an urgency for the world to change. Because I know enough to know I don't know anything, I dropped into meditation and asked God. What he shared was that *humanity is at a tipping point, and it is weighted toward Love.* In the vision that accompanied this message, He showed me an old-fashioned seesaw, which was weighted down on the left side by the ego, fear, greed and all else that goes along with ego-dominated living. On the right side was Love. The seesaw was tilting toward the side of Love, and as it did, all that was on the side of ego came tumbling down toward the side of Love. I could see that this transition caused extreme amounts of chaos and turmoil for individuals, and for nations, as the balance of the seesaw shifted. The seesaw came to rest at a point that was not completely weighted on the side of Love but certainly weighted more to that side than toward the side of ego—and it is moving more in that direction all the time. The sense was that there is no urgency. This beautiful unfolding is happening as quickly as we are able to absorb it. For it to happen any faster would be far too painful.

Everything has an incubation period. Nothing can, or should, be born before its time, whether it is a butterfly, a fetus or a new humanity. We are not to rush the birth of anything, including peace. One day, when I asked Jesus what he wanted to deliver through my *Global Peace Movement* Facebook page, he told me to write, *I love the world as it is, as it will be, as it is becoming.* That was hard because, given the state of things, I was afraid people would be incredulous at the phrase, "*I love the world as it is.*" Anyway, I got over my ego hang-up and shared it on Facebook. In fact, humility is the key to doing this work. As Jesus explained it to me while I was sitting in meditation in the empty St. Catherine of Siena church, *Humble Theresa, be humble. Love needs no adornments.*

Every day I ask God, "How can I be of service today?" And most days His reply is: *Love my children.* As you know, that is not always easy. I have prayed for all humanity for many years. But I am not sure if I am loving His children the right way. I used to send love to my children and my family **first**, and then to all of God's other children on earth. Try as I might, I had never been able to put strangers' wellbeing on equal par with that of my children. Then, one day in meditation, after God asked me once again to love His children, I spontaneously saw the entire world coming into my heart on my in-breath as if it were funneled in on an upside down Hershey Kiss. Amazingly, there was unlimited room in my heart to accommodate the whole world. My heart and my stomach burned in extreme pain. I let God guide the process and trusted that He wouldn't leave me in such a state. Once the work was complete and the world was immersed in love, the process reversed and the burning and pain instantly disappeared. There was no negativity left in me on the out-breath because it was my heart, in complete unity with the Divine heart, which took in the world and loved it. God's heart loves the world so much that He loves it and offers it free will at the same time. I have learned with God's help how to be Love. And no, I am not Love all the time. Just like you, I have good days and bad days. Sometimes it is easy to be Love, and sometimes it is not. All I can do is practice and pray every day for God's help.

We all contain within us some level of love and compassion, but with practice, those levels can deepen to levels we never thought possible. Personally, I never thought it was possible to love anyone more than I love my children, whom I love unconditionally. As a result of the internal work I did at the Sacred Activism workshop, I find myself not loving my children less but loving everyone else more—so much more that I can feel myself loving others without condition. I have done this work long enough to know that, with the grace of God, this will be an everlasting change. But even if it wanes, I will be grateful for having had that feeling for even a few days. It brings a state of inner peace like no other. It allows me to be fully functioning in this world while feeling completely united with all of humanity. It did not make me feel like I condoned all atrocities and that all was bliss. It made me feel like I loved all people, not all people's deeds. In meditation, God extended the following invitation to me and therefore to you:

Join with Me to sow the seeds of love.

This got me thinking about the time God asked me to tell everyone *God loves you.* My response was: "Everyone will think I am crazy." God replied, *everyone who speaks the truth is thought to be crazy.* Is it any crazier to speak about love than to speak about war? Why is it that we can speak with impunity about war to resolve conflicts, but the minute we shift to love, and its potential role in healing global conflict, everyone thinks we are crazy? What **is** crazy is that we have never found a better way to resolve conflicts than with wars. What **is** crazy is that we have never tried love. What would have happened if, during the two-year preparation for war following September 11, 2001, all the world's citizens, with all of their compassion for the senseless devastation, directed their love not only to the victims but also to the responsible terrorists organizations? This doesn't mean we condone their actions. What it does mean is that we recognize them as fellow human beings who are in need of a change of heart; the only way to change a person's heart is **through their heart**. The energy of **love** speaks to the heart. So call me crazy because I am suggesting that we try sending love, before sending our sons and daughters, whom we have carefully nurtured and loved, fed and fretted over, whose emotional joys and heartbreaks have become our own, to be slaughtered in battle. If that is crazy, then I am glad to be counted amongst those rare individuals.

Maybe Dr. Martin Luther King, Jr. was right when he said, "Returning hate for hate multiplies hate, adding deeper darkness to a night already devoid of stars. Darkness cannot drive out darkness; only light can do that. Hate cannot drive out hate, only love can do that. Hate multiples hate, violence multiples violence, and toughness multiples toughness in a descending spiral of destruction. So when Jesus says, 'Love your enemies,' he is setting forth a profound and ultimately inescapable admonition. ... The chain reaction of evil—hate begetting hate, wars producing more wars— must be broken, or we shall be plunged into the dark abyss of annihilation."[29] As Dr. King also said, "Love is the only force capable of transforming an enemy into a friend." We all have the power to change the world, one thought, one word, one action at a time, and that time is now.

If you want to be a sacred activist, begin by taking the time to *sow the seeds of love* in your own backyard. Send the following *Sowing Seeds of Love Declaration* to your friends, family and politicians, and ask them to vote "YES for Love" by submitting a response to the *Everyday Mystic* Blog at http://globalpeacemovementnow.com/blog/sow-seeds-of-love/. Share the link on your Facebook page and on any other social media. If I hear from enough of you, I will submit this to Change.org and ask that our message be delivered to all the world's leaders. God said to me: *It takes a lot of love to run the world.*

Global Peace Movement
Sowing Seeds of Love Declaration

We the People of the World, in order to form a more perfect union with each other, insure tranquility and promote the general welfare of our posterity and ourselves, do ordain and establish that:

We will no longer allow our children to be killed, maimed or destroyed to resolve conflicts.

We want our leaders, elected, appointed or self-selected, to find a better way.

We no longer find war an acceptable solution to conflict resolution.

We the people of the world dedicate ourselves to solving all the world's conflicts with Love.

To begin:

We the People declare ourselves free from terrorists.
We send them love.

We the People declare ourselves free from violent criminals.
We send them love.

We the People declare ourselves free of hatred for one another.
We send each other love.

We the People declare ourselves free of inner turmoil.
We send ourselves love.

We the People send love to all those in need regardless of our own religious or non-religious affiliation.

Jesus Was a Sacred Activist

Jesus started this revolution, and it is up to us—those of us who have awakened to the call of Love—to finish it. Jesus told me that this *is an internal revolution.* So, we have no excuses for not allowing ourselves *to be ruled by our soul, not by our mind.* Just this one step, executed by each and every one of us who choose to listen, can shift the world toward love because that is what our soul knows; it knows Love.

Jesus asks that we: ***Be the rain of love that falls down upon the parched earth. There is no element the earth needs more.***

CHAPTER 9

Love: The Key to the Kingdom

When your love for yourself matches God's love for you, you will have achieved the kingdom of heaven within you.

- God 7-4-11

How do we give birth to a new world other than by giving birth to our inner Self? God's last prophet was not born 2,000 years ago. His prophets are all here now, and they are us. I heard Jesus say: *The first mistake of mankind was thinking he* (Jesus) *was special. The second mistake of mankind was forgetting his* (own) *divinity.*

While Jesus spoke these words, he allowed me to **feel** how deep is the chasm between Jesus' message and people's misinterpretation through the millennia. Although words will forever fail to accurately convey the feelings that accompany these messages, I will try to describe them through this simplistic example. Consider that my clients sometimes think I am special or that I have a special gift because of my ability to receive direct revelations. The implication, in spite of the fact that I tell them otherwise, is that they could not do what I am doing. Now, if people are capable of thinking I am even a little bit special, imagine how they would react in the presence of Jesus. They would think that he was extraordinary. They would never believe him when he said that they could do what he did and greater. They would end up worshipping him—holding him up as special, and missing the point about the Divine being inside of each and every one of them. They would misunderstand that what Jesus was showing them, through who he was, was their own Divine Self. In meditation it was revealed to me that when Jesus said you reach God through him, he did not mean for us to take that literally. He meant that we reach God through his **teachings,** through his words and actions—by doing what Jesus taught, not by worshipping Jesus.

I'd love to have talents that are not easily duplicated, like those of Sting or Madonna. But for the majority of us, no matter how hard we try, we will never be that talented. Yet, 2,000 years ago, along came Jesus, one of the few in all of history who said that the amazing things he can do, you **too** can do. This one man, who performed all kinds of miracles, had God streaming live, and above all else, embodied unconditional love and compassion told us, "The works that I do, ye shall do also, and greater works than these shall ye do." As Jesus said to me: *I don't need perfection. I need you—you with your faults.*

I'd like to digress a moment here in case you are wondering about the veracity of the messages I receive. You can be sure that if I were to conjure up messages from Jesus, in my imagination, they'd start out by saying I was special. I'd like to be special in my ability to hear God, but I'm not. I'd like to be special in my ability to align myself with God's will and to let it flow through me, but I'm not. I'd like to be special in my ability to surrender myself to God's will, but I'm not. The point is that in our ability to do these things, to embody the teachings of Christ, to embody the Christ consciousness, **we are either all special or no one is special.** These are not talents, which like a fabulous voice, you either have or do not have, coded in a strand of DNA. Your ability to embody Christ, to find your own divinity, is a part of who you are as a spiritual being.

Join the Revolution

While in meditation, Jesus said to me: *The new world...starts from within. It is an internal revolution. In the new world...you are ruled by your soul, not by your mind...*

We are already a part of this new world by virtue of the fact that we are alive. In that, we do not have a choice. It is our choice, however, to join the revolution—the one Jesus started. This revolution frees us from the bonds of our ego. It gives birth to our divine Self so that we can usher in the Age of Light, which Jesus described to me this way: *This is the Age of Light. This is the Age when the light of the heart and the light of the soul shine brighter than the light of the mind.*

To usher in the Age of Light, we must follow our heart. *Go nowhere your heart doesn't lead you. Always love yourself first because in that action all else follows. You cannot give to another what you don't have. For only firmly rooted in love can you give love. Give love to yourself and you give love to others. Withhold love for yourself and you withhold love from others. Go nowhere where love does not grow...and it will grow everywhere you are if you know first how to love yourself.*

Loving yourself is a key component in recognizing your divinity. It is a message that Jesus has been asking me to deliver to my clients. To one client he said: *Love yourself. It is through self-love that everything else falls into place. No sooner do you love yourself than all the dominoes stand back up in place. For everything that heretofore fell will be righted. Do not underestimate the power of love.*

It does no one any good for you to undervalue yourself. You can only be valued by others as much as you value yourself. So it is incumbent upon you to value yourself as God values you, which is the same as saying to love yourself as God loves you.

The emphasis is on value—value for yourself. So much emphasis in the finance world is placed on valuing an asset, and you are to look at yourself in the same way. You are the asset, and you don't want to undervalue yourself. An asset that is worth unconditional love—that is your value.[30]

I got a message a long time ago about the new currency being love, peace and joy. And if you were to value yourself in the new currency, you would be worth unconditional love, unconditional peace and unconditional joy. And that is how God values you, and that is how others will value you when you value yourself that way. It starts with you. It actually starts with God, but He's already done His piece. He's waiting for you to do yours. And your piece is just to recognize what He already knows. And when you do your piece, everything else falls into place.

So waste time not—in loving yourself. Let it begin now because the world needs you. The world doesn't need you as half a person; it needs you as wholly loved by you. It's like the friendship necklace. A heart you give to your best friend and you have the other half and when you put them together, they fit like the pieces of a puzzle. So here's the deal: It's like God is one half of the friendship necklace, and you are the other half, except you can't fit with his half until you recognize your divinity and love yourself unconditionally. That's the key. That's the key that enables you to fit your piece of the puzzle with His—and then it's perfection. It's like these two pieces come together in this beautiful, bright, divine white light, and this light just shines out in every direction and makes you whole. That is what God is waiting for with each of us. He is waiting for us to recognize ourselves and to love ourselves unconditionally the way He does so that our piece of the puzzle can fit with His, and this divine healing can be born.

Each of us holds the other half of that friendship necklace with God. He wants so badly for us each to recognize ourselves as lovable, as unconditionally lovable, and worth the value of unconditional love, unconditional peace and unconditional joy.

So, the question is, what will you do with your half of the necklace? You are the necklace. You are that half of the necklace. Your whole being—your body, your mind, and your spirit—are half of the necklace but to make it fit you have to love yourself the way God loves you. I don't know how many other ways to say it. It is always the same message for everybody. It's the same message for everybody in the world. For everybody on this planet, it's always the same.

Just live that message, and you won't have to think about anything else. Just focus on that message and do it. Everything else will fall into place. There is nothing else to do. There are no other questions to answer.

At this point in the client's session, Jesus' message ended, and I saw a vision of Mother Teresa. She said she appeared at this point, *because she loved the world so much. She loved even the most unlovable of God's children—at least in the eyes of the physical world. She was here to show the world that they are not unlovable. She, like Jesus, came to show unconditional love.*

She said to my client: *Dear child, you are not the least of God's children. You have been blessed so many times over. Take those blessings and spin them into the gold that is you. God's love knows no boundaries. He is with you always. He resided inside of you. He resides through you, and He resides outside of you. You cannot be separated from His love.*

It came to me shortly after the above session that when Jesus said, "Do unto others as you would have others do unto you," that this was a loaded statement, and not for the obvious reason. Others cannot do unto you what you would not do unto yourself. In other words, if you don't treat yourself with unconditional love, then others cannot, and will not, treat you in an unconditionally loving manner. So, "Do unto others as you would have others do unto you" starts with you doing unto **you** only loving things. It starts with you speaking to yourself with unconditional love, if you want others to speak to you that way. It starts with you treating your body and your psyche with unconditional love if you want to be treated that way by others.

So Much Love

Jesus told me: *There is no world that cannot be saved. The shift to a higher level of consciousness has already begun. Everything you see as a small step is a large energetic step. For each person who attends the Meditation,[31] tens of thousands of angels are in attendance and meditating with us.*

I was shown how, all around us and in us, there exists a beautiful field of Love. *It is an energy that is everywhere, and all we have to do is stop and "look up." Everything is already here. There is nothing we have to do but stop and feel this Love—sense it all around us. It is so simple. People tend to think life is much more complicated than this, but Love is all there is. If we would just recognize this, the world would simply disappear because our lessons would be done. It is all about Love. The field of Love is so beautiful. We need to remember this—what it looks and feels like, so we can help others to know and feel it as well...People need to know what we saw ... that this Love also flows through us—through our veins and through our nervous system. The only thing that prevents us from seeing it or feeling it is our mind. It gets in the way. The last* message I received was: *Nothing exists but that which is in the minds of men—change your mind.* The feeling was that the "nothing" referred to nothing other than Love. The "men" referred to all of humanity.

Clearly, the difference between heaven and earth is **perception**. Yet we tend to get so caught up in *that which is in the minds of men*. We live it and breathe it until it becomes our only reality. We are bombarded by it through every form of media, and since we live in a world in which media is ever present, it is easy to forget what is important. But Jesus continues to remind us: *It's all about love; don't get sidetracked. Focus on the love that exists in each one of you. (It) shines out in all its glory. No explanations are needed. Become the Light. That Light shines in all of my children. By recognizing yours, you are helping them to recognize theirs. Go out into the world with that Light shining forth; that Light should precede you no matter where you go. There is an unlimited amount of energy. This is the bottomless well. There is so much love that exists everywhere. Only fools believe in the power of the darkness, that darkness has more power than love. And when people ask you what energy you are working with, you tell them LOVE—it is the energy of love. That's it. It is easy to understand. And that is what it is. And then they will not be afraid.*

Go with the energy of love in your hearts, and know that is all you will ever need. There is nothing that will protect you more in a battle than love —

Love for your enemy. This is what is meant by turning the other cheek. It is showing them the face of love. Always show them the face of love. This is how they will know that God is in you. So little is known of true love in this world. Yet truly that is all there is. Go now to that place of love that exists in each of you. See it and feel it. This is your center. This is who you are. Remember this and only this as you walk forward into the world. People think they carry the weight of the world on their shoulders, but you know that you carry the world in your hand. When the world is full of love, it is weightless and floats above the palm of your hand. That is how we heal the world— through love.

Who You Judge, God Chooses

As I worked on a client, God once again guided me to simply be Love. I had no idea how this was helping my client, but I had faith in God's instruction, so I obeyed. I stayed fully joined to His Love, trusting that in that space my client would get what she needed for her own healing. In fact, the field of Love that I was a part of was so enormous that I felt many more people were benefiting than just my client—but that was none of my business. I was to focus on being Love, and if God wanted more people to benefit from my being Love, then He would take care of that. At some point during this experience, I had an epiphany, declaring to God, "You put us into the world and asked us to be ministers to each other." I am sure God is up there hitting His head against a wall saying to Himself, "OMG, can she be any slower!" My dim-wittedness not withstanding, at that moment, it seemed so clear that God deliberately placed Jesus **amongst** His people, as one of them, as opposed to cloistering him in a monastery. God asked Jesus to minister to His people from **among** them, just as He is asking each of us today to minister to His people from among them. There is a role for everyone. Some may be called to be ministers, monks or nuns but many more are called to be citizens of the world—to live, eat, sleep and breathe along with the rest of the population. This perhaps is the hardest task of all.

Spirit said to me long ago: *Who you have judged, He has chosen.* The "you" in this sentence refers to each and every one of us who would dare judge who God has chosen to do His work. Who He chooses is not always affiliated with a religious institution and is not always identifiable by a particular dress code. So, don't be surprised if God's servant shows up dressed in rags or in Gucci. It could be either. I beg you to remain open to the infinite possibilities born of faith in a Divine plan, which may not correspond to plans ordained by some religious order. God did not, after all, entrust His plan to the rabbis but to Jesus, an outsider. Jesus did not dress like the rabbis and did not eat with the rabbis. The biggest shift in human thought, and in the human heart, came from outside the system.

Very early on in my Reiki career, I had a client who after her session, which included some powerful emotional healing and direct messages from the Divine, said to me, "I didn't know people **like you** could do this! I didn't think you could be the real deal." She had in her mind what a "healer" should look like, and I didn't fit the description. Certainly, to her, healers could not have worked in finance, they didn't wear the clothes I was wearing, and they didn't live in my neighborhood. At least she was honest in telling me her prejudices and then admitting she was wrong to judge me.

This crucial point in our evolution is no time for preconceived notions of what God is going to look or sound like when He arrives. The arrival you are waiting for is here and it is you. God is waiting to be recognized in each and every one of us. *Who you judge, God chooses* is a powerful message because whom you judge is everyone, including yourself. The message is telling you that God is choosing you too.

Releasing judgment to reach the level of unconditional love will involve some of your hardest lessons. The Universe will put in your life people who are difficult to love. Then it will wait patiently as you struggle with your feelings—not that the Universe wants you to struggle. It wants you to reach a level of consciousness, whereby you can love unconditionally. The struggle is within you. It need not be a struggle if you can put aside **judgment**. *It is not and never has been our job to judge others, thereby deciding if they are "worthy" of our love. If you believe in an All-Loving Presence, and the person you judge is good enough for God to love, then who are you to decide otherwise?*

You may decide you don't like one's **actions** *but must learn to separate the actions from the person, who is a child of God. Once you shift your perception in this regard, you will find it easier to feel compassion, and in feeling compassion, you learn to love unconditionally. Once the lessons are learned, you will find you are no longer confronted by "people who are hard to love." This is your gift from the Universe. Once the lesson is learned, you will not be "tested" again, at least on a personal level. The lesson, however, may be expanded to a community-wide, national or global level.*

Know that every situation you read or hear about, even if not in your immediate sphere, is a chance to learn; a chance to stop judging; a chance to show compassion, forgiveness and love. Try it. Take a situation and try shifting your perception. Start with someone in your life who is difficult to love. Know they carry with them a lesson made-to-order by the Universe. Begin by no longer judging them. Acknowledge them as one of your "teachers," and thank them for taking on a role that may be particularly odious. You will know when you've accomplished this because you will automatically begin to feel compassion. With compassion comes love, and with these feelings fully entrenched, you reach a state of consciousness called unconditional love. This is a higher vibrational level that brings more peace and joy into your life; even a life that is already filled with peace and joy may benefit. For lives already rooted in peace and joy, this practice will bring you to a more blissful state than the one you currently enjoy.

The beauty of this process is that you have nothing to lose. If this does not resonate, (ignore this suggestion) *and you'll know that was the right thing for you to do, if you don't think of this again. If you try the process outlined above and it doesn't work then you've lost nothing but some time trying to be nonjudgmental. On the other hand, if it works for you, you will have elevated your own state of consciousness and believe it or not, uplifted the life of the person whom you were judging.*

Sending Love and Being Love

My daughter, along with her teammates, was responsible for selling trinkets to raise funds for her local sports team. There were three co-captains, two of whom lived near us, and a third who lived about 30 minutes away. When the ordered trinkets arrived, we received a phone call instructing us to drive 30 minutes to the house of the co-captain farthest from us to pick up the trinkets my daughter had sold. It may seem like a small thing, but I was furious that with two co-captains within five minutes of us, each girl at our end of town had to drive the 30 minutes to pick up the trinkets they had sold. What was the purpose of having all those captains, when they couldn't perform a simple, logistical task, like delivering the trinkets to their end of town?

This was very early on in my spiritual journey, so judgment was still my first response. My daughter intervened, wisely stopping me from phoning the parent of the co-captain 30 minutes away to express my anger. Having time to reconsider gave a chance for the "sending love" option to surface ("being love" was not yet in my purview). So, instead of ranting, I sent love. Within two minutes, the phone rang. It was the parent of the captain I was going to call, telling me that he'd deliver the trinkets to our house. Ah, the power of love and the wisdom of children.

Applications for sending or being love in our ordinary world are ever present. In this instance, I was on a flight with a crying baby. We have all been in this situation, which is why I invested in a set of noise cancellation headphones. Unfortunately, this time the crying was piercing. My son had been colicky, so I know what it's like as the parent. But until now, I don't think I had as much compassion for the child. In early motherhood, I was too consumed with my own unmet needs, primarily lack of sleep, to feel compassion for yet another crying spell. This time, with the benefit of 16 years between my child's last colic episode and me, I felt differently. All I could feel was compassion for this child whom I couldn't see, but I could certainly hear.

I closed my eyes and became conscious of **being love**, as God had asked me to do. Within moments, the crying stopped. When I went back to reading and lost focus on "being love," the crying would start up and I'd go through the exercise again. Obviously, I was not able to multitask "being love" and reading at the same time, so I remained focused on the child. I never did get to finish reading my book on that flight, but the child not only stopped crying, he started laughing.

By being love, you are the pebble in the pond sending out the vibration of love to humanity. By being love, you are giving yourself as a gift to God, to yourself and to all humanity. Operate from a place of self-love that does not leave anyone out. If we love ourselves fully, then we love others fully, no matter who they are or what they have done. This is the love God has shown me. Forgiveness then becomes implicit in the completeness of unconditional love. Unconditional love cannot exist without forgiveness. Love unconditionally and you have already transcended the need to forgive. If you need steps to follow, start by forgiving yourself, then everyone in your personal life, then progress outward until you forgive those who transgress globally, and don't stop until you have forgiven everyone whom you find egregious. You will then get to unconditional love. Let your gift to God be to recognize Him[32] in yourself and in everyone you meet. As God said to me for the benefit of a client: ...*Go to that place in yourself where love lives, and there you will find heaven; there you will find the Promised Land—the land so many have been searching for has always been within your reach. Push aside your judgment, your preconceived notions; these are the brambles that hide the garden where My Love grows in its infinite glory. Go there now. Be a part of that landscape. Whether you live in the Promised Land or the land of your own making is your choice. Choose wisely.*

Forgiveness Releases All Karma

Forgiveness releases all karma. Over and over again I heard these words as they were spoken to me. *That's why Jesus' last words on the cross were Forgive them Father, they know not what they do.* In deep meditation at our *Channeled Grace Healing Circle* on December 12, 2012, I was taken, in a vision, to the scene of Jesus' crucifixion. I was profoundly saddened looking up at Jesus as he hung from the cross—then everything changed. I could see through his eyes and feel what he felt. Jesus had taken me into him so that I could experience the crucifixion through him. Oddly

I felt no pain, but I did feel his deep peace as he looked out upon the scene before him. I wanted to stay in that place forever. As he did not speak to me, I will have to share what I learned by attempting to translate into words what he allowed me to feel. I pray that these words do the experience justice.

When Jesus spoke his last words, "Forgive them Father, they know not what they do," he wiped the karmic slate clean for all those present at the crucifixion. He did not intend for you to carry the cross. Put down the cross. You are forgiven. Forgive everyone in your life right now, including yourself! You cannot carry unforgiveness any longer. The unforgiveness in your heart is magnified; the world cannot take it any longer. It has to go. Jesus spent his whole life talking about love, and his last words were about forgiveness. Why? Because when people don't understand that forgiveness is implicit in unconditional love, they need to hear it as a separate, last and final statement—his last words. Forgiveness is so important that Jesus used his last breath to give us the secret code, the answer to the test, the key to the puzzle. Forgiveness. If you missed his messages about Love that he spent his life spreading, then you need to get the message about forgiveness. He was giving everyone another chance. He wiped everyone's karmic slate clean, and he is asking you now to put down that cross you have been carrying. Forgiveness releases all karma.

Jesus spoke in simple words because the message is simple. Love. Forgive. That's it. What is so complicated about this? Why am I writing an entire chapter about this? Because we need help putting those two words into practice, and we need to know that ordinary people are capable of the extraordinary life that follows when you follow his guidance.

Having said that, I know that people struggle with how to forgive. I now know what forgiveness feels like, but how does one get there? That was the subject of an email I received after I sent the above message to those who had attended our *Channeled Grace Healing Circle.* Does forgiveness imply that we condone atrocious or hurtful behavior? Do we just need to let go of past transgressions? How do we define a transgression? Does it require that we stay in the existential realm of "there is no good or bad—all events are neutral and as they should be" or admit that we are all human and that there are events that wound us deeply, such as the tragedy in Newtown, Connecticut, which occurred only a few days after Jesus' message on forgiveness?

I don't have easy answers to these questions. They did, however, get me thinking about what it was Jesus allowed me to feel when he took me inside of him. I am going to go out on a limb here and interpret further—I did not feel like he was condoning the events (of the crucifixion). I don't know what scholars would say; I only know what Jesus teaches me directly, and I am sharing that with you. I looked up forgiveness on-line in the Merriam-Webster dictionary and found that the definition was a good place to start to answer the questions in the email. To forgive you must a) give up resentment of or claim to requital for, and b) grant relief from payment of.

Based on what Jesus allowed me to experience, forgiveness means you release from your heart all judgment of the accused. I heard Jesus say: *When you judge you are so condemned. You are not meant to carry the weight of that judgment.* In this case, forgiveness means to let go of your judgment. *Put down the cross.* Don't hold another person hostage to your notion of wrongness, trapping them and you in a karmic web. Jesus' wiping everyone's karmic slate clean was palpable once I was united with him. Seeing through his eyes, I saw that the air was crystal clear in an unnatural sort of way; there was not a speck of dust floating, even though the ground was covered in it. The people, inside and out, were pure. There was not a speck of dust on their souls or in their hair. Everything was new again. It felt like everything had just started out—as if all present were just taken out of the box, newly unwrapped gifts unto themselves. That is what forgiveness looks like. It clears the air. It feels like you can breathe again. It feels as if no one has ever wronged you—because, after you forgive, there is no such thing as being wronged, for who is to judge wrongness? In the vision I had, I was deeply and profoundly saddened by the senselessness and brutality of Jesus' crucifixion, until I saw through his eyes, and then all that sadness disappeared. After being taken inside of him and allowed to experience the effect of his last words, all I could feel was profound peace. There, inside the son of God, are we all, just waiting to forgive and accept the forgiveness that has been offered to us. By his example, we are given a model to live by.

Forgiveness is how we get from here, back to love. It's the path; it is the road we must follow.

CHAPTER 10

Bringing Heaven to Earth

Christ consciousness is an expression for how a man lived who embodied God. He brought heaven to earth. You each have this capacity within you.

- Holy Spirit 12-2-09

Glimpses of Heaven

In 1996, I attended a group Reiki exchange at the Glenville Civic Center. There were 15 to 20 Reiki tables lined up in the center of the gymnasium. The concept was that anyone who was a trained Reiki practitioner, of any level, could attend to receive and give Reiki. Many of the people there seemed to know each other and had practiced Reiki for many years. I, on the other hand, was a Reiki Level I practitioner and knew no one. I was paired up with a middle-aged man who was kind enough to allow me to first receive Reiki. I lay down on the Reiki table, as did all the other people who were to receive energy work. All those who were giving Reiki began working. I was completely new to this whole Reiki thing, so this could have been a very distracting environment for me to have a meaningful experience, not that I knew what a meaningful experience would look or feel like, or that one was even possible.

Within minutes of this man (whose name I never knew and whom I never met again) working on me, I had a sense of no longer having a body. I was no longer a physical being in the gymnasium. At some level, I was conscious of a part of me being in the gym, but the essence of who I am, was not there; or more accurately, it was not just there in that gym but also in another dimension at the same time. The body that was "me" was now pure, unlimited white light. I could see the beauty of life. I saw how simple life was. Jesus had pulled me across the veil that separates my world from his. I was in his presence. A tear formed in my eye, which made me once again aware of my physical body. I felt as if I was glowing or as if white light were emanating from my entire body. Jesus said to me about the meaning of life: *It is so simple. It is all about love.* And through this experience, I was shown what it is like to die. This is where we go when we cross over to the other side, which seems to exist parallel to us here and now. It is beautiful. There is nothing but unconditional love. It is a **feeling** and a "place" in which I wanted to remain indefinitely.

I was never religious, and although I called on Jesus in times of crisis, I never really knew what to think about him until he spoke to me. Although I use the word "spoke," it is inaccurate. I use it for lack of a better way to explain the message and feeling that came with it. What Jesus gave to me was the gift of knowing what these words **felt** like and through that feeling, I was able to ascertain their meaning. The message was clear—that the meaning of our lives is pure love. All he wants is for this love, which in its deepest and truest form is the Divine within each of us, to be extended to everyone without exception. Extend it as if the person opposite you were the son of God, because he or she is. And no matter how he or she chooses to live his or her life here on earth, God loves him or her no more or no less than He loves you.

Apparently, I stayed on that Reiki table for an almost indefinite period. Because I was with Jesus, I had no sense of time or of my physical surroundings, so I unknowingly laid there throughout the entire Reiki exchange. The man who worked on me was kind enough not to nudge me to get up when it should have been his turn to receive Reiki from me. He never got his chance to receive Reiki because I never came out of that state of grace until the lights were turned on in the gymnasium and it was time for the tables to be folded up and for everyone to go home. I have always felt badly about this, and if he is reading this now, I offer my deepest apologies and my deepest gratitude. For it is through him that I had one of my most profound, life changing experiences. God worked through this man to show me my first glimpse of heaven.

When Jesus explained the meaning of life to me, he was answering a question I'd been asking all my life. I hadn't asked it while I lay on that Reiki table nor had I even asked it that day. Why he chose to answer my question when he did is still a mystery to me. Maybe I had to stop talking long enough to listen. Maybe I had to be at a point in my life when I would actually think about what he said. Although it wasn't obvious to me how life could be so simple, or how I would apply this new knowledge about love to my personal relationships, I was at the beginning of a journey that would lead me to the answers.

I would go on to have many more glimpses of heaven, but one in particular, came from my grandfather just hours after he died. He told me that he was in the "innermost chamber," a reference to St. Teresa of Avila's Interior Castle, meaning he was as close to God as one can get. He told me it was more beautiful than I could know. When my mom asked me if I wanted to say anything at the funeral service, I told her that I had nothing worth saying that didn't come directly from God. So I asked God and Grandpa, since he was in the innermost chamber, if they had any messages. Grandpa said, "To all of my family, my love is boundless. It was boundless then (meaning when he was alive), and it is boundless now. I found every reason to forgive transgressions. I tried to live a life of integrity, and although I may not have always led a life of humility, I tried my best.

"Know this: we are not without faults, but they are forgiven if we are truly repentant. I did the best I could, and although I was not always able to show my love and affection, I always felt it. I was truly blessed to have been surrounded by women (a reference to his wife and daughters) in my life…—You will never be alone. You weren't when I was alive and will not be now that I am in spirit. My spirit will be there to guide Sarah (his wife) in death as in life. Fear not, Sarah, for where you are going, there is only love. There is no pain, no sorrow. The heaviness of the flesh is not even a memory. What remains is love. I feel it now. It is all that is. It is all that will ever be.

To anyone who can't feel it, I want you now to close your eyes…Close them, and sit quietly until you see the Light. That Light is your God. He is in you now; He was in you yesterday; He will be in you tomorrow. You and He are one. In this state, you can experience His love for you and recognize the unity amongst yourselves and all of humanity."

When Grandpa finished, Jesus spoke: *Walk not in fear or sorrow, my children, for I have always been at your side, and I will continue to guide you and to cherish you. I ask only that you cherish me. Not your jobs, not your belongings, not just the things that are right with your life but everything. For in cherishing everything, you cherish me. My life was a guide to you, an example of how I want you to live. (Grandpa's) life, too, was a guide for you. He showed you how to live in the face of adversity and in good fortune. Now I beg you not to dwell in the sorrow of his passing as he is with me, as I have called him to be. His essence remains. You can feel his spirit and his love all around you. As he said, it is boundless—as yours should be. As above, so below—on earth as it is in heaven, my will be done. Go in peace. I love you all.*

As often happens, my grandmother died a few months after my grandfather. God and Jesus spoke to me again.

God: *It's so simple—it's all about love. Don't judge who you should love. Love all those you see. Love those that are easy to love and those who make it difficult to love them. My love for you knows no bounds as your love would know no bounds. Go forth into this world carrying My light—the light of love and compassion. Grandpa and Grandma shone that light when they were "alive," and they radiate it now in spirit. You have only to look inside yourselves to find it. Once again I ask you to close your eyes. See the light that is you. You are Me personified. We are one, and in so being, you are one with each other. Love Me, and you love yourself. Love yourself, and you love one another. There is no place for judgment or exclusion. I have not asked you for that. One of you is not more or less worthy than the other –just as neither Grandma or Grandpa was more or less worthy of My love. They are both with Me now and will be here when you arrive. They are your guides. They love you no less now than when they lived amongst you. Every loving thought you have is immediately received by them. So, think not that you have lost them. They are with you as they have always been. To perceive them now, you must quiet your mind. Know them in their true form, which is your true form, which is one with Me, your Father, your Creator—the All that Is. Remember our unity and it will set you free. Blessed are the children who walk in My Light.*

Jesus: *And in me, they will dwell. Know that they* (my grandparents) *are well taken care of in "heaven." They are one with the God consciousness. Amen.*

May the peace that resides within be yours without. May the peace that is me within you be reflected onto all of life around you. For it is in that reflection that you will see a new world—a world free of suffering.

Look for me in everyone you meet. For when you see me there, I will be reflected back to you. You will see not that person's "faults" you will see only me—this is as it should be. I give you these opportunities to bring "heaven to earth"—seize them—they are all around you.

I leave you with love and the knowledge that you and I are one—now and forever. Amen.

This Way to Heaven on Earth: Recognize the Christ Within

It seemed that Jesus was always trying to point me toward heaven on earth, but it is only in looking back at his messages to me that I see this is true. One day Jesus said: *I want you to recognize me in everyone...* If you are like me, you will know that is easier said than done. You will also recognize the potential for bringing heaven to earth should we all share, with **everyone** we meet, the **light and love** that is the God within. I prayed ardently over the years to know my divinity completely and thoroughly. I prayed to see the Christ in me. I prayed to see the Christ in everyone I met. I prayed for peace among all people. And one day Jesus answered: *Give me your hands and receive my love and guidance. It's all about love. Remember that message.* A few months later, he asked me: *How can others be what you yourself do not yet believe you to be?* It's true. If I can't see myself as divine, how can I expect others to see their divinity? If I can't behave as if I am filled with the love and light of God, how can I expect others to?

Messages at St. Catherine's Church

I received an email from a client telling me that, while she was praying, she received guidance that I had to go to St. Catherine's church and meditate in front of the tabernacle. Since I don't typically resonate with religious services, I made sure to go when Mass was not in session. I don't know what a tabernacle is, so I did not know if I was in front of it. I felt, however, that it was my intention that mattered most to God. I found the frigid temperature in the empty church distracting, but once I settled in, Jesus appeared and gave me the following messages. Some of this is pretty wild and I apologize if any of it sounds blasphemous but, I assure you, it didn't come from me. I would not actually say some of these things and others I would be embarrassed to write.

...All I want is for you to love one another. What happens in Revelation[33] you do to yourselves. The war, the famine...is already upon you. This story is not about a point in time. It is a lifestyle choice that my children are making, (and) have been making for thousands of years. There are always those with more and those with less. You have yet to figure out how all can have what is needed. I have given you tools and technologies, yet you exploit them for the beneficial gain of the few, not the many.

Close your eyes and see what the world could look like. Would you ever imagine a world where a group of people had not? Where you set aside hundreds of thousands who you said would get no food, no clean water and no shelter? Of course not; yet that is what you have done. It pains me to see my children fight. (At this point Jesus stood in front of me and gave me the host and wine.) He continued: *It is symbolic of how I live in you and through you. I am in every cell of your body...I don't need perfection. I need you—you with your faults.* (At this point, I saw Jesus and someone else baptize me.)

Now you are perfect because you are born again in me. That does not mean you are without faults. That is your choice—how you behave as you go through each day, each circumstance, each interaction. Always look to me for guidance.

St. John of the Cross is a servant of mine. He has served me well, and he will serve you well. He has already spoken to you in your dreams, and he will continue to speak to you. Pay attention! Stop hiding yourself. Go forward with strength and confidence. You have more to give. Help me choose to save my people, and yes, they are ALL my people. I exclude no one based on religious creed.

I then asked, "What do you want me to do?" Jesus continued: *Just recognize the power within. Become familiar with it. Own it. Practice with it. You must be so grounded in it that you go nowhere, and do nothing, without being fully aware of my presence within you—then you will be ready. Amen.*

You are one of the few people who realize you are not special and who realizes that I am not special. **I am all of you made manifest in all your potential glory.** *Go now.*

Okay, so there it is—not all that flattering about me, but that is what he said. I will try to do as Jesus asks and just recognize his presence in me because that is my power. It is all of our power. What he says to me, he is saying to each one of us. That is why I share these messages.

Reentering the Garden—Reclaiming Our Selves

I was invited to share my personal journey with a group called the Passion Project, a grassroots, non-profit organization that welcomes women who have followed their hearts to tell their story. I was a bit uncomfortable knowing that most of the speakers were quite accomplished and many had published books. But the Project's founder, Polly Simpkins, thought I had a story worth telling, so I reluctantly outlined my unlikely path from finance to energy healing. The funny thing is that I did feel like a book would come of this speaking engagement. What I didn't know is that it would be Linda who would ask me to write it.

On the day before my Passion Project presentation, I had an energy healing session with Heather Cumming to help with the ongoing work of diminishing the presence of my ego. She told me that in a prior life, I had operated at a much higher level of consciousness than I do now; however, I was persecuted for what I knew and for who I was. She said that I was meant to live at that higher vibration in this lifetime, and that it would be okay, because in this lifetime I chose a path that was gentle.

The following day, I did my Passion Project presentation as planned. There were about 30 women present, more than three times the expected number. About three-quarters of the way through my talk, a woman in the back of the room, who had bounded in only moments before, raised her hand and asked, "Where do you get **your** power from because there are only two sources of power?" When I asked her what those two sources were, she became aggressive and said, "You mean you don't know?" as if the fact that I did not know the two sources **she** was referring to made me some sort of a fraud. She continued more along the lines of an attack versus questioning until it came out that she wanted to know what **I** called my source because, according to her, the only possible source that I could access was the Holy Spirit. God and Jesus were, in her mind, not available to me. She further insinuated that the "other power" was that of the "devil."

After explaining that my source is God, a term I use simply to apply a name to an otherwise unnameable Source, a name I use purely for the sake of convenience, she continued on a diatribe about the Trinity and how the Holy Spirit is the "right" source and how my source can't possibly be God. She then went on to "ask" if I believed that *The Bible* was the word of God. I explained that I thought that what is written in *The Bible* are the words of God as chosen by the Council of Nicea, and that the *Gnostic Gospels* may also contain the words of God, as she continued to talk over me about *The Bible* and the Holy Spirit. I believe, at this point, one of the attendees raised her hand and emphatically asked, "Could we get back to the speaker?" Others in the room seemed to concur, and with that this agitated women picked up her belongings and ran from the room, as if being chased. After she closed the door one woman said, "We were just talking about the ego, and there it is!"

The unity of purpose of the other attendees along with their higher vibration of love simply provided too much light for this woman to stay. No one asked her to leave, nor did anyone give the indication that she should. During the exchange I felt no anger, frustration or persecution, although she clearly was trying to expose me as a "fraud" or a "nonbeliever" because I did not adhere to her belief system. I suspect, as in the story of *Joshua* by Joseph Girzone, that had Jesus himself appeared and spoken directly to her, she would have denied his existence. She would have held firm to her belief that **only** the Holy Spirit can communicate with her. She does not accept that, in my experience, God speaks to us **all the time** if only we have "ears to listen," which was the basis of the entire talk that day. I was sharing the way God speaks to me. I was making no assumption about the way He might choose to speak to others. I have no "power" other than that of knowing that Jesus and God are within me as they are within you. Either we all have this power or no one has it.

That night I got into bed thinking I would finish an enchanting book written by two of our students, Annabel Monaghan and Elisabeth Wolfe, entitled *Click: The Girl's Guide to Knowing What You Want and Making It Happen*. I decided, instead, to follow my intuition, which was telling me to pick up *Blessings of the Cosmos* by Neil Douglas-Klotz, a gift from Linda. What Douglas-Klotz does is to go back to the original Aramaic and describe how Bible passages might have been understood in their original language. I started reading where I had left off several months before. The title on the page was "A Particularly Bad Day." What followed astounded me. I include the text here knowing that the connection to the day's events will speak for itself.

"Blessed are ye, when men shall hate you, and when they shall separate you from their company, and shall reproach you, and cast out your name as evil, for the Son of Man's sake." (The words as they appear in *The Bible* in Luke 6:20-26 King James Version.)

Klotz explains how this passage may have been heard to Aramaic ears when spoken in Aramaic:

> "You may not think so, but it can be blessedly ripe,
> just the right thing to discover your true purpose,
> when people see you in a bad light,
> coloring your true colors with their own

inner hue and cry;

when people single you out for abuse,

because of the wounds they have felt inside;

when you are conspired against and

things get said behind your back;

when your good name gets tossed about,

shut out, and carried here and there

as if it were a waste of time to mention you.

All this happens because people see in you someone

who is trying to fulfill the divine image,

who lives according to their real purpose.

Yet in the distorted, fun-house mirror

of a heart they currently carry within,

they see you backwards,

which is the way they see themselves."[34]

Several years after this, Linda was pressed by one of her friends to explain what I do. And similar to my experience at the Passion Project, the intimation from her friend was that I was a fraud, or worse. She too was asking about my Source. She was questioning whether it was safe for Linda to associate with me, since, in her friend's mind, it was possible that I was not speaking **her** truth and might be tempting Linda with false or even "evil" teachings. Oh, pleeeeease. Linda explained to her friend the work I do in these words: "She has reminded me that the Christ consciousness is already within me. She has helped me to recognize the Light of Christ within me. Theresa's message is that the Light has always been there."

So it seems that everyone knows THE TRUTH and that they must make sure that only **their** version of the truth is taught. What seems to make people fearful is when someone teaches that an individual can find divine truth, or divine revelation by seeking a direct relationship with God. Do people really think God is such a nitwit that He can't speak directly to His creations and make Himself understood? Do they think they will be tricked? Do they think that God has chosen some special people to be the keepers of the truth? Well, all I can say is that if He has, the world is pretty darn confused about who they might be and what the message is. The

Divine that has shared messages and visions with me, in all their many forms has one, consistent message: Love. So, if you are wondering if it is God's words you are hearing, ask yourself if they are about love because God loves everyone and everything, without exception.

We think we know so much…we know what God meant when He said love your neighbor. Really? So why is it that people don't love their neighbor if their neighbor is of a different race, religion or sexual orientation? Is that what God said? I know little, but I am pretty sure that sentence was "Love thy neighbor as thyself." Perhaps the problem is that we can't love our neighbor because we don't yet fully love ourselves. *We are already the Christ consciousness—the Light. For it to shine through, we need to get rid of the "me" (ego).*

The Light cannot shine through us if we throw a dark blanket over it in the form of our own prejudices and preconceived notions. Let them go and see how bright your light shines. To attain Christ Consciousness means to attain the same state of consciousness as Christ. If in Christ's state of consciousness he recognized his unity with God, then to achieve Christ consciousness means for us to recognize our unity with God. That is what Christ knew. God consciousness is implicit in Christ consciousness because what Christ knew is that he was one with his Father in heaven.

Jesus taught that each of us is the presence of God on earth. Jesus was my path to unification with God consciousness. He may or may not be yours. Whatever the case may be, I urge you, as I urge my children, not to turn away his teachings.

Jesus said to me: *Have the courage to say what you need to say. He who sees me as his path is saved, but I am not the **only** path. There are many paths that lead to my Father's Garden. Choose the path that is right for you. Then walk it until you reach the Garden. You will know the path that is right for you because it will bring you peace. It will bring you joy. It will bring you love. The closer you get to the Garden, the more stable these states will become. Once in the Garden, you will **BE** peace, joy and love. It is the only state you will know. Trust me when I tell you this is who you are already; but you do not yet know that. Peace is what grows in my Father's Garden—inner peace, love and joy. Why stay away when you can have it now? Begin your journey— do not delay. The Garden is the earth itself and it is in your heart. Ask yourselves, "What have we done to our Father's Garden?" Reclaim the garden. Weed out sorrow and pestilence. Tend to the seeds of harmony and forgiveness. This Garden was given* to all the inhabitants of earth. *Think not that you have dominion over any of it. It was meant to be shared.*

In another meditation, Jesus said to me: *...Every thought, every intention brings us closer to peace. Wager not your bet against me. For I am your Savior, your guide and your light...Fear not this coming contraction. For all life will become one. Life is at its beginning and its end at the same time. Do not look for the "start" of peace for it is already here. For thine is the kingdom and thine is the glory.* (This is Jesus saying the kingdom and the glory is ours as well as his.) *There is too much to mention, but know that you will see peace in your lifetime and the lifetimes of your children.* I asked Jesus if he meant inner peace, and he replied: *All peace. They are one in the same. There is no one who dies unnecessarily. Peace is upon us. Don't look back, and don't ask how. For when thine peace comes, you will know only in hindsight. Fear not the details of how my world comes to fruition. For there is only one way—by the Hand of God. So too you will know peace in my garden...You all live in my Father's Garden if only you have eyes to see. Open your eyes, Theresa. For only through your eyes can others see. Life is a course in the miraculous if only you have eyes to see! Life is miraculous. Miracles abound when you are looking through me. Through my eyes, which can't leave anyone out.*

There is so much done and so much still to do. Honor yourself, Theresa, and your ways of knowing—for never has there been so much courage and so much power in the world at one time. You know because I Am, so do not let another day pass where you do not love yourself because it starts there. It starts within as the seed of knowing...It is all about LOVE. Spread my word. I said: "Oh Jesus, this is when the trouble starts." *Not this time.*

About six months later I heard God say: *...My Light is within you now. What you have asked for has been given. And what has been given cannot be taken away. I do not give half a gift, so you can see that you and My son are whole in Me. This is true for everyone. I await their recognition. They do not have to come through My son, but they have to come to Me. They have to come to Me with full abandon. They have to abandon all else they hold dear. That doesn't mean they will lose all else they hold dear. It simply means that to enter into union with Me they must be **willing** to let go of all they hold dear. That willingness allows you and I to form the complete whole.*

On Earth as it is in Heaven

Praying The Lord's Prayer, as I often do, I dropped into meditation while focusing on the words, "Thy will be done on earth as it is in heaven." I was focused on how to do that when I heard God say: *Your job is to be love and to send love to all you meet.* To "be love" is to be a fully actualized or fully realized human. This is what Jesus was. He was a fully realized human. So when God tells me to "be love," He is telling me to be no less than Jesus was—a fully actualized being capable of reaching her full potential. I know I am capable of being love because I can feel that state while in meditation or when focusing all of my attention on being love for a designated period of time. The hard part is to carry it through one complete day. Jesus came here to show us how to be love in this world. He taught us by his example. He showed us how one who **is** love acts, even under the worst of life's circumstances. He loved unconditionally and he forgave even those who crucified him. **There is no drug as powerful as forgiveness**. Forgive yourself, and forgive those who trespass against you. I believe that if Jesus did it, then so can we.

I wanted to do my part to bring heaven to earth, and I was waiting for God to assign me a "to-do." Instead, I got a "to-be." He is saying to me that to bring heaven to earth, I must **be** love. This is not just my assignment, but is, ultimately, the task for each of us. Can you imagine all 7 billion people on the planet **being** nothing but love? If each of us were to embody unconditional love all of the time, we would have heaven on earth.

CHAPTER 11

Mother Mary, Grace and the Divine Feminine

It is by the grace of God that you are here. It is God's grace that you must send out to His children. You are awakened to His call to be the embodiment of His love and His will here on Earth. Withhold the message not.

— St. Teresa of Avila 5-1-07

I was doing Reiki on Linda many years ago when my hands starting shaking uncontrollably, tears filled my eyes and I fell to my knees. A voice said to me: *You are channeling grace.* I didn't know what grace was, so being the scholar that I am, I went to Dictionary.com and found this definition: "the freely given, unmerited favor and love of God." Well, I got the unmerited part right. I felt, however, that for the Divine to ask me to channel grace was highly unlikely, so I thought I must have misunderstood the message. Then during a Reiki session, I saw Mother Mary enter me, and once she and I became one, we together worked on my client's heart chakra. My hands shook as they moved with extraordinary speed through my client's energy field. It felt as though my hands were made of rubber. When I was done, my client told me she saw Mother Mary (I hadn't told her that I too had seen her and that she had come through me) and that her heart chakra felt as if it were "new"—totally clear and full of love. Then the words of the prayer, "Hail Mary, full of **grace**..." came to me, and I realized that perhaps I had heard correctly...I was not only channeling grace, but it was coming through me, through Mother Mary.

In another session, I saw St. Thérèse of Lisieux enter my body along with Mary, and this is how I practiced "Reiki" for quite some time. It was no longer Reiki, of course. Clients frequently reported feeling energy flowing through them, and some reported feeling as if they had had "surgery." They sensed the "surgery" that I was witnessing while I was working on them, although I hadn't disclosed any of what

I was seeing to my clients until after the fact. All this happened without my hands touching the clients' physical body. On some occasions, Mother Mary would surround or enter my client's body or both. I made no promises that this would happen for everyone, as I was not in control of the work being done. I always trusted that Mary and St. Thérèse were doing whatever was needed for my clients' greatest good, in accordance with Divine law. When I looked back at my journal entries just before and during this time, I could see, once again, that what I thought was a random series of events was actually a Divinely orchestrated plan.

How it all Began

I attended a healing circle at Starvisions, a spiritual retreat center in Chappaqua, New York, led by spiritual healer and Divine channel, Roland Comtois and shaman, Bear Walker. I went with my friends Linda, Kim and a few other women. I was fully prepared to be passed over for a healing as this is what typically happened to me in group settings. This time, however, was different.

Roland called me to stand up in front of the room, which was filled with about 30 other attendees. He held my hands and told me I was to heal many people. He said I have always known the truth. He then was guided to sing *Amazing Grace*, which he did in the most heavenly voice. He let go of my hands, and I started shaking. He put my shaking hands down by my side and then told me to send Light to everyone in the room. My hands began to rise, without any assistance from me—my knees and hands were shaking, and I sent the Light. Kim said she saw my hands turn to white light, and that light was streaming out of my body and my heart as if I was cracked open.

Grace is the word that came to me when it was over—this was **grace**.[35] Kim, watching this spectacle from her seat, heard the same message from Spirit. Bear Walker said he could see my light shining clear up to the heavens. He said the hardest thing would be to keep me here on this earth plane. I needed to keep my feet on the ground, or I would "take off"—a message Linda had gotten for me many times over the years. Roland said, *You were never lost. Stop asking "Why me?" and accept that you are to heal many people.* I am not the type of person whose first response is, "Why me?" I am painfully aware, especially when things go wrong, that my circumstances are usually the result of my own decisions. I have only asked, "Why me?" once in my life, and that is why I remember it so clearly. I was commuting to my corporate finance job, when, while stopped at a traffic light, an elderly man hobbled with great difficulty, across the street in front of my car. As he did, I burst into tears and asked God, "Why me?" as if I knew that at some point in time, my future and his were bound together—that somehow I was to help him, or many others like him, in a way I did not yet comprehend.

Roland asked me where I thought the light that I was sending out from my hands came from. I started to say it was channeled through me from "out there," and then I realized that it came from within me and shone outward. It came from that place inside of me where God and I are one. Apparently, that is what Roland saw too.

About a week after my experience at Starvisions, Linda, Kim and I got together for our weekly Reiki exchange. Kim and I began working on Linda when my arms, body and hands started shaking, and Spirit said through me: *And so it is done.* None of what I said was in my voice. After the healing was complete, I was told that I was channeling grace—and the feeling humbled me to the point of tears, yet again. I heard the message: *...and there is God. He needs no fancy palace. He needs only your heart and an open door to let him in.* Channeling grace left me in a state of complete bliss. While Linda and Kim did Reiki on me, the words, "I am complete. I need nothing" kept going through my mind. So I was a bit disappointed to hear Jesus say in meditation that night: *You're not done. You have just begun.* Oh for Pete's sake! Does this journey never end?

Accepting, Believing, Acknowledging

In a meditation, God asked me to open my heart to fully accept my channeling of grace. I have to **accept** it and **believe** it for it to have its full power. I had trouble fully opening my heart, even though I wanted to. I asked for help, but God said I had free will—the insinuation seemed to be that I was somehow preventing my heart from opening fully. I kept trying. Then He said, regarding an upcoming Reiki master class that I would be teaching, *you are going to tell everybody in that room that you have been asked to channel grace. Then you will ask if they will allow you to do so. You can say you don't know what will happen. This is part of your accepting this challenge. You must publicly acknowledge what has been asked of you.*

You have to understand that it is one thing for me to acknowledge my "full power," whatever that is, with Linda and Kim; it is quite another for me to acknowledge it in a broader setting. It would be very embarrassing for me to explain what God had asked of me, and then stand there and channel grace, especially with the way my arms and hands started shaking. Concerned that I might be a narcissist for even thinking that I heard such a message, I asked God if it was my ego that thinks He has chosen me to channel grace. His reply was: *It is your ego that thinks you can stop Me.* Which reminded me of my fear of surrendering my will to the will of God. I was always afraid God or Jesus would ask me to do something too difficult and seemingly insane, like dragging a life-sized cross across the country. To this concern, God asked if I was *so vain to think that my path will be easier than the one Jesus chooses for me?* Mmmmmm, good point.

Hail Mary, Full of Grace

A few days after the above conversation with God, while channeling grace to a client, my head got so light at the start of the session that I felt as if I wasn't even there. I saw Mother Mary's face just above my client's face. (The client later told me that she saw it too.) I was being forced to lean closer to the client, and then Mary and I became one. As this happened, my hands, which were on the client's face, began to shake. I could feel Mary's energy throughout my entire body, and I heard the words, "Hail Mary, full of grace" run through my head. Once my hands were lifted off the client's face, they moved to her heart chakra where they began to move back and forth at an extraordinarily fast speed. My hands, once again, felt as if they were made of rubber. They shook wildly above the client for some time and then swooshed energy away to either side—then the session was done. Her heart chakra was cleared and glowing brightly. It was as if she were made anew, which is how the client felt afterward.

The following week, during our Reiki exchange at Linda's house, I really wanted the opportunity to channel Mary, St. Thérèse of Lisieux, or anyone else Jesus chose for me. I was about to begin work on Linda, but I knew that if I laid my hands on her head, it was going to be a traditional Reiki session. So instead, I went to Linda's left side and just stood there with my hands slightly raised—simply waiting. I was getting the message to be patient. I stood still for a long time then was guided to place one hand a few inches above Linda's stomach and the other above her heart. Soon, one hand started shaking. The rest of the session was completely guided by Mother Mary, who took over my body. I was still in my body, but she was there too. She moved my hands so very fast through Linda's energy field. I was given no indication as to what was being worked on. At one point, I was guided to kneel, as St. Thérèse of Lisieux worked on Linda's right arm. I hadn't told Linda that I was seeing and working with Mother Mary, but as if to confirm Mary's presence, Linda saw a crown at the beginning of the session, which she knew to be a symbol of Mother Mary.

I had gotten used to Mary and St. Thérèse working through me, but I was wondering why my arms and hands vibrated and moved back and forth so fast. I recalled a Reiki session I had done on Linda, many years earlier, when my hands started vibrating and shaking. Instead of lifting them off her body to allow them to shake and vibrate in her energy field, I forced them to remain very still on her body. The tremors happened numerous times after that, but each time I was determined to shut them down since I thought it might signal the onset of Parkinson's disease. I'd seen those tremors in my grandfather, and I wasn't about to let them manifest in me. Now I realize that it was probably Mother Mary and St. Thérèse knocking at my door. My deepest apologies go to Linda for delaying any healing that may have occurred. Had I known it was Mother Mary and St. Thérèse of Lisieux, I would have let them in immediately.

Channeling grace brought a new client to my practice, let's call her Gina. Gina was very religious and a devotee of Mother Mary, but she was skeptical of my ability to channel Mother Mary. Unbeknownst to me, during our first session together, Gina silently prayed to Mother Mary, asking her to "hold her hand" if she was really working through me. As Mother Mary would have it, at that very moment, she told me to *hold (Gina's) right hand*. Mother Mary gave Gina the proof she was looking for. It wasn't bad for me to have that confirmation either.

Where Did I Go?

Mary's presence continued to grow stronger. In one instance, I sat down with a client after her session ended but found I could not speak. Mother Mary's energy was still in me and that made it almost impossible for me to function. I had to force myself to "come back." The following afternoon, I was on Linda's Reiki table and, again, felt the presence of Mother Mary and St. Thérèse in me. They stayed with me all that day and through the night until I woke up the following morning at 4:00 a.m. On yet another occasion, I described to a client at the end of her session, how Mary and St. Thérèse came through me. As I explained this, I started to cry because I could still feel the presence of their pure, unconditional love. It took me a long time to be able to converse, and once again, I felt their energy for the rest of the day. Exhausted, I slept that afternoon, and when I awoke, I had the distinct feeling that there was no more "me" left. I wondered at this point if the entire ego self was gone. But writing this years later, I can assure you that there is still more ego work to do.

Speaking of the ego, I wanted Mary to explain to me what she and St. Thérèse were doing when they worked through me, waving my hands through a client's energy field as if I were a puppet. As my hands sliced the air, Mary would ask me to deliver messages, which, because of the physical exertion with which my arms were being moved, sounded as though each word was an exclamation. I had to warn clients beforehand not to worry about what was happening to me. I was fine, but it seemed that when Mother Mary came through me, the energy level was so high it was all I could do to stay standing. I would often not be able to speak for some time after she left. She told me not to ask for an explanation. I had the sense that there was no possible way to condense what she was doing into our language of symbols and sounds. Since so many of my clients had seen profound changes in their lives after our channeled grace healing sessions, I thought I had better heed Mary's advice.

Unstable States

I loved working this way. Sometimes I would channel Mary, but it could also be a combination of Mary and St. Thérèse of Lisieux or Mary and Jesus. Other times, St. Teresa of Avila would enter me. There were very distinct differences in the energies of Mother Mary and Jesus. Where Mary's presence would make my hands and arms shake wildly, Jesus' presence would make my body completely still. I would collapse to the floor many times, after these sessions ended. During my transition, sessions would be a combination of Reiki and channeled grace or simply channeled grace. It was completely outside my control. Or maybe it was just my doubt that made Reiki part of the mix at all.

During a Reiki Master Class that Linda and I were teaching, we did the *Meditation for World Peace*. Just before it ended, I dropped into an extraordinarily deep meditative state where my hands started shaking as well as my left leg and torso. I could not stop the shaking, and my heart was beating very fast. The energy flowing through me was tremendous—more powerful than anything since that first evening with Roland. Then, I started channeling grace to the room but was unable to stop when the meditation ended. When I finally did stop channeling grace, I was unable to speak for a long time. Thankfully, Linda was there to continue the class. I listened to the students discussing and asking questions, but all I saw was perfection. I had no response, not only because I couldn't speak, but also because I could see that at that moment everything was perfect in their lives; no response was necessary. When I finally did regain my faculties, one student in the class told me that for about 30 minutes after the meditation ended, my eyes changed. She said it was as if they were two endless blue oceans.

In his book, *Power vs. Force*, David Hawkins describes the state I had experienced as follows: "The ecstasy that accompanies this condition isn't absolutely stable; keep in mind that there are also moments of great agony...It finally becomes obvious that one must transcend this level or constantly suffer excruciating 'descents from grace.'" [36]For me, the trouble started at the end of the day when ordinary reality took over. I had descended from grace all right—right into cooking dinner, picking kids up from after school activities, helping with homework and scrubbing pots and pans. My eyes, I am certain, were no longer endless oceans of blue but more like blood-shot pools surrounded by dark circles.

My New Job Description

With Mother Mary working through me, I was ready to launch my *Global Peace Movement* website. I asked Mary how I should describe what I do, and she gave me the following job description: *I channel grace as has been requested by God. I channel grace through Mother Mary and St. Thérèse of Lisieux. Also working with me are Jesus, Archangel Michael, St. Teresa of Avila and St. Thomas Aquinas. I have been asked to use this grace to help the world. Mary says that her children have strayed too far, and she needs to bring them back into the fold of love.* Neither Mary nor St. Thérèse speak of religion—they speak of love.

Mary to all: Open your hearts, and let in the Light for it is there that you find Love. Love is all there is, and it is already inside of you.

*I have asked Theresa to work with you to help you to find this Love. She will do **nothing you can't do yourselves**. She is a **temporary** guide under my mentorship. I will work through her to bring you to me and to God (Love). I have enlisted St. Thérèse to help me. We both work through Theresa as she is a clear and open channel. Trust her—we do. May you have a blessed journey back to Christ.*

Hearing that I was a temporary channel was deflating, to say the least, and I like permanent—not temporary—work. We also like to hear that we have talents that others don't have. Well, apparently that is not the case with me. I have been assigned a job that can be done by you too—and Mary wants you to know that. She has made sure I am easily replaced, leaving me with no job security.

I asked Spirit why God chooses certain people to do His work, and Spirit said: *Who you have judged, He has chosen.* God works in paradox. Those who we think aren't worthy, God chooses to do His work. I would definitely put myself in the unworthy category, so if that is the only job requirement, I guess I am qualified. As luck would have it, that one job requirement qualifies most of us.

Kim had a vision in which I channeled grace to a large group of people who were sitting in meditation. Since I'd just launched my *Meditation for World Peace,* and I trust Kim's visions, I invited a group of women to a morning of Meditation and Channeled Grace. When the *Meditation for World Peace* ended, I had each participant sit for a few minutes in the middle of the circle while I allowed Mother Mary to work through me as a channel of her grace. When everyone had received Mary's grace and the music had ended, I tried to thank everyone for coming, but I couldn't speak. No one could move. Mother Mary's energy put us in a trance-like state of pure bliss. She was there, and we were all a part of her love.

Eventually, my Reiki practice was completely replaced by Channeling Grace and in mid-2011, in addition to private sessions, I started offering *Channeled Grace Healing Circles* to larger groups. By this time I was not seeing Mother Mary coming into me, but I would often see her, Jesus or them both in the room as we channeled grace to a group. I had no ability to suppress the tears that would sometimes roll down my face as I channeled grace or as I tried to describe a message from Jesus after the session ended. I had to get used to my arms and hands moving through the air as if I were a puppet on a string, held in the hands of the Divine. Fortunately, by the time I was conducting the group sessions, my arms and hands were moving very slowly, almost imperceptibly, through the air. The Divine would have me stand with my arms outstretched for most of the hour-long *Channeled Grace Healing Circle.* I am quite the weakling, so under normal circumstances, holding my arms out for less than a minute causes me pain. Oddly, while channeling grace, they could stay extended for as long as the Divine wished, without muscle aches. Actually, I couldn't feel my arms at all. It is as if they became weightless. I had to get used to the fact that, even after the grace session had ended, I could not return to a normal functioning state. Instead, I would stay in a state of unified bliss with the Divine as people got up to leave, walking past me or talking. If I tried really hard, the talking actually helped me to come back to this reality. If I weren't trying to come back, I don't know how long I would stay in those states. I don't know how it all works, but attendees seemed to benefit from these sessions. My experiences channeling grace convinced me to replace our Reiki classes with another workshop I developed: *Channeling Grace—Healing Yourself and Others.* Of course, I thanked Mother Mary for awakening me to grace, for without her grace, none of this would have been possible.

So What Does Grace Look Like, and Why Do You Want It?

The 13th century Flemish Mystic, John Ruysbroeck says, "Grace touches everyone, for it is given by God but not everyone responds with a free conversion of his will and a purification of his conscience." For those who believe in a Higher Being, it is never exclusively through ourselves that we are saved but through our efforts combined with God's grace. The paradox is that it seems we still have to **do** something. We can't just sit on the couch eating bonbons and say God's grace will keep us from getting fat. The trick is that we never know when or where God's grace will appear in our lives, so we must always do what we can, at all times, to help ourselves and each other.

Through example, I will share with you how grace has shown up in my life and, with their permission, in the lives of some of my friends and clients. Grace can be subtle, so if you are not looking for it, you may consider it—as I did most of my life—good luck. I don't think the nomenclature is important, but the difference for me has been an overriding feeling of inner peace versus the lack thereof. When I thought I was simply "lucky," there was always the underlying feeling that my luck would someday run out. Now that I see the Hand of God, I realize I have a partner who cares about me and for me, every day. He seamlessly wove Himself into my life and into me, and I have responded with a conversion of my will. I don't think I am there yet when it comes to the purification of my conscience—I am not really sure how that happens.

God's Grace at the Airport 9-30-11

I arrived at the airport to find my flight, which had been on time when I left home an hour before, was now canceled. The reason? Weather. What—the blue, windless skies above? I reminded myself not to get sarcastic as I was being told that I couldn't get on the earlier flight, even though there were empty seats, and I was there in plenty of time. Apparently, if they had put me on that flight, I would have had to pay additional charges, and if the earlier flight had been canceled, I would have lost any possibility of getting out that day. I was told by the ticket agent to go sit outside and enjoy the day (yes, she implied that the weather was perfect) while waiting the three hours for a later flight, which she had rebooked me on. I sat outside for a while until my husband called and convinced me that I should engage my dormant type A personality and demand whatever it was I felt entitled to. As I approached the ticket agent, I heard God tell me to go directly to the gate where the **earlier flight** was in the process of boarding. At the gate, I handed the person my ticket, which was for the flight three hours hence and was allowed to board the earlier flight, at no extra charge. God spoke, I listened. There was no luck involved. This was grace in action.

The Treasure is Within 2-8-12

I am forever questioning God, but I ultimately do what He tells me. Maybe because I made it as far as the night before I was supposed to sign the real estate contracts to sell my house, God gave me another grace. As if to verify the veracity of the messages I had been receiving regarding the sale of my house, God gave me feed-back on a message I had delivered to my cousin, Mark, weeks before. On the night Mark's brother, JP, died from cancer, JP's spirit appeared to me and said to tell Mark, "It's in the canister in the cupboard." I was shown a Ziploc bag in a canister. Before delivering this odd message, I asked Mark if it was possible that his brother might want to tell him the location of something. Mark's eyes widened as he explained that, during his brother's long battle with cancer, he'd been meaning to ask him where he hid the coins that their deceased father had left them. He had never had the chance to ask. I conveyed JP's message to Mark, along with the vision, and sure enough, Mark found the coins.

My mom was very excited about this message and the subsequent discovery of the coins, so she asked if I was going to put the story in *Everyday Mystic*. I hadn't planned on it. I told her I had countless pages of messages from Jesus, Mary and Holy Spirit, not to mention a few saints. Why would I include a message from my cousin JP about the whereabouts of a bag full of coins? Because, although the messages from Jesus, Mary, the Holy Spirit and the saints may not always have the irrefutable proof that came with the message of the coins, their messages are lead-ing us to forgotten, hidden treasures. When Jesus, Mary, the Holy Spirit, the saints or angels tell you to love yourself, and you do it, it is like finding the treasure in that canister—the one you knew was there but couldn't find. God is pointing you in the right direction, but you have to do the work. If He tells you to love yourself, then work at loving yourself. If He tells you not to judge or to forgive, then work at those things. The treasure is in you, and it has yet to be discovered. The treasure is your ability to love yourself and others unconditionally.

You Will Be Provided For 2-9-12

While Linda channeled grace to me, I had a vision in which Jesus showed me what he meant when he said to "give a person your coat and more, if he asked for it." I was shown that this teaching does not always have to be interpreted literally. It means for us to be able to let go of everything we own. It is a way of telling us not to be attached to anything we own. And, as a very wise teenaged client reminded me the following day, God will always take care of you if you put your trust in Him. This young man walked away from everything he knew with just the clothes on his back. When I asked him if he was scared he said, "sometimes," but then he would remember a message I'd delivered to him in which Jesus said he *loved him so much*. He reasoned that if Jesus loved him so much, he would take care of him, and he did. He found a small amount of money on the road and used it to buy a sandwich, which he shared with a stranger. That stranger's friend came along and later bought my client a meal at an all-you-can-eat buffet. God will take care of you, but you need to put your trust in God. You can't give away your coat thinking you will be without a coat. You give it away with the **knowing that you will be provided for**.

On Retroactive Insurance and Creating Your Own Reality 8-9-12

I was stopped in traffic on the local interstate highway when the car behind me, never noticing that three lanes of traffic in front of him had stopped, smashed into the back of my Mini Cooper. I was on my way to visit Linda with some freshly baked banana bread on the front seat, so while we waited for the police, I walked back to this young man's car and offered him a slice. He declined. I think he thought I was a bit weird. After all, he just slammed into the back of my car. Clearly, he was in the wrong; there were any number of ways this could turn out, none of which involved being offered banana bread. The police arrived, and we found out that the young man's insurance had expired long ago. I did not react. I had insurance. Why should I get angry with a guy who did not have any? To me, that only indicated other problems—maybe he couldn't afford it and was doing his best to get by. Who knows? It is not my place to judge, and as I have learned, "Who you judge, God chooses." So, I was at peace. I did have neck and back problems as a result of the accident but found a great acupuncturist, Dody Chang. She cured me, and to this day, remains an important part of my life. For that, I am thankful. Several months after the accident, I received a call from the driver's insurance company saying that they wanted to compensate me for my days without a car and any medical expenses my insurance did not cover. Huh? Apparently, the driver got insurance, **retroactively**. This is unheard of, as far as I know, and the money was inconsequential, but the miracle was not. Call me delusional, but I am convinced that if I, for one moment, fell into a place of victimization in the months following the accident, I would never have received this phone call. God's grace is out there waiting for us to let it in. It's your choice to block it with negativity or to open your heart and let in the free flow of divine love. I am not here to convince you. If what you are doing is working for you—great, keep doing it. But if you find you could use a little more inner peace, then give this approach a try.

Love Yourself, Love God

In the case of one client, God told her to love herself, but as God knows, that is easier said than done. So, as God would have it, during one of her Channeled Grace sessions, she was shown her own divinity. She was able to see herself as a divine, blinding, radiant white light unified with God. In that state, she could see clearly that when she doesn't love herself, she doesn't love God—and she loves God so she now loves herself. God's grace helped her to have the same compassion for herself that she showed for others.

Channeling Grace

Channeling = Asking + Allowing

Channeling is such a new age term that I thought I should define it in the context in which I use it. To me, channeling grace is about asking and allowing. I ask God to allow His grace to flow through me, and then I step out of the way and allow it to happen.

Channeling grace is also about healing with love. When you ask for God's grace to come through you, you must first see your heart as joined to the Divine Heart of God. You are not using your heart's love. You are using the love that joins you to the Divine Heart—the Sacred Heart. That is the Heart Jesus carried. It is a Love and a Heart that is always there for you. To prepare yourself:

Ask in your prayers to love the way that God loves.

Ask to love yourself the way that God loves you.

Ask to love all God's children the way that God loves them.

Ask to love the earth and all that lives upon it the way that God loves the earth and all that lives upon it.

Make yourself available to God, and be humble. Tell Him you are available to allow His grace to flow through you. Know that the decision is His; God will be in complete control of how His grace manifests. Know too that God wants His Love to flow between His children. To allow grace to flow through you, you want to free yourself from yourself—in other words, release your ego. You are to make no claims because nothing miraculous will be of your doing. *All glory belongs to God.*

Ultimately this all comes down to two jobs for you: **ALLOW and BE LOVE!**

The Redemption of the Divine Feminine—Finding Balance Between the Divine Masculine and Divine Feminine

Mother Mary worked through me long enough for me, and many of my clients, to feel and to respect the power of the divine feminine. At this critical juncture in the evolution of humanity, we are being asked to redeem what has been lost for thousands of years: the divine feminine, which exists in each of us, both males and females. Being born female does not guarantee that one's divine feminine is present, nor does being born male presuppose that it is absent. Both male and female alike have repressed the divine feminine.

When Linda and I began exchanging Reiki on a regular basis, there was a recurring theme for me: to get in touch with my divine feminine side. First of all, I didn't know what that meant. Second of all, I had always associated traditional feminine qualities with weakness: lacking power, being a bit too sensitive and pursuing frivolous activities. I am sure there are numerous psychological theories as to why this is so, from my personal upbringing to the then-prevailing worldview of women. Entering the work force in the 1980's, when women tried to be like men to prove they could do it all, had its impact on me. So let's just say I didn't see any good reason for me to get in touch with my divine feminine. My personal experiences and societal norms told me that I was better off being in touch with my divine masculine. It wasn't until much later in my journey, when Mother Mary started working through me, that I began to understand the subtle power of the divine feminine. I learned how we all benefit from maintaining a balance between our divine masculine **and** divine feminine qualities. It was not a matter of being either/ or. The ways of the divine feminine should not be hidden but instead be honored by both men and women. How can there be peace on earth if there is not peace within and between men and women?

I am not suggesting that we replace the current male dominated society with a female dominated one, as that would only lead to a host of other problems. I am suggesting, however, that it is time to create **balance** by inviting the divine feminine back into our lives. How do you do that? By simply **allowing**; by honoring the earth upon which you rest and from which comes all of your food, water and air; by honoring the natural cycles of the earth, the solar system and yourself; by connecting with your higher Self before speaking or doing.

The divine feminine resolves all tensions before they become anger. Every issue must be "on the table." The divine feminine does not hide things. It is free of vanity. It serves and heals at the same time. It serves and leads at the same time. It is at the bottom and at the top at the same time. It is at the beginning and at the end at the same time. The divine feminine trusts in higher guidance and does not always seek a rational explanation. The divine feminine is intuitive and will not always be able to rationalize an action with a spreadsheet analysis. Is there ever a rational explanation for a miracle? Miracles are the resulting physical manifestation of the feminine earth energy joining with that of the heavenly masculine energy. One cannot attain a miracle on his or her own. The miracle of inner peace and global peace is within our grasp. As the *Meditation for World Peace* says: *The power of peace lies within. It is a state of being that already exists. It is up to you to see it and as you see it, you project it into or onto the world.*

The Garden of Eden

In a vision, I was shown and retold the story of the Garden of Eden. It was in the Garden that women were first demonized—where Adam was made to look like a victim of a woman. I was shown that **both** Adam and Eve took the apple and ate of it **at the same time**. Men have been carrying Adam's victimhood instead of saying, "Let's try this again." Women have been guilty of accepting the blame. What both Adam and Eve failed to realize is that God forgives. Why do they walk away in shame, carrying an apple, when they can have the whole Garden? The Garden and heaven on earth are one and the same thing. Walk back into the Garden yourselves.

It has never **not** been there. All we ever had to do is to *turn around and walk back in*. I am asking you to do that now.

We are tempted every day to buy a new car, clothes, a watch, or a certain lifestyle—to spend more than we have. Isn't that the story of Adam and Eve? Wanting more than they had? Look at the housing crisis. Borrowers were tempted to borrow more than they could repay. Oh, and by the way, advertising and finance are male dominated industries. Are men the new Eve? Have we allowed Eve to be maligned as a temptress and then allowed the temptress archetype to be hijacked by men, for profit, as if it were the most natural thing in the world? Think about what has happened here. Women accepted the blame and lived with the shame, while men capitalized on the temptress. They called women evil then went on to make money by embracing her "evil ways," while avoiding being labeled evil themselves.

It is time to reunite the divine feminine and the divine masculine in a balanced and harmonious relationship where neither is victimized and neither is guilty.

There is No Man Without Woman
About seven months after the Adam and Eve vision, I was driving to pick up my husband at the airport. On the way, I decided to listen to *The Gospel of Thomas* by Elaine Pagels, an audio book given to me by Linda. As I listened to the author say what I have heard a million times before—that Jesus was the Son of God—a thought struck me. God the Father chose for His Son to be born to a woman, completely bypassing **man**, and in this case, Mary's husband Joseph. There is no Jesus without Mary. There is no Jesus without a woman. Yet Mary is almost completely overlooked in biblical writings. She is ignored in the gospels of the New Testament. How is it possible that the woman so important to God's plan is overlooked? This is a sin of omission. This is the ego of men in action. They realize there can be no Jesus without a man but his birth was **impossible** without a woman.

Men of all time have realized the creative power of women, and therefore, cast her as second best to maintain male superiority. Women must recognize their own importance and not allow themselves to take a backseat. Of course, history also ignores what appears to be Joseph's **acceptance** of Mary's role. There is always a sense in his character of playing a supporting role in God's plan. He never competes and never takes center stage. Why don't we spend more time talking about this? Why isn't Joseph the archetypal male?

God could have placed Jesus here in any form He chose. He could have had Jesus come into our lives fully formed, but He didn't. He was born of a woman, showing the Jewish community of which she was a part, how important the role of a woman is. Women of the time never capitalized on their role—and Christianity further perpetuated the sin of belittling women, especially in its early years. How did this happen? Who were these people throughout history to ignore whom God had chosen?

God said to me: *I have chosen a woman because a woman is indispensible to My plan. There is no man without woman. Woman is My flesh made manifest.* So I asked God: "What about woman being begotten from Adam's rib?" God replied: *God created man and woman. They are both a manifestation of Me. I AM both and neither. I AM you and your brother. Do not assign Me a gender for I AM above and beyond that. It is asked of you not to focus on the duality. One (male or female) was never made to represent Me more than the other. Take this to heart: men and women are in My eyes equal. They are different aspects of Me. Never has it been said that women and men are not equal. Their unequal stature has come from you. Only when men recognize their strength will they recognize the strength of women. Until then they live on the false idea of superiority.*

The Equation of Life

How could we have gotten this so wrong for so long? How could humanity be so messed up? I cried for the lack of truth. I cried for women having been maligned for thousands of years. Then I cried for myself for being asked to give up my privacy to deliver this message. And if that sounds like self-pity, it was, but it didn't last long. Jesus, Mary, St. Thérèse of Lisieux, Archangel Michael and too many others to identify stood behind me for support, but still I cried because they are there and I am here. I understand how volatile a subject I am dealing with in this book and this message about women is no exception. Without women, the equation of life cannot be balanced. It is hard enough, even with women, to get the equation to balance—but without them it is impossible. God gave us the equation and we threw away one of the variables. Then we wondered why we could not get it to compute. Wonder no more. And just in case this is not clear, it is not just about equal pay for equal work; it is much, much more. The equality has to saturate every aspect of society. There is no area of life where God sees women as not worthy of the same stature as men and visa versa.

Both Jesus and Mary were visible as I heard these words: *...men and women need to take back the co-creative force of the divine feminine. Women were never meant to be demeaned. God loves both men and women equally. See not the differences before you but the wealth that comes from joining forces. Embrace the divine feminine and the divine masculine within each of you. It is through the divine feminine that you gain cooperation and veneration for all living things.*

CHAPTER 12

Sweet Surrender

...The reason for the nonlinear nature of life is to force you to make decisions constantly because each decision you make is an opportunity to surrender your will to God's will.

- Mother Mary 4-1-09

For years after I began this journey, I resisted surrendering my will to the will of God. Why? Because I was afraid God would ask me to do something extreme, like build an ark in my backyard. Could I really trust God? It was a long process, one that would try my patience again and again, but with the help of God and my angels, ultimately, I did surrender—not completely, but enough so that my life substantially changed. Looking back, I realized that what God asked me to do was extreme in that it got me in touch with unconditional love. It got me in touch with my spirit Self. It got me in touch with the notion of unity. It got me in touch with miracles. I guess these requests could be considered extreme, but in a way that was truly a blessing to me and to those around me.

In the midst of my struggle, St. Teresa of Avila appeared to me and said: *To make it to the interior chambers is not easy...it is not your intelligence that will get you there. Surrender. Surrender to the will of Jesus, and he will guide you through the passageways to the place where unconditional love resides. We want you in the interior chambers. There are many there that welcome you with open arms. Get a recent translation (of the Interior Castle). I know I do not write clearly. Humility is a gift, and I will grant it to you if you really want it. Be humble. Look at a baby. Everyone loves a baby because he has not ego! Ego is learned when we think that who we are is not good enough. Think you that God made you not good enough? If you are one with God, then is God not good enough? I know you don't believe this, so why live it? Humility, my children. Humility, humility, humility.*

After receiving the above message from St. Teresa of Avila, I tried even harder to surrender my will to the will of God. I chose to journey through my "interior castle" via weekly Reiki sessions and twice-daily meditations. I received a lot of help from St. Teresa of Avila and St. Thérèse of Lisieux, who appeared to me regularly in 2005 and 2006. I also chose to work a bit with the practices and teachings presented in Caroline Myss' *Entering the Castle: An Inner Path to God and Your Soul,* which is based on the writings of St. Teresa of Avila.

Too Afraid to Surrender

Through this work, I realized that my heart has always known what it wanted, and it is my heart that speaks God's language. Most of my life, however, I was too afraid to follow my heart. In doing my own interior castle work, I discovered that in the past, my fears had dictated my choices—specifically a fear of failure and a fear of humiliation. This is why I didn't pursue my passions for architecture and photography, and instead, followed the safer route of economics and finance. I'd reasoned that I could make a good living in finance then pursue photography as a hobby. I guess I thought reading *Architectural Digest* magazine would satisfy my design urges. Finance did provide a decent living but didn't allow any time for hobbies— something I hadn't counted on. Anyway, my first mistake was that I had reasoned at all. Following higher guidance, the language of the heart or the path of God, rarely, if ever, follows reason.

I continued following St. Teresa of Avila's journey into the mansions of my own interior castle. In the first mansion, I found all kinds of humiliating experiences I'd long forgotten. It was painful to go back and feel the humiliation and sadness, but it also helped me to get in touch with my lost passions. I tried to accept and surrender to the pain, understanding finally that it is all part of life and growth. Where I found anger at others or myself, I released it, and I released those persons I was otherwise holding "hostage" to my anger.

Since I was so concerned about achieving and maintaining my own humility, I made a list of those characteristics that were important to me, such as kindness, compassion, unconditional love and the ability to forgive. In my meditations I also discovered that poverty is not a necessary condition of humility. This is significant to me because I struggled for a long time with this question: "Do I need to renounce all creature comforts and live a life of poverty to be humble?" I made a list of those people who I thought embodied humility, and it was surprisingly long. It, of course, started with Jesus but included many people whom I am blessed to be surrounded by on a regular basis, some rich and some barely scraping by. Based on my list, I could see that there is no correlation between humility and money. Some extraordinarily wealthy people were more humble than the poorest people I knew.

I meditated on my fears about doing my own soul work, especially surrendering my will to God's will. I was still afraid that God would ask of me something humiliating, like what I am doing now—writing this book and sharing messages from God and the saints with you. Then it happened. My fear materialized when my trusted friend, Linda, approached me to say that she had received spiritual guidance that I was to publish the messages I'd received, and worse yet, include my personal story, explaining how I went from corporate finance to receiving messages and channeling grace. I trusted Linda enough to let her type my journals, but God knew I would need more proof that the message she received was real before I would consider "going public." He gave it to me in two completely unrelated instances.

First, well-respected mystic and best-selling author, Andrew Harvey, heard some of the messages and said to me that I "must, must, must get them out into the public, even if I had to self-publish." Then I attended an intimate group channeling session hosted by Roland. Before arriving for the session, while in his hotel room, Roland sat silently with each of our names in front of him, connecting with each person's energy. During that time, he received the following message for me: *You are the God Light. You know the truth. Mother Mary is in you and around you along with the Sun/Son. Record your words! You have the higher heart.* Once he arrived at the session, he channeled more messages for me: *Mother Mary, with the most beautiful and great light, is standing all around and within you and is pushing you forward on this path. Mother Mary gave up so much on her journey—you resonate with her. You have to recognize you have the essence of her light. You can't believe it. Accept it. Pink light of compassion and nurturing is all around you. This is the truth of who you are. You will be able to carry out your mission with humility. You are all this truth. You want to ask the mundane questions, like when, how, where... You are not supposed to be dancing around in spirit floating from cloud to cloud... You have to be here in the physical world to bring energy forward... **You have to write the book.** Mary wants a chapter. It will be sacred to them who need to receive these messages. **You are to write the book. Get going! Write the book. Tell the story!** You are telling a wonderful story.*

Lead others forward. Step into God's connection and light without any reservation. Immerse yourself!!! You are surrounded by God's Light. Instruct everybody else how to find that place...[37]

In a meditation after this session, I had a vision in which I was shown how I created a bottleneck by not accepting the full extent of my personal power, which then prevented the people around me from accepting their own personal power. I was shown how important it is for each of us to expand our consciousness to allow room for others in our lives to expand theirs. If we don't expand into our full potential, we become the cork in the neck of the bottle that contains all those people who incarnate with us, whose lessons and growth are interdependent on our own. I had no interest in expanding my consciousness or anyone else's by writing a book, but I relented, and unprompted, these two authors independently confirmed Linda's message. God knows my weaknesses, and so He knows what He needed to do to keep me moving forward with His plan to get me to reveal the messages He has shared with me. He knows that, unlike His saints and great mystics, I put up too much resistance.

I try not to intentionally humiliate myself because I am perfectly capable of humiliating myself in less calculated ways. Yet, despite my opposition, it does appear in rereading my journals that, on several occasions, I did put aside my ego long enough to surrender to God's will and do what He asked of me. Aside from writing *Everyday Mystic: Finding the Extraordinary in the Ordinary*, here are some of the more prescient examples.

Painting: St. Thérèse of Lisieux as My Art Professor

In the midst of doing my interior castle work, both St. Teresa of Avila and St. Thérèse of Lisieux were appearing and speaking to me. On March 28, 2007, after delivering a message to Linda from St. Teresa of Avila, I heard St. Thérèse of Lisieux say to me: *Theresa, paint.* She was very specific, giving me the sense that it was to be abstract—color only. I told her that I didn't paint, but she didn't respond to my comment. I stayed open to the possibility that a non-artist like myself might be able to paint but wasn't sure exactly how this would come about. I didn't know how to paint; I didn't know what kind of paint or brushes to buy, and I didn't know anything about mixing colors. Not a week after she issued her directive, I received a flier in the mail for a class called "Painting from Within." I thought this must be the class St. Thérèse wanted me to take, so I enrolled. Although the class description said no prior experience necessary, I found myself to be the only one out of seven or eight students who had never painted. The others in the class were painting the sort of things I might buy at an art show. I am sure they were not thrilled when the instructor had to take class time to teach me about mixing colors and cleaning my brushes. We were sent home with our first assignment, which gave us broad leeway, as the only requirement was that the painting be in black and white. Uh oh.

I had the canvas and the paint but no easel, so I set my canvas up in the crotch of an old tree in my backyard. I sat on the ground, closed my eyes and asked St. Thérèse to show me what she wanted me to paint. Not only did she show me the design, but she also told how to make the brush strokes. What she was saying seemed counterintuitive, but I did as I was told. It worked well until the wind blew small dead leaves and bits of dirt from the tree and the ground onto the wet paint. I just kept flicking them off the painting the best I could. Each painting I did would start with a meditation in which I asked St. Thérèse to show me what to paint. She would show me the design and the colors. All the paintings ended up being similar in style.

By the seventh week of class, the teacher said for all the class to hear, "Theresa, it is too early in your career to develop a signature style!" Her scolding reminded me of my childhood experiences in Catholic school. However, instead of being humiliated and shutting down my internal guidance as I'd done so many times in the past, I responded so the rest of the class could hear, "I paint what St. Thérèse of Lisieux tells me to paint, and this may be the only style she ever guides me to paint." When class ended I packed up my belongings and never went back. To this day, I am still following St. Thérèse's guidance, and to her credit, the finished pieces sell as fast as I can paint them. I have sold everything except the first painting I did, which I keep as a reminder of this story and my surrender to God's will through one of His most precious flowers, St. Thérèse of Lisieux.

Kiss Her Feet, A Lesson in Humility

I liked being in control of my life—at least if something humiliating happened, I usually had an excuse like an evening out indulging in one too many drinks. In the ordinary course of my day, being in full control of my faculties and willingly surrendering to God, allowing Him to use me to do His will, was risky business of a different order. Surrendering myself to God's will leaves me with no excuses. I am laid bare. When I carried out His will in this instance, all I could do was steady myself for the reaction that was bound to follow.

I was doing Reiki on a client who'd been to see me only two or three times before. As often happens, I saw Jesus as I worked, and I delivered his messages. That part is embarrassing enough because I rarely if ever know how the messages will be received. This time, however, he told me, *Kiss her feet so she'll know it's me.*[38] Really?! I resisted, as I am sure most everyone other than the saints would do. In this day and age, and where I work in the suburbs of Wall Street, we don't go around kissing people's feet. I guess God took me at my word when I said I wanted to surrender. St. Teresa of Avila must have been there too, working on my humility, because I did surrender. I overcame my ego, kissed her feet and told her what Jesus had said. To make sure my humiliation was complete, my client's only response was to say that she was unsure what to do with messages from dead people. What was left of my ego was in tatters.

It needs to be understood here that I don't need to subject myself to this kind of humiliation; I have choices. I have a degree in economics and an MBA. I voluntarily left my job in corporate finance to stay home with my children, and as I was safely away from the harsh demands of the workforce, to work on these principles of unconditional love, forgiveness and the dissolution of the ego. In addition, I pursued my interest in Reiki, which seemed to be a compatible practice. When I left corporate finance, I left behind the respect that accompanied me at work, and to some extent, respect in my community. At least initially, I suspect those in my social circles accepted me more for what I once did than for what I was now doing. Surrendering myself to God and relinquishing my ego is my choice and it can be painful. At times I wonder why I just don't go back to the comfort of a good salary, doing a job that is revered by those around me.

Buying a Car: God as My Auto Dealer

Traffic was standing still in all three lanes of the Interstate highway, and my Mini Cooper was the last car in the left lane. The driver of the car that hit me never realized that the traffic in front of him had stopped. Several weeks after the repairs were completed, I had a dream in which I was told that the Mini was "cursed." Well, I don't believe in curses so I ignored the dream. I drove the car that day and I was hit again from behind. My acupuncturist, who was treating my injury from the first crash, recommended that I read *Healing Beyond the Body* by Larry Dossey, in which he tells the story of cursed objects. I read it and became a bit more concerned. So, I began to meditate on the issue, asking the Universe if it was trying to tell me to get a new car, and if so, which one. I was, however, hoping to be told to keep my Mini.

It was the end of 2008, and a lot of money was being lost in the financial markets. Like everyone, we were affected. My rational mind was not aligned with the message I was receiving in meditation, which was to buy a new car. Choosing my rational mind over the spiritual guidance, I decided against a new car and started driving an old SUV we had. The eight year-old SUV was my primary car for many years and had never been in an accident. The first time I drove the SUV following my decision not to act on my guidance to get a new car, the SUV was hit. I drove it back home and bought the new car. My husband was incredulous, as we really didn't know how we were going to pay for it. I energetically cleared the Mini before trading it in for my brand new car, which I've had for four years now, and it has never been hit. My son now drives the SUV, which has not been hit since he started driving it.

God's Will Be Done: Lessons Through My Daughter

Many people have asthma, so in and of itself, that is not so unusual. What is unusual is that my daughter was a tri-varsity athlete who was strong and healthy up until she became asthmatic in her senior year of high school. The condition was so bad that she couldn't even walk down the corridors of her school without gasping for air. She started with a congested cough for which the first doctor gave her antibiotics and an inhaler. The illness only got worse over the ensuing months, in spite of visits to specialists in New York City, Fairfield County and New Haven. At the same time, I brought her to various energy healers, including a shaman. No one could get to the root of the problem, and none of the treatments worked. Most often, we were able to drive her to the emergency room ourselves when she couldn't breathe, but one time we had to call 911. This did not happen all at once. It was a grueling unfolding, where each day was worse than the day before. In addition to all the doctor visits, I prayed endlessly for her wellbeing.

I had been thinking a lot about free will during this time and had concluded that the ultimate use of mine was to surrender it to the will of God. So, while on a practical, worldly level I continued to search out medical doctors who could cure her, on an existential level, I gave my free will to God and asked that His will be done. I told God in no uncertain terms that my will was for my daughter to fully heal and that I would never give up trying to cure her using any combination of means at my disposal. What became clear to me in the process is how my daughter was separated from this life and the next by one single breath. If she could not breathe in after exhaling, and I could not get emergency medical help to open her airways, I would lose her. And so it is that the hardest thing I have ever had to do was to pray for her life, but in the end, to know that I would have to surrender to the outcome. We are designed to die, not to live forever. We all know that—yet that knowledge never makes it easier for us to accept death, especially when it involves a child.

I prayed incessantly for the life of my child, but in the end asked that God's will be done. I understood that as much as I wanted my daughter to live, I wanted it only if it was aligned with God's will. After all, how would I know if my will is the best thing for my daughter? I can't possibly know. My daughter fully recovered with the help of a naturopath and some very talented medical doctors. I thank God, but I also thank the brilliant minds who created the medicine and medical equipment that enabled her to breathe when she could not. I am a proponent of energy healing and God's grace, but I am a staunch believer in traditional Western medicine as well. I have seen God's grace heal diseases that Western medicine could not, and I have seen Western medicine heal diseases that God's grace did not. Or maybe the Western medicine was God's grace in action. I do not believe we should throw out the baby with the bath water. God gave us brilliant minds, and he also gave us free will. We can use both.

Surrendering 101, Again

No matter how long I practice surrendering my will to the will of God, it seems that I need to retake the introductory level class, which God is only too willing to teach. This one came in the Whole Foods parking lot six years after the above incident with my daughter. I passed an elderly man in a handicap parking spot, having trouble starting his old beat-up car. He grimaced as he turned the ignition to no avail. I felt bad for him, so I asked God to help him start his car, and just like that, the car started. I thanked God until I saw what followed. The elderly man proceeded to back up into a car that had pulled up behind him! Luckily, the other driver's loud honking prevented an accident, but it reminded me that sometimes what seems to be a bad thing to us can be a good thing overall. Praying, instead, for his car to start, **if it were God's will**, could have made all the difference.

I Surrender—You Win…

Many years after the asthma incident, my daughter fell off her bike and sustained three compound fractures in her wrist. It took two surgeons four hours to repair her wrist, which required inserting three metal plates and 17 screws. Looking at the "life-as-lessons playbook," I tried to figure out what my lessons were around her accident. I thought I'd done everything I was supposed to do as her mother. I tried to allow her to journey in whatever direction life took her. I was on the other side of the country and endlessly worried about her when she was on her 1500-mile bicycle journey from Los Angeles to Vancouver. I was relieved when she returned home to the East Coast unharmed. I could rest easy knowing that now she was only riding her bike a few miles a day between home and work. Her injury happened in the town in which we lived, while I was across the street at the supermarket. I get it—I am not in control, and I cannot protect her even when she is close by. I surrendered, yet again to God's will, except at an even deeper level this time. I had no choice. During a predawn meditation, I said to God, after a short conversation with Him about my children and myself, "I surrender. You win." God replied: *It is in your surrender that you also win.*

Just When I think I've Got It

April 22, 2011 was the first day of a workshop I attended at One Spirit Learning Alliance hosted by Andrew Harvey and Rev. Diane Berke. In deep meditation during the class, I saw and felt my complete—and by then I knew, momentary surrender to the will of God. In the vision, I collapsed at the foot of the cross, exhausted from my resistance. Jesus and Mother Mary stood in front of me, along with others whom I could not identify. Jesus told me that I didn't need to be crucified, but I wanted to be. I was ready. I didn't realize it was Good Friday, the day Jesus was crucified. Even if I did know it was Good Friday, it wouldn't have meant anything because I didn't know what Good Friday symbolized.

In deep meditation during day two of Andrew's class, I felt myself surrounded by peaceful stillness as if I were in a space with no light. After a very long time, God said to me: *Bear My son.* But even after the extraordinary experience of surrender I had felt the day before, I couldn't say, "Yes." I had failed my first test since thinking I'd **completely** surrendered my will. I came out of the meditation, and Andrew explained that in the tomb after his crucifixion, Jesus was impregnated with a light that would transform history. I tried not to look too anxious as I silently called out to God, "Come back!!! I made a mistake. I get it now. I can bear Your son if You mean for me to carry his light." I was afraid that what He meant by "bear His son" had something to do with another baby, and I couldn't possibly entertain the thought of a baby now, with my youngest going off to college. I felt so weak. Twenty-four hours before, I had completely surrendered, and then I found myself saying "No" to God.

Later that day I went into another deep meditation and found myself back in the tomb. There, in the tomb, was Jesus, Mary, St. Thérèse of Lisieux, St. Francis of Assisi, and someone I could not recognize surrounded in divine light. I forgave myself for running away from God's request to "bear His son." Then I recognized that I could agree in this present moment to bear His son. Next, I made mental notes of all the ways to "bear His son." I could carry His messages forward as I am doing in this book, carry His light, or as Andrew says, serve the growing Christ in each person.

I was thinking about my inability to surrender, when God asked me to bear His Son, which just to be clear, I never took to be the equivalent of the Immaculate Conception. I was, however, concerned that God wanted me, at my advanced age, to raise another child. Jesus said to me: *...you are honest with me. I have many followers who would never test themselves like that. They think they could do those things.* I just said, "God I'm weak," to which He replied: *No, Theresa, you are strong. It is your strength that allows you to get up every time you fall.* Even though God said that I am strong, I kept thinking of how weak I was compared to someone like Moses who led an exodus. God said to me: *You are leading My people inward to themselves and to Me. It is not a physical place they must get to but a state of being. Shy away not from the task I have assigned to you.*

So, clearly, I'll never be a saint or a mystic on par with St. Teresa of Avila or any of the other greats because, as you can see, I failed God's test—one I am sure they'd have easily passed. It's humiliating enough for me to write this book, which to me is tantamount to building an ark in my backyard. I don't have the kind of faith of the great mystics, but I work on it, taking one step every day, no matter how small. God knows whom He's dealing with, so He is more than happy to help by meeting me wherever I am. That's the thing about the God I have come to know and the God I have introduced in these pages: He shows nothing but unconditional love of all and for all.

God allows me to have extraordinary experiences in my ordinary life, as He will allow you to, if only you ask. You may already be having extraordinary mystical experiences, but if not, ask. Ask to have that relationship with God, and know, as I know, that He loves you as much as He loved the mystics. He wants you to have these experiences, but you earnestly have to want them. You have to make time for them and for God. You have to stop talking and surrender yourself to Him. Until you surrender, **you** will be in charge, and **you** can't make mystical experiences happen. The more you surrender, the closer you get to God. I heard God say to me: *There are so few mystics not because they can't, but because they won't.*

I have not read *The Bible* in its entirety, but I am aware that in *Revelation*, it warns against false prophets. I am also aware that some of you reading this will think I am a false prophet. I am not a prophet, false or otherwise. I am an ordinary person like you. All I am saying or encouraging is for you to have your own relationship with God. I am telling you that He is listening to you and answering you, if only you have "ears to hear" and "eyes to see." I am an ordinary person who has extraordinary experiences when I surrender myself to the Divine.

Knowing and Not Knowing

In a message channeled by Martha Hamilton Snyder, I was told that I was to surrender to the point where knowing and not knowing were to become the same thing for me. At the time, I had no idea how I would ever get there. Knowing and not knowing were never the same to me; I couldn't imagine being indifferent. I am just now beginning to understand the following message, which Martha delivered to me so many years ago:

*...It has been important, you understand, that you NOT have full awareness—full vision —until you are at the point where **knowing and not knowing are all the same** to you. Because all you need to know is the moment and the love within the moment, which is pure communion with God. When you are set free from the needing to know, from the desire and urge to create security or to try to control your path or future, then the flower of knowledge will open fully and be present in your minds eye, like a beacon of light ever guiding you to that which you have come to assist God in...For you, dear one, the path ahead is indeed one of being the Light and allowing the Light of Christ to Flow through you and permeate the sentient beings near at hand. Being at one with the Light of Pure Love within you is central and is all that matters in your life...To willingly surrender any thoughts that are of the ego, such as fear of loss or of not succeeding at your goals. Your gift is your ability to align your open heart to the Christ energy and to allow this to flow through you without interference. Your challenge is the very human need to be able to direct this energy and this ability to create things in your own life that you think you need or want. Your greatest Strength is your*

desire to release all and surrender all in absolute faith and to live in complete peace without fear on any level.

I have no idea what the future holds. I don't know what Jesus' plans are for me now that he has uprooted me from my community and my friends. However, the interesting thing is that now "knowing and not knowing" are truly the same to me. When Jesus appears during my healing sessions, his love transfuses me, and I have no need to know what is being done. Paradoxically, Jesus taught me even more after I surrendered my need to know. The less there is of me, the more room there is for him.

The Ultimate Surrender: Trading Your Life to Save Your Children

During the entire hour that Linda and I channeled grace at one of our healing circles at Wainwright House, I saw Jesus and me on the cross as one being. It was an odd scene since the image of the crucifixion has never resonated with me as a symbol of Jesus' love. I lost my sense of the people sitting around us. I surrendered to the experience and trusted that whatever healing needed to be done for them was being done. Jesus explained to me, in the way he does—without words—the importance of that image and why it was chosen as a symbol of his love. He started with a question: *If you could trade your life to save your children, would you do it?* Of course I would, without hesitation. Jesus explained that he allowed himself to be crucified because he loved us all as much as I love my children and then even more than that. I still don't understand how that saved us, and he didn't explain that part. Maybe just showing us how a person can have that much love for people who are not his biological children is a lesson in itself. Maybe allowing oneself to be crucified is a lesson in the ultimate act of surrender to God. Maybe Jesus knew the details of God's plan or maybe he simply had to trust God. Either way, his act of love is unfathomable. Jesus taught me that: *He used his life as an example in a final glorious act of surrender and unselfishness. He sacrificed his own life to teach us true love and forgiveness. When will we learn? The point is not that we have to suffer. The point is that we have to love so much that we are willing to give our life.* Trust me, if we lived like that, it would be the end of most suffering.

Your Will Minus Your Ego = God's Will

I spent more than a decade trying to surrender my will to the will of God. Then, in an unexpected twist of fate, I found that what I want, **free of my ego thoughts**, is what He wants. God made it clear that I AM inseparable from Him as together we dance the waltz that is the co-creation of my life. The big lesson came when my doctor discovered a suspicious looking cyst in my left breast. I was ambivalent about the outcome—it will be whatever it will be I thought. A biopsy was scheduled. Linda, while doing a channeled grace healing session on me, saw that I was not to be ambivalent. Being ambivalent is not the same as surrendering my will to God. Ambivalence implies that I really don't care. I needed to deliberately set my intention for the outcome I wanted. I had to express my will with the condition that it be fulfilled, if and only if, it is also God's will. So I prayed, "God, my will is to be cancer free, if it is also your will. Your will is my will, and my will is your will only when my request is free of all ego."

But how can any request I make be free of ego? Does not the request itself indicate the presence of an ego? Is it possible to make a request that is not generated by my ego? To resolve this potential conflict, I use the free will that has been granted to me to make my request, to own my role in the co-creation of my own reality, and then to acknowledge God as the ultimate arbiter by asking that my will be fulfilled if it is for the greatest good of **everyone** who might be impacted by my request. In my case, the cyst turned out to be non-cancerous.

I then tested this theory on a more benign level—the weather. We have all dreaded the possibility that our vacation plans might be affected by rain. I love a warm, sunny climate, and thanks to the generosity of a dear friend, my daughter and I got to spend a weekend in Miami. While there, we were hoping to take an airboat ride in the Everglades. We were at the marina waiting for another friend to meet us, when he called to say that he had to turn back toward his home due to heavy rains. Being a yacht captain with many trips across the Atlantic under his belt, he was no stranger to weather patterns. So, when he told us the storm was headed our way, it was hard not to believe him, especially since there were dark clouds above our heads. I decided that this was a good time to test my ability to make a request free of my ego.

A few raindrops had fallen, but I tried not to buy into the "illusion" of what I was seeing. I could **feel** that my request for no rain was coming from a place below my neck and above my sternum and spanned the width of my chest. How bizarre that it was not coming from my mind. It was as if my mind was only there to register the fact that I held a request, but somehow, the request circumvented my ego and came directly from my heart. I can't explain it any better than that. Since I was testing the theory that my will, free of my ego, is God's will, I wasn't sure how it would turn out. I did, however, have to hold the faith. So here is what happened: other than the few raindrops that tried to entrap me into thinking I had failed, the rain held off for our entire airboat ride. As we drove back to my friend's apartment for lunch, it began to rain heavily. When we were ready to go out to the beach after lunch, the rain stopped, the skies cleared, the humidity was gone and there was a beautiful breeze blowing. At the beach, a stranger approached my daughter and said in a voice that conveyed his astonishment, "This day is magical!"

My will to sunbathe, at any given time, may not be in the best interest of the farmer whose crops need rain. I may not even know if a farmer is in the vicinity, but God does. I trust God to find a solution to meet not just my needs and those of the farmer, but the needs of all those affected by my request for sunshine. This is a simple example, which I have tested often, so I know it works. And I can say that, since that time in Miami, I have been able to feel a distinct difference between a thought that is generated by my mind or my ego self, and a feeling completely free of ego that is generated by my heart or spirit Self. Those feelings are generated from a place where God and I are one.

God gave me free will and wants me to walk the razor-thin line of using it, free of ego. This means using it for the greatest good, not only of me, but also of all God's creations. My will, free of my ego, is God's will. God's will is my will when my ego is absent. And so I pray that if my will is aligned with God's will, that He please allow it to manifest. What I can't be is ambivalent about any aspect of my life because ambivalence creates chaos. I believe that had I continued to be ambivalent about the outcome of my biopsy, then, perhaps the doctors would have found cancer. What I must do is love myself unconditionally and relinquish my ego. The combined forces of unconditional love and a self free of ego, are powerful beyond our wildest imaginings. Linda, channeling grace to me recently, heard: *You are who you are.* Said in the first person, that translates to, I am who I am, which reminded me of God's reply to Moses when Moses asked who he should say was speaking: I Am that I Am.

> *You are who you are.*
> I am who I am. I Am that I Am.

When I disburse the seeds of my ego, God's will can flow through me unencumbered. He has waited more than half a century for me to understand this. The ego is insidious, as St. Thérèse of Lisieux told me, so I must diligently guard against it. When I surrender, I surrender not in ambivalence but in the knowledge that God will choose that which is for the greatest good.

PAINTINGS INSPIRED BY ST. THÉRÈSE OF LISIEUX

CHAPTER 13

The Everyday Mystic

Enlightenment is not a linear progression. It is a process that turns back on itself to burnish the piece of coal that is you into the diamond that God knows you to be.

- God 12-2-11

Mother Mary appeared weaving her energy into the physical body of my client, a person for whom she appears regularly. I could both see it and sense it happening. When she finished, it was clear that he (yes, **he**) was carrying Mother Mary's energy into the world. She said to my client, let's call him Paul: *...and don't worry if you are holy enough...you're not. We don't look for perfect.* Then she instructed him to keep living his life as he had been—as if nothing had changed. He was to continue being a father, husband and businessman. Mary was instructing him to carry her energy, which is the same as saying to carry her love, into his everyday life.

I use this example because it so clearly illustrates how we are asked to be Everyday Mystics. We have to go on **living our lives**. We are not being asked to become monks in a monastery. Most of us aren't being asked to leave our families or our communities. God's work can be, and is, done in subtle ways as well as in the grand ways with which we have all become familiar. What we need to begin recognizing is how God works through people. In this case, He chose my client Paul, a middle-aged man, to carry Mother Mary's energy into the world. And by the way, Mary told me that Paul is not the only one carrying her energy. There are many more like him—and no, I'm not one of them, and I don't know who the others are.

You must pay attention. God has plans for you too, which may be, and most likely will be, woven into your everyday life. They will therefore require you to be **living** your life every day—trying your best; putting one foot in front of the other day after day; figuring it out for yourself; and asking Him for guidance while listening for the answers. God may lead you directly to a door transitioning you from one phase of your life to another, or He will have you knocking on door after door until you find the one that opens. He may even have you go back to retry doors you thought were locked to see if you can try a different technique to get it open. Your job is to do all you can to get to the door. Then your job is to do all you can to get the door to open. God's job is to allow the door to open—or not. You will not know which door He is going to swing open for you until you have made the effort to get to the door and turn the handle. Only you can get yourself to the door, and when one door fails to open, it is **you** who must get yourself to the next door and the next and the next. And once you find a door that opens and you walk through, you must embrace the journey that will inevitably lead you to the next door and the one after that. Rest when you need to, ask for help along the way, but don't give up on your journey.

The pace at which things happen in your life will be determined, in part, by how much effort you put into getting to these doors. What is behind these symbolic doors can be anything you think you want or have been working toward. It can be that job you were hoping to hold onto or the new job you were hoping to get; that house you wanted to build or buy; that new car; that vacation you were saving for before your savings were eaten up by a health crisis; that unconditional love of yourself or others; that disbursing of the seeds of your ego—our desires are endless. And yes, I am embarrassed to say that I have been known to arrive at a door that was locked to one of my dreams, and after trying to open it by gently knocking and turning the knob, I would resort to metaphorically pounding, kicking and screaming, and expending all of my energy on resistance and indignation before finally slumping down at the foot of the door, defeated. It was only then that I would accept that this particular goal was not going to be realized. In frustration, I'd walk away and start again. Now that I understand that the last step is taken by God, I am much more accepting and forgiving of myself when the door doesn't open, since even without the desired outcome, I did my part. The journey sometimes is the destination.

Everyday Miracles

I'd woken up at 5:15 a.m. and was starting to meditate when I heard my 14-year-old dog walking around downstairs, knocking into the kitchen chairs. I arrived too late; I had to clean his poop off the kitchen floor and then stand outside in the northeastern December chill while my dog walked in circles trying his best to finish relieving himself. Who knew dogs could get dementia? I trudged back upstairs, and trying not to wake up my husband, crawled back into bed in the dark. Well, that didn't go so well. I proceeded to knock over the notepad and pen I had on my nightstand. Fumbling in the dark, I found the pad of paper but could not find the pen, so I felt around for a pencil I knew I had close at hand and settled in to begin meditating again. Something had come to me that I wanted to write down. So, in the darkness, I reached over for my pad and pencil and to my surprise the **pen** was there, crossed over the pencil. I asked God if He'd placed the pen there, but I didn't get much of an answer. Then I remembered that St. Thérèse of Lisieux had done this for me once before while I was doing energy work on Linda, so I asked if she'd placed the pen there. I knew the answer before she responded because my eyes started to fill with tears. I acknowledged her love for me, and for all of us, and she replied: *If only you knew.*

Using the pen, I started to write the thoughts that were coming to me even though, at some point, I realized that they were my words and not the words of Spirit. My journals are reserved for revelations from Spirit, so it was unusual for me to record my thoughts, but I kept writing anyway. Then, feeling as if the pen was running out of ink, I switched to the pencil. When the sun came up, I could see that everything I'd written with the pen was not there—the only notes I had were those I wrote in pencil, and for the most part, they were the words of St. Thérèse of Lisieux.

I tell you this story in hopes that it will help you to overcome any lingering prejudice you may hold as to what the day of a 21st century mystic may look like and to help you to recognize and to interpret a miracle or some intercession from God, even a small one, like the appearance of my pen on my notepad. Opening to mystical experiences doesn't exempt me from the humbling, everyday tasks, like cleaning up dog poop. It does, however, enable me to recognize everyday miracles. When I found that the pen had miraculously appeared, crossed over my pencil, I assumed that God wanted me to write with the pen. Selecting the pen, I proceeded to write three and a half pages. When I saw that the pages were blank, I laughed. It is not that God didn't want me to use the pen; He very much did. He just didn't want my thoughts. I switched to the pencil just in time to capture the words of my higher Self and of St. Thérèse of Lisieux. An alternate reaction might have been for me to get angry at the pen for not having ink, at myself for having a pen with no ink or at God for misdirecting me. Any of those reactions would have caused me suffering.

God does have a sense of humor, and He knows what He is doing. You can thank Him for sparing you from my thoughts. Here is what I wrote with the pencil and what He wanted me to share with you: *...We have to pray. But don't just pray. We have to be like a child who bounds into the kitchen and declares, "Hi, Ma!" and fully expects his or her mother to answer. God will be there if you expect Him to be, just like a child expects his mother to stop what she is doing and attend to his or her needs and to be embraced by her, to be fed by her and to be loved by her. And so it is that although I speak of God as the Father, He responds like the Mother. I come to God as a child, expecting Him to stop what He is doing and take care of me, and He does. I have a childlike knowledge of God, Jesus, Mary and the few saints I've heard of or whom I learn about after they have appeared to me. I had no idea that any of them would be anything but as accessible as the quintessential mother, and that is how I approach them. I do not use an intermediary any more than I would ask my children to use an intermediary to get to me. I expect my children to bound into the kitchen every morning full of life and wants and needs and desires, disappointments, loves, trials, joy, excitement—and I will be there to respond. God will be there to respond to you when you show up with your life at His door or the door of one of His servants, and they are happy to serve. The gang's all there. I call them my peeps, short for my people. They are the people standing in the kitchen when I bound down the stairs with my life and say, "Hi, God! Hi, Mary! Hi, Jesus!" God in His unfathomable love for me, and His unfathomable ability to be "God the Father" yet embrace me like a mother, listens patiently and answers. He and the gang are there for you too.*

After receiving this revelation I said to St. Thérèse, "I am feeling the love of each of those in heaven for each of us on earth. If only we knew how much they loved us. If only we knew how we are watched over. If only we knew they were there for us 24/7." St. Thérèse of Lisieux replied: *Our love for you is profound. Our love never leaves you. If you want to know us, be still with me. Enter into the simple place of your heart. Once there, join the powerful force that is God. You may see God as Jesus. You may see God as a vast stillness of space. Dwell in your heart, unified with my Father and yours. When you do this, you will find your heart full to overflowing with the love of Christ. For he dwells where my Father dwells. You will find them together. Go not in your haste, forgetting what I have said. For this world counts on you to love—to love yourself, to love God, to love one another. Do as I say, and your time will not be wasted.* I said, "St. Thérèse, I love you." She replied: *Love God.*

Loving God

In a meditation prior to me receiving the above revelation, I asked God what it is I am teaching, and Jesus replied: *You are teaching people how to love God.* I don't know that I know how to love God other than in complete childlike simplicity. Love Him like a child loves her or his mother—like you expect Him to be there for you every time you fall—like you expect Him to love you no matter how many mistakes you make, no matter how many times you have to ask how. And then know, as I know, that God loves you with all your faults and failures. And know that *enlightenment is not a linear progression. It is a process that turns back on itself to burnish the piece of coal that is you into the diamond that God knows you to be.*

My love for God became apparent to me late in my journey, through an unexpected experience I had while doing Reiki on my mother. As I channeled healing energy to her, a strong feeling washed over me making me sob. The feeling was accompanied by a loud and very clear realization, "I do this work because I love God." It was so odd because there I was working on my mother, whom I love, and yet the insight was so powerful that there was not a question in my mind that the session was not for my mother but for God.

I am not at all like the saints—those individuals who so clearly loved God and dedicated their lives to Him. Is it possible to love God and not be a saint? Is it possible to love God and not dedicate your life to Him? Is it possible to love God and just go about an ordinary life—being a teenager, drinking, doing stupid things, growing out of that stage, marrying, raising a family, and on and on? I have read how some saints chose death rather than recant their faith in God or in Jesus. I love God, but if someone gave me the choice between burning at the stake and saying out loud that I didn't believe in God I'd choose the latter.

I can also tell you that, on a practical level, my loving God so deeply doesn't always translate into me being the best possible person. I get cranky, bicker with my husband, and get annoyed by or lose patience with others. I recognize that even St. Thérèse of Lisieux got annoyed with the other nuns, at times, but maybe dedicating her entire life to God offset any failings she might have had. I don't have that offset, but my love for God is palpable. Like a fish longs for water, I cannot live without God. And yes, I do wish it would translate into my being some kind of extraordinarily kind and perfect being all the time, but it doesn't, mostly because that darn ego of mine gets in the way. So, like you, I have to keep getting on that bike, and yes, I keep falling off and sometimes I crash and burn. This struggle for mastery over the ego is part of our humanity. We can look to Jesus as a role model for what a human life looks like when someone has mastered the ego, is in alignment with Divine will, and is **living in the world**, as opposed to in a monastery or a convent. There are others who, for me, are models of God consciousness, like Gandhi, Mother Teresa and Dr. Martin Luther King, Jr.—so we know it can be done. I know they had their personal struggles, but what they did for humanity was to put Jesus' teachings into action. We are at a point in our evolutionary history where this must be done again, by all of us.

The Choice is Ours—Personally and Globally

I realized, only in retrospect, that there were a series of dreams, visions and meditations that led up to Jesus' life-changing message on November 14, 2011 telling me that it was time for me to sell my house and move to the country. The personal messages were interspersed with global lessons about love. In reading through them, you will see how God may reveal instructions to us that affect our personal lives as well as teach us lessons about the global community.

In the first dream, which occurred on October 25, 2011, I had to pass through a series of strange doors as I was leaving a party. I walked through one door that led to a bridge-like platform that was suspended from above by one thin wire. I was tightly holding on to the wobbly platform with one hand while grasping a pair of green, strappy high-heeled shoes with the other. A male guide told me that I would never make it across the platform bridge while holding on to those shoes. I was waiting to drop them but there were boats crammed with people, drifting aimlessly in the water below. If I dropped the shoes, I would hit someone, but I couldn't hold on to the platform any longer with just my one hand. Since I couldn't hang on to the platform, and I wouldn't let go of the shoes, my guide took me to see a therapist who asked me about my unresolved issues. This is where the dream ended.

I was able to analyze the dream with the help, once again, of Diane Berke. In the dream there was a split second when there were no boats in the water below me when I could have dropped the shoes. However, I hesitated and missed my opportunity. The green strappy shoes were a metaphor for a lifestyle that, at some point, was no longer going to serve me. The message being that I had to drop that lifestyle when God asked me to, and there would be no time to hesitate. The dream was followed by a visitation from Jesus. In this visitation, I was wearing a simple white tunic that went from my neck to my feet and kneeling in an empty church in front of an altar, praying. Jesus appeared and took me behind the altar to a place flooded with God's light where he told me that I was not to get bogged down in the details. I was to have **faith**. As he spoke, we were bathed in golden light from the heavens. Little did I know that this dream and visitation would prove to be prophetic. The prophecy would be revealed and fulfilled step-by-step. I did not know that Jesus' November 14, 2011 *Sell now, I will find you something* message was only weeks away; and I didn't make the connection between this dream and that message until after I had already moved.

In my daily predawn meditation on November 9, 2011, I saw myself drop the pair of green strappy shoes. As soon as I did, the wobbly platform that formed the bridge stopped moving and seemed to lock into place. I walked across to the other side where I saw a beautiful white light. It felt like heaven but without dying. I entered this space completely surrendered and unencumbered.

Three days later on November 12, 2011, I had another dream worth noting. I awoke at 4:39 a.m., intending to meditate. Jesus, however, instructed me to go back to sleep. After a few unsuccessful attempts, I questioned His judgment. He kept giving me the same answer. I tossed and turned and forced myself to sleep as instructed. When I awoke, I could see why he wanted me to sleep. The "dream" that followed seemed to be a mix between a dream and a vision of my children's pre-birth planning session,[39] whose meaning became clearer with the meditation that followed. The experience was amazing—yet another example of how, when I follow God's guidance, even the seemingly incongruous directions bear fruit.

The "dream" was set alongside the river behind the house I grew up in. It was a sizable river, which at one time had enough water flowing in it to generate power for a factory. There were boat trailers and big groups with guides who gathered along the river. Even though we were not part of this paid expedition, my kids joined right in, mimicking the movements of the guide as he instructed the group we joined on how to navigate the rapids. He explained, "These are class IV rapids and very cold." The participants had to wear special, rather expensive life vests to stay safe. The group we joined had watched a DVD on how to navigate the rapids on this particular river. We missed the opportunity to watch it, but I knew that the DVD showed the participants, as they flowed down the river, the **precise moment** that they had to push off rocks, to their left and right, to avoid certain disaster in the heavy rapids. At this point, my daughter looked at the life vests, acknowledged their usefulness, and decided that, indeed, she should have one. She signaled to me that she would either save her money to buy one or ask for one as a birthday gift. After a question from my daughter, the guide explained that you could die if you did not properly push off the rocks at the precise moment it was needed, as shown in the DVD. Wow, I thought to my self, "I was just going to take my kids out on the river with no training, no preparation and no special gear. And to think I grew up on this river going in it with no guidance at all." Someone asked a question, and the guide admitted again that some people died doing rapids like this. Listening to the dangers, I realized it was a miracle I had survived as a kid on this river.

I felt uncomfortable participating in the group because we hadn't paid, but somehow my children felt perfectly at ease joining in regardless. The guide accepted them as if they were part of the original group of people we came across. He never asked them to leave or singled them out for not paying. He included them in the training and completely and totally accepted them, as if no payment was needed.

I share with you a meditation that followed this "dream" because it is here that God shifted the lesson from my personal life to the global stage. God does not always make it easy to follow Him, which is why it is sometimes only in hindsight that we can see the full picture. In the meditation I was shown the meaning of a recurring vision, seen by both Linda and Kim, of a tidal wave hitting the East Coast of the United States. That image is a metaphor for the destruction that will result if we don't change our current way of life. We need both action and faith more than ever to stop that wave. The actions required are as varied as the problems. In addition to our actions, we must have faith that we can and will push back this wave that is destroying the fabric of who we are and destroying the earth.

This boils down to one thing we can all do: **love**. We need to love ourselves enough to save ourselves. And it is here that I realized the link between my meditation and the "dream." In the "dream," the guide told the group **the precise moment that they had to push off of rocks, to their left and right, to avoid disaster. The guide explained that one could die if this is not done right as they would have a hard time surviving the white-water rapids combined with the cold temperatures.** In the "dream," I marveled at the precision needed to navigate these rapids. I marveled at my daughter who examined the highly specialized life vests and decided, in spite of their high price and her anti-consumerism, that she should have one. However, upon further reflection, the message to me was clear: her life was worth the cost, meaning she loves herself enough to take care of herself and to prepare herself for the journey. We must value ourselves likewise. We must also know that God (or you unified with God) is our river rafting guide, and He accepts us into His group, no questions asked. We are expected to jump right in and **participate** in the lessons. The environment, the economy and humanity are all at a tipping point. We still have time to push off those rocks and avoid disaster, but we must pay attention. Start by examining the analogy within the context of your personal life, and then take it to the national and global levels. The world can't wait much longer for love.

I am holding the belief that *miracles are God's medicine.* I am holding the faith that there can be the miracle that humanity raises its level of consciousness, so that compassion for one another and for the earth comes alongside profits. I am holding the faith that government exists to ensure fairness and compassion. I am holding faith that unconditional love of all, for all is the modus operandi in our personal lives, our businesses and our governments; and that that holds true not only in the United States of America but for all countries.

> *I have faith in God.*
>
> *I have faith in miracles.*
>
> *I am God's servant.*
>
> *He has shown me to put up my hand to stop the oncoming tsunami.*
>
> *I will stand at the shore, hand raised against the tide and*
>
> *I will trust that He who asked me to do this will deliver the miracle He promised.*
>
> *I do that now. There will be no fear because my relative smallness belies the God that exists in my heart.*

The choice is ours: Destruction or De-Construction. Destruction comes when the wave hits the shore. There is devastation at every level of society: social, psychological, economic and spiritual. De-Construction is the step-by-step dismantling of the old paradigm, with cooperation from businesses and governments, to make way for a society whose value and currency are love, peace and joy. God doesn't want a tsunami of change that destroys us, but He honors our free will, so He can do nothing if we bring it upon ourselves. It is incumbent upon us to wake up now and make the necessary changes.

We must reach for the impossible while things are still possible.

A Lamplighter

I was told that the guide in the first dream is a reflection of my own golden shadow,[40] which I seem to have a hard time accepting. The difference between the guide and me is that he fully accepted or "owned" his job. He didn't shy away from it. I don't know how many times Jesus, Linda, Kim and others have to tell me that I am a leader, a way-shower, a lamplighter, before I say "yes." Way back in 2004, Linda, while doing Reiki on me, had a vision of people standing on a stone bridge over water holding unlit torches. The message she heard for me was: *Guide them to the light. You are the lamplighter—light the torches so that they may see the way.* In another session she heard: *You were a lamplighter. Continue your work. Light the light that leads to love.* In meditation I saw Jesus hand me what appeared to be a long tube of light, but I couldn't understand why people would need a "lamplighter." If I could carry the light, couldn't everyone else? My belief was and is that they could. I was concerned that accepting my role as a way-shower might somehow be mis-construed as me setting myself apart from those who had not yet recognized their own light. God's response was: *...you are being asked to do this in My name. I have asked you to be the way-shower, the lamplighter. How can you not do this that I ask of you? In denying your "gifts," you are denying Me. In denying Me, you are denying My children the opportunity to see Me and **know** Me.*

Two days after the river "dream," on November 14, 2011, the Divine shifted my focus back to my personal life. This is when I was in the meditation that precipi-tated the sequence of events that irrevocably changed my life. I heard Jesus say to me: *Sell now, I will find you something.* Believe me, this was a big deal, so I kept ask-ing for verification—I needed to be sure that this was the right thing to do. I loved my house and since it was Divine Light that brought me there, I needed to be crys-tal clear that it was the Divine who was asking me to leave. I asked Jesus to send me a buyer. I also asked for a sign that this was the right thing to do. Soon after, we had dinner with friends who told us that they had just bought a farm. This conversation seemed to have come out of left field, as they had never spoken about looking for a farm before. Still, I did not want to do anything until I knew that I was following God's will for me as this decision would affect my entire family and at this point, my husband was not aware of the message I'd received from Jesus. Given that we did not want to leave the area, I believed our first step might have been to start looking for rentals in and around our hometown so that we could be prepared for when we sold our house. I trusted that Jesus would tell me, or show me, what he wanted me to do, but I also knew that I had to start acting on his guidance as, oftentimes, more guidance comes only once we are brave enough to take the first step. As you know, I received **a lot** more guidance.

No one is forcing you onto God's jet stream. Stay on that old trolley line. There is plenty of track and there are plenty of engineers, conductors and others who have a vested interest in your continued participation. The track is straight and safe. God's jet stream is not for everyone. It crisscrosses the cosmos, so strap on your seatbelt because you will go for the ride of your life. You will definitely not be staying on an earthbound one-way track. As God knows that I love to get validation of the messages I hear, the day after receiving this message I read something similar in St. Teresa of Avila's *Interior Castle.* "Their love is not strong enough to overcome their reason; I wish it were that they might not be content to creep on their way to God; a pace that will never bring them to their journey's end!"

Although it can be, the path God puts us on is not always the easiest one to follow. But "easy" is not the determining factor. Sometimes God puts us on a path that causes us to struggle; but whether we are at peace or in turmoil on that path is up to us. Mostly, it depends on whether we choose to accept or resist the obstacles we encounter, whether they are physical, mental, emotional, real or imagined. Following guidance is further complicated by the fact that, as Kim pointed out in one of my sessions, God never gives us an exact map. Very early in my spiritual journey, I had a vision in which I was walking on a path whose stepping stones only became visible one at a time, as Jesus lit them for me. Only as I took each step, did he illuminate the next one.

If you are not content, and you want your life or the world to change, it is up to you to do something about it. Sometimes you will clearly hear the voice of God, either through a divinely guided message or through a sign you may have asked Him for. When this happens, **listen up and act** on that new information. Take each step as it becomes illuminated, trusting that God will provide the next one when the time comes. Even if you don't trust God to give you the next step, you can be assured that taking the first step will lead you to something interesting. And maybe that something is better than the something you have or are doing now. Just like in a soccer game, once the coach gives you the play and puts you out in the field, you are expected to do the best you can especially when the play doesn't go as planned. During those times when you are not receiving divine guidance, it is up to you to do the best you know how.

I was perfectly content in my Fairfield County home. I struggled a lot after receiving the message to sell my house, and I struggled for a year after moving. Not because anything was bad. In fact, everything was really good, but I tortured myself by getting stuck in the past or by looking at what might have been. I just as easily could have looked at the present, which was truly glorious. But I didn't always do that. Maybe it is human nature; maybe it was just my ego that wanted to hang on to old familiar images and places. Just before moving out of Fairfield County, I backed out of my driveway on a crystal-clear day. The Long Island Sound glistened in my rearview mirror. My gardens were lush and weed free, unlike the ones I was moving to, which were wildly out of control. Was I out of my mind leaving this beautiful place I have called home for the past 21 years? As I drove away with tears in my eyes, I said to Jesus, "I need your help. Being human, I can only see what is in front of me. Please send me a sign that I am doing the right thing by moving to what seems to be the middle of nowhere." In less than seven minutes I received a sign from my radio. NPR (National Public Radio) was reporting on rising sea levels, and specifically on a "hot spot" where sea levels will rise faster than in the rest of the world. Where is that hot spot? On the East Coast from North Carolina to Boston, which would include my coastal home. Apparently, in this area, the higher sea levels will exacerbate flooding.

When I say I struggled, I don't mean to insinuate that I lacked inner peace because, by then, "struggle" had taken on a new bent. I was more of an observer of my own emotions. I observed the absurdity of my self-torture. I could look on in amusement, and once in a while, I would indulge the sadness. Yet, there was a detachment that prevented the sadness from causing a lack of inner peace. When I couldn't maintain this detachment, and I needed grace, it came either in the form of a sign from Above or in the form of help from Linda, Donna, Kim or in the following case, JoAnn Wolff.

We were preparing to move out of our house in July, my favorite time of year in Fairfield County. I watched the young children riding their bikes to their various summertime activities. It reminded me of happy times. I was sad knowing that where Jesus was sending me, I would not see these kids. In fact, there are barely any people. Does God always ask us to leave what we love? In tears, I asked my friend JoAnn if perhaps I had heard Jesus incorrectly. Maybe I wasn't supposed to be moving. I was with JoAnn for a John of God Crystal Bed Treatment.[41] She told me that if this move were not meant to happen, I would have been blocked from moving many times over. The first obstacle would have been that my husband would never have done an about-face and agreed to it. She was right. I wondered at my weakness. How did Mother Mary and Jesus do it? How did Mary give up her son, and how did Jesus give up his life? I can't even give up my hometown. As my friend Monika explained, everything I am going through is meant to break me down so that there is nothing left of my "me." Ah, the ego work, again. With each layer of "me" that is peeled away, I can get closer and closer to the me that is one with God.

I know I do this work only because I love God, and therein lay the difficulty. It is my choice to follow His lead. However, it would have been easier for me to move because my husband's job required it. At least following a job, and presumably the money, is rational. The fact that I willingly gave up a life and a house that I loved to move to a part of the country that I don't love, to follow Jesus' command, is completely irrational. And then Andrew Harvey's words ran through my head. I remembered him saying that if we could do something to help the world, why would we be so selfish as to hold it back. Is my personal life and where I live more important than the miracles that have occurred since I bought this new piece of property? Would I trade the health of those who have already been healed for keeping my life in Fairfield County? Would I trade the growth that has occurred in some lives as a result of my obedience to God? The sad truth of the matter is that I had to think about the answer to those questions. You know where I came out, but I am telling you that our human nature is to satisfy **ourselves**. It is always a tug-of-war between our ego and our divinity. I can see why there are so few saints and so few Mother Teresa's. And I can see why there is only one Mother Mary and only one Jesus. Who can do what they did? Even if we can be divine and human at the same time, or as Jesus said, we can do as he did and greater, this stuff is really hard. God knows that I am weak, so, yet again, the day ended with another of His graces. My husband came home and announced that even though our new home is 71 miles away, in another town with another area code, we would be able to keep our old phone number. It may seem insignificant to you, but these little things helped me to know that God is by my side supporting me at just the right time, in just the right way. Sometimes all I need to get me back on track is a gesture that small. And so another day passes in which I fall and God picks me up.

God is My Religion

While on a trip to England the summer before we moved into our new home, we visited the Church of St. Materiana. This is where Jesus taught that you could have a direct relationship with God. I could feel the gentle energy here as we approached and then entered the church. People used to sing here, all day, every day of the year to call the essence of God into the church. This is one of only a few churches in which I have ever felt the energy of love and peace. I saw a past life in which I walked the path to this spot with Jesus. I was guided to lie on the floor where I had slept in that prior life. Lying on the floor of the chapel, this message played in my head over and over ... *Your love for Christ will guide you.* I was shown how the balance of good and evil, light and dark, opulence and simplicity—all the dualities—play out in our hearts, in our individual lives, and how each time we choose, we are choosing for all of humanity. This is what I am being asked to do now with my move. Choose God's way over my way. This is as it should be. As our trip leader, Jude Currivan explained, the dark and the light are both conceived in love and should be embraced equally. We are designed to do this dance.

Days before we moved into our new home, I was standing in my new bedroom with my husband, asking if the windows faced due east, which they do. I was thinking of the beautiful sunset views we had just seen at a friend's vacation home. Oh well, I guess we'll have to settle for sunrises, believing that they would not be all that spectacular. The next morning, I received a photo of the sunrise outside my soon-to-be bedroom from my contractor. It was spectacular! Whose contractor shows up before dawn and sends photos like this? I think his photo was yet another message from Above. As I looked at the photo, I pondered the difference between sunrise and sunset. At sunset everything is already illuminated and then dims. While at sunrise, what was formerly dark becomes **illuminated**. Kim, while channeling grace to me, heard that I should read John 9:13, which meant nothing to either of us, so I was surprised when I read: "They took the man who was **formerly blind** to the Pharisees." For me that one phrase was the affirmation I needed to know that I, like the man who was formerly blind, was meant to watch the veil of darkness lifted from the earth as I awoke each morning.

We finally moved into our newly renovated home on September 13, 2012 and Hurricane Sandy hit on October 29, 2012. We had no damage to our new property or in our section of town, not even a loss of power, but there was damage to other towns in Litchfield County and to my old neighborhood in Fairfield County. My old neighbors were used to flooding; on every other such occasion we'd responded to storms by venturing out to see what the waves were doing. Hurricane Sandy was different. There were no neighbors kayaking in the streets the day after the storm. The fun was gone. Houses that didn't typically take on water were flooded. Houses a few streets over burned to the ground. Fortunately, in my old house there was only a small puddle of water that seeped in under the basement door, otherwise it was bone dry. Another house at the same elevation didn't fair as well.

Many friends were left without power or heat. So when one friend called to see if she, her two children and their dog could stay at my newly remodeled home, my answer was "yes, of course." Then my husband invited his friend to come as well. I didn't think anything of taking these folks in when they were in need. However, a client pointed out to me that such generosity is not necessarily the norm, and that is the only reason I am writing about it. I was told about a family who turned away someone in need during the storm due to their inability to accommodate the refugees in a fashion that would not infringe on their own privacy and rituals. These are good, loving people who intellectually know Jesus. But what I heard Jesus say was that one does not really know him until one acts like him. I find it hard to imagine that Jesus would have turned anyone away for any reason but especially for reasons of inconvenience. Maybe storms like Sandy are opportunities for us to learn a new way of being in the world—a way that tears down the illusory barriers we build to distinguish ourselves from others by way of rituals and perceived order. Maybe Sandy actually tore down walls of homes and exposed us all to each other because, in the end, that is how we stand—exposed to one another in our vulnerability and in our strength. Our humanity has to extend beyond the walls that have been erected to keep the unruliness of life at bay. Stay aligned with Christ consciousness, and you will always know what to do. Jesus will guide you to a loving solution if you can stop your thoughts long enough to listen to what he, or your heart, has to say.

Christ consciousness is not a concept; it is a way of being in the world. I heard Jesus say: *To know Christ is to be Christ.* In a recent visitation, Jesus said to me (this is paraphrased): *The notion of me as you is nothing if it is not reflected back to all you see.* If you think you know him, but you don't act as he would have acted then you really don't know him. At the very least you must admit to yourself when you are falling short of the mark. And the beauty of Jesus is that you don't have to see him as "the Son of God." If you do, that's fine. If you don't, then all you have to do is see him as a man who modeled your full human potential. He modeled unconditional love and forgiveness. Two qualities, which embodied by each and every one of us in each and every circumstance, would shift the world to a higher level of consciousness. That would be a world worth modeling to our children and a world worth leaving to future generations.

In the late winter of 2012, Roland, not knowing about my years of communications from Jesus, delivered this channeled message to me: *Jesus thanks you for being his pupil—thanks you for being a devoted symbol of his light. You have made every decision as you were supposed to...And you have absolutely no idea how big your aura is. Your humility and your ability to hold onto that vibration of energy has allowed you to excel on your spiritual journey. That's the reason why you are where you are on this day. Standing with you is an enormous team of souls, extraordinary beings of light. But you have absolutely no idea where your life change will take you. You changing—from here to there—goes beyond anything humanly possibly, it's spiritually real. It was all part of some divine energy, and I kept hearing that your intuitive, spiritual connection and link is opening the door so that millions, millions of people will find refuge. You are about to have, and you have already had, amazing life changes. You are about to take another journey forward on an extraordinary path. When I thought about you today, your aura was bigger than my hotel room...*

When you drove on the property, the angels said, Welcome home. And as you stood there, you looked back at your property here and you said to them, "But my life is there." And they said, But we have a thing for you to do. We have something for you to do. And with your trust and your obedience to your spiritual guides...And so as I thought about you, I saw this amazing journey that you have taken from your awakening to this present moment. And whether it was a narrow road or a wide road with peaks or valleys, you have fulfilled, up until this moment in time, your divine purpose. You were summoned here in this life to create a place where the light would shine; where souls could heal; where many would find refuge, and they will.

The journey ahead brings you opportunities that you never even dreamt of. You have never dreamt as big as I see this. This is not presented to you to cause you stress. It is not presented to you to cause you fear. It is presented to you because they are in a state of gratitude for you—for your contribution to humanity. Oh, your husband will be beyond delighted to know that he has contributed to this experience as well. And they are equally thankful to him.

Roland said I have no idea what is coming, and I don't, although there have been several miracles that I can attribute to the farm, which may be the subject of another book. Kim, while channeling grace to me heard: *You will show them that God's church is within. Instilling God's church in them…each person becomes their own House of God. They come to know there is no place they need to go, except inside. This is what you will be doing for the world.*

Roland also told me that he felt Mother Mary's energy at the farm, but Mother Mary is not just at the farm, she is **everywhere**. Just like God and Jesus, she is where your heart is. One Christmas season, as I stood on line outside our favorite pasta store, I looked up and across the street, I saw Mother Mary looking down. She was there gazing down at the whole lot of us who were standing in line, freezing as we awaited our turn to cram into a tiny Bronx, New York shop to get our homemade pasta. There she was, not in some far-off place famous for Mary sightings, but right here in this gritty corner of New York City. She said nothing. Her presence showed me once again that we don't need to look far for "our gang." Mother Mary was there as God's agent, looking down and watching as we went about our business. She is always there, in the Bronx, in you and with you, wherever you need her to be.

I am in no way special, and God is talking to me, so he must be talking to you too. The only difference may be that I am listening. I am an ordinary person having extraordinary experiences with God, and these experiences are not unique to me. For those who believe in God, these experiences are waiting to be recognized. For those who do not believe in God, they are there as well—call the source your higher Self.

As for religion, I don't have any, but I am not trying to dissuade you from yours. Jesus did speak to me as I sat in an empty church a few times, but I rarely sit in a church. Mostly he speaks to me outside of church—at home, in my car, at the nail salon. This is the basis for *Everyday Mystic*. I suppose if I were pressed to describe my belief system, I would tell you what I heard in meditation: *God⁴² is my religion. It has only one tenet: Unconditional love of all for all. This one tenet does not allow you to harm anyone or anything, including yourself, with words, thoughts or deeds. Just do this. No other dogma. No other rules.*

As Jesus said to me at the start of this journey,

It is so simple. It is all about love.

EPILOGUE

It is so simple. It is all about love.

- Jesus 12-2-96

I don't like the smell of farms. Before buying one, the closest I would get is a good farmer's market, and as much as I like to cook, I would find myself making a beeline for the farmer who had turned his or her crop into some sort of prepared food. I also dislike old houses with low ceilings. So you may be wondering how my husband and I are doing since we moved into our 1760's house on 55 acres of farmland. We found the local farmer's market, but around here they do not sell as much prepared food—mostly raw ingredients.

The move taught me a valuable lesson about throwing out all preconceived notions about farms and farming. My husband found a Farmer-Landowner Workshop sponsored by the Westchester Land Trust, which I expected to take place with us standing knee-deep in mud. I did not expect what I found at Amba Farms in Bedford, NY—Amba being Sanskrit for Universal Mother. I did not expect to meet farmers dedicated to the land in a practical as well as a spiritual way, nor did I expect to meet such extraordinary landowners. These people were dedicated to turning unused suburban land into useful farms, while providing young people with an opportunity to make their living as farmers in an otherwise prohibitively expensive area. The farmers work the land, sell the produce and keep the profit while the owner gets to see their land used for organic farming, instead of growing grass. I am thankful to my husband, who once Jesus got him on board, led the charge to turn our property into a working farm.

The move also introduced us to Lesley and Bill King, two of the loveliest people from our old hometown, who own and run the Back Forty Farm in Litchfield County. We would never have gotten to know them had we not been on this journey. They may not know it, but they played a crucial role in Jesus' plan. It was at their farm that Peter first saw the book, *Animal, Vegetable, Miracle: A Year of Food Life* by

Barbara Kingsolver, which opened his eyes to the merits of sustainable agriculture. It was also Bill and Lesley who introduced us to our realtor Judy Auchincloss of Klemm Realty, who found the farm for us and didn't seem to judge me as I pulled out my pendulum to check the energy of each property she showed us. Chris and Larry Washington of C&L Restorations, LLC made our old home livable, including the installation of geothermal heating, solar electric and a shoe closet to hold my now seldom used strappy, high-heeled shoes; and Marcia Tucker of Marcia Tucker Interiors made the inside of the house heaven on earth. Chris, his father Larry, Marcia, and the countless craftsmen they connected us with, transformed the old 1760's house, which I hated, into a work of art, which I now love.

Had I let my preconceived notions get in the way of God's messages, I would never have had this experience. We can't hear God if we already think we know what we want or what we don't want to hear. Even those who are adept at hearing His voice can go into the selective hearing mode. It's okay. God will wait. But think of all the fun you'll be missing and of all the wonderful people you won't be meeting. Oh and by the way, the social life here is bountiful. We did a lot of socializing in Fairfield County, but we do even more up here. If I thought I'd get back to my 8 p.m. bedtime by moving up here, I was wrong—yet again.

Before moving, I had a flashback to one of the many times my daughter hugged me as we stood in our Fairfield County kitchen, saying a cheery "Hello, mama!" I implored Jesus not to take me away from that kitchen, which had been the scene of so many happy memories. Jesus replied: *I will give you something greater.* Yet, even as I sit in this beautifully renovated new kitchen, I am sometimes sad. I sacrificed my entire way of life to follow Jesus to Litchfield County, and the move has made me aware of the work I still have to do. I never considered myself as having attachment issues but now that it is gone, I am finding I was attached to my old home and community. For God's sake, I am finding I was even attached to the Whole Foods supermarket. Bizarrely, my sadness is not accompanied by the turmoil that might have been present 15 years ago. Is it possible that in doing this inner work, in surrendering and in following the voice of God, that I have found inner peace? Before this journey began, it would have taken much less than being uprooted from the comfort of my beloved hometown to leave me reeling.

In meditation one morning, before I listed my Fairfield County house for sale, I saw myself back at the edge of a cliff I'd seen in a dream. In the meditation, I unhesitatingly stepped off the edge, and as I did, the Hands of God appeared, and I walked right into Them. I said to God, "That was easy because Your hands were there." God replied: *My hands were there because you had faith.*

I ultimately did have to ask for guidance as to where I was to move **before** selling my house. That one leap of faith was too big a step for me to take. I was trusting God to take care, not only of me, but also of my children and my husband. Then God said to me: *It is no less than I have asked of others.* I can't say that was all that comforting. Faith, I find, is yet another thing I have to work on.

The move has also been a lesson in control—as in I don't have any. My newly acquired gardens are out of control. There are too many of them and each is too big for me to bring order to. The grass is unruly. Trees and shrubs are planted with no apparent rhyme or reason. What I left behind was less than a third of an acre of combined house, lawn, and landscaped, architect-designed, weed free gardens. What I got was 55 acres of chaos. I am sure God is up there laughing as I struggle with my lessons in control down here. I say laughing because it is not like things are so bad, and maybe He is up there having fun orchestrating the lesson plan as you will see in the following story.

We found a farmer to work the land à la the Westchester Land Trust model. We interviewed quite a few before meeting Derrick, a young man originally from Jamaica, who is dedicated to organic farming and has years of experience in the Northeast. He explained how he plants in harmony with the cycles of the moon and the movement of the planets. When asked if he needed us to build fencing, he explained that there would be plenty of produce to satisfy his demand as well as that of the animals. Greenhouses, which all other interviewees required that we build for them, were not necessary because Derrick had started all of his seedlings in his third floor walk-up apartment. He was like a proud parent showing us photos and even movies of the fledging seedlings. He also had his distribution outlets in place and didn't need us to supply housing, another requirement of most other farmers. As I listened to him speak, my brain was guiding me to tell him that my husband and I would discuss things and get back to him. But what came out of my mouth was, "Great! Let's give this a try." Talk about a lack of control. It was as if I were God's puppet.

I keep waiting for this story to have an end, a grand finale meditation, but of course, one never comes. There is no end because it is about a journey of consciousness, and there is no end to consciousness. It just keeps growing and changing. In meditation one morning, I saw how even after death my consciousness will change, but it will not end as it merges with the Everythingness and Nothingness I see as God. Being pure consciousness, surrounded by and at one with unconditional love, will be yet another step on this extraordinary journey. And so my physical death will be the final ordinary event in which I will once again have the opportunity to experience the extraordinariness of God and of Love. Jesus will bring me back to the place he shared with me at the start of my journey, when he pulled me across the veil into his presence and said: *It is so simple. It is all about love.* We are always at the beginning and the end at the same time.

It is so simple. It is all about love. — Jesus

Unconditional love

Of all, for all.

Do no harm to anyone or anything including yourself,

with words, thoughts or deeds.

PART III

Messages for the World

The messages belong not to you but to the world. You must share them in all humility for you cannot do our work with an ego intact... We own not the words, nor do you. But God does asks you to own the deeds. You must be the doer of the deeds, but always remember the Source; it is your Lord, God, the Holy Spirit.

- St. Thérèse of Lisieux and St. Teresa of Avila 11-26-05

The purpose of this book is to tell you that the power to have a direct relationship with the Divine is within **you**, and that anything I have to say that is worth hearing comes directly from the Divine. These messages came to me when my mind was quiet, and I could hear the Divine clearly. I have indicated the source in those instances where it was evident who was speaking to me. Follow the messages, but please do not follow me. I know nothing, and I can do nothing for you other than to tell my story and tell you what I have heard the Divine say. If you find the multitude of messages confusing, then remember this one from Jesus about the meaning of life, *It is so simple. It is all about LOVE.* Bring your entire life into alignment with this one message. All the messages from God and His messengers are about LOVE. They are about loving yourself and loving one another—unconditionally.

St. Thérèse says, "He has always used human beings to accomplish His work among souls."[43] I struggled with how to introduce you to my relationship with St. Thérèse of Lisieux, so I asked her for help, and she replied: *Look into your heart. Do you love me?* "Yes." *Then write from your love for me and your love for God. I have taught you how to love. I have taught you to honor no one and everyone. I have taught you that either no one is special or we are all special—that is what the flowers are all about. In a field of flowers, every one has beauty in the eyes of God.*

St. Thérèse of Lisieux began appearing and speaking to me in the fall of 2005 while I did Reiki on Linda. Later St. Teresa of Avila spoke to me as well. Typically in a healing session, I would receive messages from Jesus, Mother Mary or Spirit, but the messages would pertain specifically to my client. However, when St. Thérèse of Lisieux appeared and spoke while I worked on Linda, it was clear that her first message was for the world. The fact that the message had come during Linda's healing session meant that I could not claim that St. Thérèse had spoken to me **alone**, the way I could have, had I received it in meditation. I suspected at the time that St. Thérèse did this intentionally so that we couldn't attach one or the other of our names to the words. My suspicion was later confirmed when St. Thérèse said: *I will continue to talk to you two like this so that you will both be present for my most important messages. Go now. I love you both…for the work of the Lord is done in pairs to deconstruct the harmful effects of the ego…*

Both St. Thérèse of Lisieux and St. Teresa of Avila speak of humility. St. Thérèse of Lisieux goes further and explains that as she owns no material goods, so she owns none of the words she says. I have to admit, and St. Thérèse already knows this, that I had difficulty wading through her autobiography when I picked it up six years ago. She explained feast days in excruciating detail as well as her longing to join the convent. How could she have been so good? The fact that she didn't see herself as such is astounding. When I reread her autobiography now, especially this next passage, I see how profoundly inadequate I am to be the recipient of her messages.

"How can a soul as imperfect as mine hope for love in all its fullness? Why do You keep these boundless longings for great souls, those eagles which soar to the heights? I, alas, am only a poor little unfledged bird. I am not an eagle. All I have are the eyes and the heart of one, for in spite of my littleness I dare gaze at the Sun of love and long to fly towards it. I want to fly and imitate the eagles, but all I can do is flap my tiny wings. They are too weak to lift me. What shall I do? Die of grief at being so helpless. Oh no! I shan't even let it trouble me."[44]

St. Thérèse taught me, in all my littleness, how to love. She taught me how we are all special, and if we dare to gaze at the Sun, we will likely be lifted up toward It. She reminds me that even when I stay away from God and "…soil my half-formed wings in the dirty puddles of the world … "[45] that in His infinite mercy, my cry reminds Him "that (He) did 'not come to call the just, but sinners.'"[46] And so, it is with all my imperfections and the full knowledge that I am completely inadequate for the task at hand, that I offer to you the messages I received from St. Thérèse of Lisieux, St. Teresa of Avila, Mother Mary, the Holy Spirit, Jesus and God.

MESSAGES FROM ST. THÉRÈSE OF LISIEUX
AND ST. TERESA OF AVILA

Come, little children, into the folds of my garment, and I will protect and nurture you. Peace to all I see, even for an instant.

Peace to the planet, the ants and anthills, the achievers. Peace to all who seek it and to those who don't yet realize they need it. Peace to my brothers and sisters. Let the light of creation rain down upon the hills and valleys, upon the huts of mud and straw, and upon the castles. Men and women rejoice in the second coming for it is already here. Open your eyes and hearts, and you will see. It is through your sight that you manifest its (second coming) brilliance and healing power. Follow the path I have set before you. Lay down your guns and your anger. Oh, beautiful children of God, drink up the rains of peace as they fall upon you from the heavens. Heed my call.

...I drop to my knees and beg of you to follow me. We can't live without it (peace). Leave not this earth without sowing peace in your own backyard. In the second coming, the panther lies with the lion, who lies with the rabbit, and we feed on love. There is no more. Life is at its beginning and its end at the same time. It just is. It is the present moment manifest in all its glory.

How does it (peace) happen?

Lay down your swords and pick up a broom to sweep away the obstacles to peace— misunderstanding, judgment, and a sense of lacking. You lack nothing. I have provided for you everything you could possibly need. You misallocate and mismanage. There is no lack of anything but understanding and trust in me. My knees bleed I've been on them so long. Please waste time not and spread my word. Amen

The road to peace is littered with obstacles. Fear not, you two. You are my warriors, and I have prepared you well for the (upcoming) "battle." It is not a battle in the traditional sense of bloodshed but one for the hearts and minds of all God's children, and it will be fought with love. There will be no causalities but those that choose not to heed my call. I said I'd spend my heaven doing good on earth, and you two are part of the plan. Walk with confidence into the "fields of battle." I will continue to talk to you

two like this so that you will both be present for my most important messages. Go now. I love you both—for the work of the Lord is done in pairs to deconstruct the harmful effects of the ego that society has nurtured so that it is insidious; unlike in days of old where it was obvious. It is stronger than ever but well hidden. Make no decision alone. Go in peace and be blessed my holy children of Jesus. I love you both. Amen. In the name of the Father, and of the Son, and of the Holy Spirit. Amen

You are doing as I ask. Thank you for hearing my messages. It is you two who will "walk my walk and talk my talk" as you say. The world is in trouble. We need peace more than ever. Bring it forward in your breath. Breathe in destruction, devastation, war; purify it and breathe out love. This is only the beginning. The road is long and will not end with you (two). *I made a vow to spend my heaven doing peace on earth, and I am forever searching for "warriors," those good and kind souls who will* **know** *me and my Lord Jesus Christ and bring forth the message without the rhetoric. There is no place in this crowded world for rhetoric. It belongs here not and is not a part of my plan. Go in peace my children. Rest. We have work to do. Amen, and may God bless you in the name of the Father, and of Son (the child Jesus) and of the Holy Spirit.*

Oh, my children, you are back. I need to speak to you every week. You are not making me up. I am really here. We have work to do...You must both examine your every thought and word to eliminate the perception anyone might hold of you being above them, even on a plane of enlightenment. We cannot afford this misconception. My work must be free of egoic reference...Be gentle in your instructions. Don't call yourselves healers—energy workers, Reiki Masters—not healers. It assumes an outcome over which you have no control. Be humble, and even when you think you are, be even more so (humble). Be humble, but never forget that God loves you. He will take care of your needs.

Today's lesson is **humility.** *Go in peace my children. I love you and revere you for your efforts. May the Christ Child reside in you today and every day. Amen.*

There are many ways to save the world, but only one is through God, and it is guided by love—it is love.

Yes, we are talking to you as we have spoken to hundreds and thousands of people already. God chooses who we speak to. The messages belong not to you but to the world. You must share them in all humility for you cannot do our work with an ego intact. Disburse the seeds of the ego so that they nay never rejoin to form the whole (ego) again. We own not the words, nor do you. But God does ask you to own the deeds. You must be the doer of the deeds, but always remember the Source; it is your Lord, God the Holy Spirit—It is the Holy Spirit that resides in you and gives you guidance as do we (give you guidance). Fail not my child for it would be impossible when you follow our words. Look for our signs everywhere. Amen.

Me: Ok, the danger here is that now I expect you.

St. Thérèse: *And I will not disappoint. You two are in my "brigade" as generals…Now back to where I began, with you two. Love not yourselves (other than how God loves you). I will remind you over and over again of this for my work must be free of any residue of ego. Walking amongst the populace, you must distinguish between what is real and what is illusion. You will be tempted to your dying days, but you will prevail against it all for I will be your guide. I will keep your eyes focused on what is real, and it is love. There is nothing else. Love of our Lord and love of one another. Through this formula, we will bring peace to the world. Let go of your expectations of how this will be accomplished. The Divine plan need not be revealed for you to trust in it (another part of your lesson). It may unfold over many lifetimes to come, but know, as I, that you are an integral part of the plan; everyone is. Call on me any time for guidance. Now is the time to work on eliminating the ego and judgment. Go in peace you two. I love you.*

> St. Thérèse of Lisieux
> Your foundress,
> Your patron,
> Your mother.
> Amen

There is much work to do. Rest. The lion, the sheep and the rabbit await your call. They are your "army;" you will see how when the time comes. Remember their symbolism. Fear not the lion for his mane deceives you. Take not the rabbit for granted for he is

a gentle symbol of rebirth. And the lamb, ah, the lamb—he is but all of you (humanity). Power used wisely will be the rebirth of humanity. Stir them with love (the key ingredient,) and we have "as above, so below." What is "above" is already "below." You two will help the world to see that. My work is done in pairs. You will each have a role, and judge not the roles I assign. One is not lesser nor greater than the other. Do not assign order of importance to what I do, what comes from the heavens. There is no order; there is only the glory of all. We are all one with the Almighty creator of all that is. Jesus was and is a tool for all to see that. You (two) are also tools in the workshop of the Almighty creator of all that is. He will use you as He sees fit. He does not have one task that is more or less important than another. Jesus' job on earth was no more important than that of every mother taking care of just one child; of every child who manifests himself as just what he is, a child; or every grandparent that pats the head of a grandchild; and on and on. There is no end to the magnificence of each and every person or action. Think not that one is "above" and one is "below." We are all on the same level, of the same importance and glory in the eyes of God, the Almighty creator of all that is. Walk not in darkness—the darkness of importance or status to anything in life. It is an illusion. Let go of that tendency, and you will release ego and judgment. It is the way I have chosen for you (two).

Go in the name of the Father, the Son and the Holy Spirit who resides within. Amen

Remember the nuns that irritated me (in church)? Find music in the chaos. Find a symphony in the cacophony of life's experiences. This is a surmountable journey. One in which you will ultimately succeed. Feel free to question as they will always lead you back to God. You will not stray for long. I will not allow it.

As for the world, we are entering a time of peace as the holiday season approaches, a time of rest, a time of reforming alliances. Focus on your heart chakra and your family. I'll take care of the rest. Amen

Hello, girls. So your trials continue. Linda, call on me for help. I am your friend. The world doesn't stop while you two learn. You (two) have done well under my tutelage. Linda, I brought this lesson to you for without it, you could not move forward—you know that. Trust in my guidance and ask for it. I do not fail my students, and yes, in

this instance you are the student—not the teacher. You and Theresa will teach when the time is right. The world needs two people like you (learned, clear, compassionate, enlightened). There are more like you out there. I am grooming them to do my work, and my work is for the love of Christ. It is through him that we have life and through him that we have love. Your message will appeal to all faiths—it will transcend barriers between religions and obstacles to belief in a Divine presence that requests nothing but love—it is that simple. You will build on the work of the masters before you, but you are masters in your own right. For what is a master but one who has succeeded in truly understanding the message of God.

The Christ child resides within you. Give birth to his world. Birthing the world of Christ is a slow process—it cannot and will not be hurried. You must do nothing until you hear from me. Go in peace.

You have both been soldiers before and will be "soldiers" again in my army. I take no prisoners. You choose me and God, or you don't…How you deliver my message will be of utmost importance.

Me: St. T, thank you for speaking to us.

You may not thank me when I put you to work!

You (both) are doing my work. Bless you in the name of the Father, the Son and the Holy Ghost.

Blessed be the child who walks in the footsteps of the Lord, and you two are very close. You will help each other to place your feet in those marks made by our Lord, Jesus Christ. Fear not when you topple over because you have lost your balance trying so hard to stay in those (foot)steps. They look straight and easy, but they deceive you. What you think is straight is not always so, and when you see a curve don't be fooled. See with your hearts and let your feet follow. For it is the heart that made the footsteps, and it is the heart, your heart(s), that must follow them.

Fear not the brambles (on the side of the road). What's black is white, and what's white is black. The world is turned upside down (on earth). What's "real" is not, what's "not real" is. The brambles are gifts in disguise. They will bear fruit if you shine love upon them.

Oh no, I'll not stop talking to you like this. You are on a long journey and there is strength in numbers...

Remember to ask me (for guidance.)...Once you learn how I work, things will get easier. Between two worlds there is no other way for me to teach you. Remember to ask—it helps me to communicate. That is all for today. Love me.

∾

Sound the alarm. It is time for this planet to awaken from its long slumber.

Linda: How do we sound the alarm?

St. Thérèse: *Do what you are doing. Talk to them about peace. Talk to them about me and my message of love. Pray for peace. Show love and mercy in all that you do. This is what I ask of you. Blessed are the peacemakers.*

Me to St. Thérèse: Guide me to the light.

St. Thérèse: *You are the light, my child. Let your light shine for all the world to see. Amen.*

∾

Me: May I start by thanking you for the divine grace of having you in our lives?

St. Thérèse: *No, you may not. I already know.*

Me: Please heal Linda in whatever way she needs it.

St. Thérèse: *She's baked.*

Me: Do you really talk that way?

St. Thérèse: *I spent so many years cooped up in that convent. Now, I know I can be Divine, and I can be me at the same time. Yes, this is "me," this is my personality. I love Jesus and I love you (two). Nothing can change that. Not you or my inability to find the "right" word. I will get my message across, and you will understand it. You can be sure of that. There is no way that I can fail in my mission because my mission is Divinely guided and therefore so are you. Follow in the path I set before you. Look for the markers. Stay open to me. Get a Dictaphone machine. My messages will become more prolific.*

*Start sending love (to everyone). Agree on the list. Pick a time and send love every day. The power of two. This is serious business. Don't be discouraged by a lack of **visible*** *results. Have faith. Have faith in me and in the divine plan I administer. I speak not for myself but on behalf of my master, your guiding light, Jesus Christ, the most ascended of all the masters. Follow him, and you will not be led astray.*

Send love as if your life depended on it.

Blessed are the children who follow in the footsteps of the Lord...
Me: Is there a time the universe chooses for us?
St. Thérèse: *The Universe does not recognize time...Yes, weekends too. Evil (darkness/ lack of light recognition) does not take weekends off.*
Go in peace my children. I love you. Do well.

This is about the journey of the soul, which knows no bounds. Your mission, as St. Thérèse of Lisieux has told you, is from God. I am here to guide you on His mission for your souls. Listen carefully as this is a very subtle mission. It requires very little energy in exchange for what will be a gargantuan awakening. Hold my gaze! (Don't close your eyes). We will awaken Linda first (I could see St. Teresa's hands over my hands.) *She is older and wiser and will lead the way in this. You are the vehicle because you are pure love, and we have removed enough of the ego to allow for me to work through you. It matters not who awakens first, second or last. It is an order chosen by God, and all of you will arrive at your destination—that is a given—it is not by chance and it is not negotiable. Fear not the order and assign no significance thereto. Go in peace. My work is done.*

Walking in our shoes is not a task to be taken lightly and humility does matter. Practice not what you choose but what we instruct. Follow our way—the way of the Lord in your every thought, word and action. Follow us. Look up and we will be there guiding, directing, instructing.

Me (forever doubting): I want to make sure I am not making this up.

How could you? Do you not see me? Do you not feel me? Do you not love me? Put away your doubts. St. Thérèse of Lisieux put her hands over mine (I saw her and saw St. Teresa of Avila standing behind her) and she said: *You must heal completely to do my work. We have attuned you to our energy, and you will attune others.*

To make it to the interior chambers is not easy...it is not your intelligence that will get you there. Surrender. Surrender to the will of Jesus, and he will guide you through the passageways to the place where unconditional love resides. We want you in the interior chambers. There are many there that welcome you with open arms. Get a recent translation (of The Interior Castle). I know I do not write clearly. Humility is a gift, and I will grant it to you if you really want it. Be humble. Look at a baby. Everyone loves a baby because he has not ego! Ego is learned when we think that who we are is not good enough. Think you that God made you not good enough? If you are one with God, then is God not good enough? I know you don't believe this, so why live it? Humility, my children. Humility, humility, humility.

Our love we send to you. The depth of our love for you has no bounds. What you do for each other, you do for us. Continue with your work, and don't forget the rest of the world. Send it love as you send love to one another. We will continue to pray for you. Linda is a child of God. We want to work through you both. Keep up your work. The time will come. Honor (remember) our spirit of love and devotion. That's all it takes, but you must be persistent in your pursuit. Don't give up when things don't go "your" way. We have said enough. Pray for peace. Your friends, your guides, your faithful companions—St. Teresa of Avila and St. Thérèse of Lisieux.

We speak with one voice. Bless you, my children for your work has begun in earnest...Continue the work of the Lord, your God, your Guide. We will not fail you. Ask us again to be your guides. Heaven and earth will become one—they are one. Help people to recognize that. Show them the Little Way—the way of peace—one soul or spirit at a time (yes—that was from me). The time has come when we must leave. Adieu my fair ones!

...Just by becoming who you are becoming you affect thousands of people. Keep on heightening your awareness—that is all we ask right now.

And the two shall be as one. Walk amongst the people, you two, and bring your healing gifts. It is time to share. It is time to spread my word. It is time to spread the true word of the God consciousness. How? *Advertise.* Where? *Religious publications. I will find you a place to teach. Build it, and they will come. It (the people, the classes, etc.) will build slowly then reach a crescendo. You two are guides. My army of love needs "warriors" who can spread the word without personal (egoic) gain. Of course you will be recognized, but you won't need the recognition. It will be of no consequence to you. You tread a path of humility—the path that is lowest and highest at the same instance. Fear not what I ask of you, for it will all happen as it has already been ordained (in Divine Time and in Divine Order). You can't stop the tide of change. Be thoughtful in your approach. Don't be rash. Do not rush. The world evolved over millennia—so too will the change. Be patient, my dear friends. Love is on your side. I am on your side. Amen.*

...The path is not long. The time is near. Know that I am always with you, in good times and in bad. I pray for peace on your planet. I pray that more souls will listen to my message of love. The solution is love. But how do we get people to love? By loving them. Hold back from (loving) no one. This is my message for today. Go in peace my prophets.

May the peace of God be with you both as you travel the path I set before you. My path is not lined with gold, but it is as surely lined with love and will lead to love. It leads you straight into the arms of my savior and yours Jesus Christ where you will reunite with him and the kingdom of his Father. Ah yes, that (He) is a Father! For in His house, you are safe. There is balance. There is peace. There is unconditional love and kindness. When you reside in that house, these qualities become a part of you, and you bring these qualities to the world by being the embodiment of them. That's it. There is no grand plan. There is only a "grand being"—a state of being that is so "grand" it is capable of bringing peace and harmony to the planet. That is what I mean by being a "soldier of love." It is a state of being so elevated that it heals not only in your Reiki room, but it heals everyone in your path, whether you recognize it or not. This is what you are called to do. My soldiers carry no weapons. My soldiers embody love. They know they are one with the Father. They know they reside in the Father's House, which is the source of all that is good. Abide with Him, my dear ones, and know His

ways as your own. Become one. Unite, not as men unite with one another to form an army, but unite your spirit with the spirit of my Father, your God and you will be part of the greatest "army" on earth.

Ah, the monkey stays on the monkey's back. The monkey is the ego. Get the monkey off your back. The ego is like a drug. Resist every urge to let it engage—complete abstinence is the way. Each time you feel it rise within, fight it back—do not give into temptation. Just like an alcoholic, there is no such thing as "just this once." Just this once starts the whole cycle all over again. Run. Run away. Restrain from all, even the smallest temptation to engage it.

The ego creates blocks to unconditional love and blocks complete unity with your Father, Jesus Christ. Doubt me not. Release the ego, and see how quickly you realize complete unity with Christ. With this follows complete unity with one another. If you don't believe me, try it, and see if it is not true. For there is no truth greater than that of unity, and only the humble arrive. The choice is yours.

Do my work, dear ones. Do the work of Christ. The road to egoless living is narrow, but once you cross the dividing line, you will see it is smooth and easy to travel. (In this vision I could see that the road of the ego is wide but full of rocks, difficult to travel, but its breadth deceives us.) *Come off that road you have traveled so long. It is one thin line that divides my road from yours. You are one step, one thought, one breath away. Cross that line, and never look back my dear ones. Unity is the answer. All your questions disappear into the One. Be at **One**.*

My castle is open to everyone. There are bridges and doors everywhere, but we cannot force those who do not want to, to enter. You cannot force another to cross. You can only show love and compassion (and humility).

A soul in a state of grace has nothing to fear from the devil.

It is by the grace of God that you are here. It is God's grace that you must send out to His children. You are awakened to His call to be the embodiment of His love and His will here on Earth. Withhold the message not.

Peace will come my children, and the work you do is in no small part responsible. My work is done in pairs, and you have heeded well my call. It is the "pairs" that was almost more important than the work. By honoring the "work in pairs," you have brought the energy of unity to many. Yes, you still have work to do individually but you (can) see that universal work can be done simultaneously. You do not have to complete your own work to accomplish mine. Thank God!

Worry less. Enjoy more.
Think less. Enjoy more.
Celebrate life.
Let life flow to your door like the waves…
For you do not need to seek after life.
Life will seek after you.
For if God wanted you to seek after life, He'd have given you wings.
Instead you have feet. You are slow moving creatures, planted in one place for long periods of time, for a reason.
There is nothing to "figure out." That has been done for you.
You are only to listen. Set aside your demands to know why and listen to what is. It is all there for you—NOW.
There is no tomorrow. There is no "there."
There is only now and there is only"here."
Never mind what others say.
Follow your hearts, and let your slow feet lead the way.

Honor the earth as you honor your (our) Father in heaven for both are part of the divine plan right alongside you. One is not needed more or less than the other. They are needed equally to balance. It is the way of my Father to leave out no one or no thing. My Father loves the earth as He loves the heaven. He loves your body as He loves your spirit. One does not exist without the other, and so thou shalt not judge the earth

to be not worthy of your full love and admiration. Embrace it wholeheartedly. My children need a place to live, and they shall live upon the earth—it has been decreed and ordained that this will be so. Fear not the darkness (dirt) for within it lies the source of life on earth. Do not disregard the gifts of your Father.

You change the world and those around you by becoming who you truly are, but don't hold it as a condition that "they" must change—you are responsible only for your own awakening.

Ah, and so the two have become one. As it has been all along, you finally see. Spread love. Be love. Embody love. For where love goes, peace follows. Peace is not here or there, past or future; it is ever present waiting to be recognized, like a children's game where love is the decoder. (You can only see clearly when you look through the filter of love). **Love,** *that is your job. Before this you would not have understood this message. You must feel this message. You must feel and know its power to respect the message. Had I said it earlier, it would only have had an intellectual meaning. You are* **beginning** *to feel the meaning. Now* **live** *the meaning (of love). It has power still yet beyond your wildest imaginings.*

Your patroness,
St. Thérèse of Lisieux

St. Thérèse: *(In a new world)…There are no leaders. It requires everyone or no one. The others get on board unknowingly. The "train to freedom" runs constantly and does not halt until everyone is on board. As it "circles the earth," more and more people climb aboard. You two were early to board and are calling more to join you as you do our work. Some you know; others you will never meet. It matters not where they get on, or if you realize they are aboard. For it is known from here where we stand. Don't give up. Trust in what you do and your role in the divine plan. Do not be discouraged by "setbacks," and there will be a few. Keep working toward your goals and do not give up faith. This will be tested. We are your guides while you are here (on earth). You will do good work and even greater work when you are gone. Keep them boarding the*

train! Don't become afraid of the volume (of people)—the train expands to accommodate all those who desire it.

∾

The ego works in mysterious ways—be vigilant. As you sow, so shall you reap. Sow seeds of the ego and you will reap despair. The seeds of divinity are already in the ground; they need not be sown. They do need to be nurtured, watered and allowed to see the light of day. They are tender, …but they will always strive toward the light (the Father). Nurtured and caressed by their mother earth, they fear not, nor fight their presence on earth but sensibly grow toward the Father in heaven. You must do likewise.

Question not where God has sown His seed. …Honor and understand that this is where the seed is being nurtured by its Mother earth, and instead of looking at the soil in which the roots have been asked to take place, look to the Sun or Father. The roots will take care of themselves. A plant doesn't grow by "looking" down (and questioning "Why did I take root in this crack in the sidewalk?") Honor the crack. …It is the ground in which you have been asked to take root. Look toward the Sun, and begin to grow.

∾

Ah, sweet is the rain that falls upon thee; for it is the rain (lessons) that helps you grow. Lift your face to the heavens as the rain falls, and know that is falls for thee. For you alone was this rain chosen. Allow it to wash over you.

∾

There is no rest for the weary. The lessons will keep coming. They come to those who seek the Truth. So for as long as you are a seeker, you will have lessons. Do not wish them away for that will mean you have stopped searching.

∾

Our love for you is profound. Our love never leaves you. If you want to know us, be still with me. Enter into the simple place of your heart. Once there, join the powerful force that is God. You may see God as Jesus. You may see God as a vast stillness of space. Dwell in your heart, unified with my Father and yours. When you do this, you will find your heart full to overflowing with the love of Christ. For he dwells where *my Father dwells. You will find them together. Go not in your haste, forgetting what I have said. For this world counts on you to love—to love yourself, to love God, to love one another. Do as I say, and your time will not be wasted.*

Me: St. Thérèse: I love you.

St. Thérèse of Lisieux: *Love God.*

∼

MESSAGES FROM MOTHER MARY

Have mercy on him. He is a child of God.

∾

My children have strayed too far...bring them back into the fold of love.

∾

Open your hearts and let in the Light for it is there that you find love. Love is all there is, and it is already inside of you.

*I have asked Theresa Joseph to work with you to help you to find this love. She will do nothing you can't do yourselves. She is a **temporary** guide under my mentorship. I will work through her to bring you to me and to God (Love). I have enlisted St. Thérèse to help me. We both work through Theresa Joseph, as she is a clear and open channel. Trust her—we do. May you have a blessed journey back to Christ.*

∾

...The reason for the nonlinear nature of life is to force you to make decisions constantly because each decision you make is an opportunity to surrender your will to God's will.

∾

Don't let your need to control dictate your relationship with God. Allow God to come into your life in whatever way he chooses. Be ever aware of when He is there. It is not going to be obvious to you. You have some notions of what God might look like in your life. Relinquish those. Always ask what God's will is in the broadest sense. Looking at the forest as opposed to the trees. Ask what is God's will in the big picture for me.

∾

Where my son goes, there you go. Where you go, there my son goes.

∾

You do not have to reach for the "ring" of inner peace. It is already there inside you, and with it comes global peace. With inner peace comes peace on earth. Do not shut yourself off from this possibility. Only through you can God's Garden be re-cognized on earth. It is waiting to be rediscovered.

∾

Be pure of heart.

∾

The strongest trees in a storm are those that bend with the wind.

∾

Personal power does not come through controlling others. It comes through loving yourself.

∾

MESSAGES FROM THE HOLY SPIRIT

Decisions made in fear will result in a situation to be fearful of.

～

*Listen to the universe when it speaks to you! Your **mind** is too limited to imagine all the possible outcomes. Even if you don't get what you hoped for, the universe has something even better in store for you. Believe, trust, love and learn.*

～

When all else fails, try love. Have compassion for yourself. Sing praise to the Lord for all is good.

～

If you can have just one noncompetitive relationship on earth then you have manifested heaven on earth.

～

Throw away the self-deprecating for the happiness of what is. Accept the gifts that God has given.

～

True healing lies in true forgiveness not "brushing off." True love is resplendent. Love with conditions is tainted—a poor facsimile of the whole (love). True love, forgiveness and compassion are in you—let them out.

～

Look inside yourselves for peace. Be one with your Divinity, and you will be free. Recognize that you are not a separate entity from God. You are the Divine made manifest. Walk your journey with this knowledge.

～

I want you to know peace and love.

Every person, every situation is there for one reason—to teach you how to love. This is why we have diversity; because without it you could not learn unconditional love. All the multiplicity, all the complexity boils down to this.

Pain is like a river. You must let it flow past. You cannot hold on to pain just as you cannot hold on to a river. If you do, the river becomes swollen.

You carry knowledge within—inside the God consciousness. The knowledge does not come from outside of you. Just like a seed that contains all the information it needs to grow. So do you. Look within. Start talking to the Christ within. Acknowledge your ability to perform miracles.

God is a concept. You are the God made manifest. You needed Jesus to show you what God made manifest looks like—and he looks like you. He is you.

If you are the manifestation of the God consciousness, then you need to set your intention, and know that your intention will manifest. This is why you can manifest—because you are the God consciousness, and as such have all the powers you have historically attributed to God. God wants you to know Him by being Him. Jesus was a son, but so are you a son of God.

There is no healthy portion of the ego. (The idea that we would) need to call on "ego" in certain situations assumes that divine nature is incapable of handling all situations. This is a false assumption. Intellect does not equal ego.

Releasing judgment to reach the level of unconditional love will involve some of your hardest lessons. The Universe will put in your life people who are difficult to love. Then

*it will wait patiently as you struggle with your feelings—not that the Universe wants you to struggle. It wants you to reach a level of consciousness, whereby you can love unconditionally. The struggle is within you. It need not be a struggle if you can put aside **judgment**. It is not and never has been your job to judge others, thereby deciding if they are "worthy" of your love. If you believe in an All-Loving Presence, and the person you judge is good enough for God to love, then who are you to decide otherwise?*

*You may decide you don't like one's **actions** but must learn to separate the actions from the person, who is a child of God. Know you not that God has asked this child to act as he or she does just so you may have the opportunity to learn to love unconditionally? Once you shift your perception in this regard, you will find it easier to feel compassion, and in feeling compassion you learn to love unconditionally. Once the lessons are learned, you will find you are no longer confronted by "people who are hard to love." This is your gift from the Universe. Once the lesson is learned, you will not be "tested" again at least on a personal level. The lesson, however, may be expanded to a community-wide, national or global level.*

Know that every situation you read or hear about, even if not in your immediate sphere, is a chance to learn; a chance to stop judging; a chance to show compassion, forgiveness and love. Try it. Take a situation and try shifting your perception. Start with someone in your life who is difficult to love. Know they carry with them a lesson made-to-order by the universe. Begin by no longer judging them. Acknowledge them as one of your "teachers," and thank them for taking on a role that may be particularly odious. You will know when you've accomplished this because you will automatically begin to feel compassion. With compassion comes love, and with these feelings fully entrenched, you reach a state of consciousness called unconditional love. This is a higher vibrational level that brings more peace and joy into your life; even a life that is already filled with peace and joy may benefit. For lives already rooted in peace and joy, this practice will bring you to a more blissful state than the one you currently enjoy.

The beauty of this process is that you have nothing to lose. If this does not resonate, (ignore this suggestion) *and you'll know that was the right thing for you to do, if you don't think of this again. If you try the process outlined above and it doesn't work then you've lost nothing but some time trying to be nonjudgmental. On the other hand, if it works for you, you will have elevated your own state of consciousness and believe it or not, uplifted the life of the person whom you were judging.*

Many blessings to you—to those you learn to love and to those that, for now, have sacrificed their own happiness to teach you.

~

You live through your past; you do not carry it with you.

~

Love is what will keep you alive, not fear.

~

Be love, see love, and everything will fall into place.

~

Fear doesn't keep you safe. Love does.

~

The difference between heaven and earth is perception.

~

We are already the Christ consciousness—the Light. For it to shine through, we need to get rid of the "me" (ego).

~

Don't let your mind undo what your soul has accomplished over millennia.

~

*When Jesus said you reach God through me, he did not mean for us to take that literally. He meant that we reach God through his (Jesus') **teachings**; through his words and actions—by doing what Jesus taught (not by worshipping Jesus.)*

~

The trilogy—Father, Son and Holy Spirit—is also what you are. Jesus showed you who you are through who he was. He never meant for you to think only he was the inclusion of the Father, Son and Holy Spirit. He meant that you are too.

❧

The reason we are afraid to let God choose is because we think He will choose poverty and a life of hardship for us.

❧

...and there is God. He needs no fancy palace. He needs only your heart and an open door to let him in.

❧

...you try too hard. Everything you look for on a physical or spiritual level can be found by giving over to the will of God. Perfect health and contentment are already present.

❧

Why does God choose certain people?
Who you have judged, He has chosen.

❧

God is Love. God is not a human-like figure. God is the "energy" of love. He is the "active" version of Love that exists everywhere.

❧

*If gold is **solely** what you wish, you will have gold and nothing else. Prosperity is much deeper than just money.*

❧

Miracles are God's medicine.

❧

Christ consciousness is an expression for how a man lived who embodied God. He brought heaven to earth. You each have this capacity within you.
You have to know your heart to let your heart be known.

❧

*What **you** say or do is not the cause of the reaction in another. Reaction is completely the domain of the person reacting.*

We must resolve all tensions before they become anger. Everything must be "on the table." The divine feminine does not hide things. It is free of vanity. It serves and heals at the same time. It serves and leads at the same time. It is at the bottom and at the top at the same time. It is at the beginning and at the end at the same time.

The pendulum swings side to side before it comes to rest in the middle.

Know that true wealth comes from within. It comes from the goodwill you have created...

Glory belongs to God. It belongs to no man. It is only when you realize only the God in you, that the glory belongs to you too.

There is one God, and He or She has many different faces. What He or She looks like is you. You are God made manifest. Close your eyes and invite yourself to recognize your own God essence.

They will know you in your humility.

Regardless of your belief system, you will be offered a place with God. If you choose to believe "there is nothing," then that is what you choose. There is not "punishment."

Embrace yourself—even your perceived imperfections. Jesus perceives none of them. He perceives you in all of your perfection. Imperfections are the ego's perception of yourself plus others' perceptions, which permeate your field.

Glory belongs only to God. Glory belongs to no man until he is unified with his creator, and then it belongs to them both.

There is no drug as powerful as forgiveness. Forgive yourself, and forgive those who trespass against you.

You are the Light. You are one with the Father. You are unified in Christ consciousness. The forces of evil cannot hold a candle to you.

*The devil **tempted** Jesus. He did not **scare** Jesus. Nor should you be scared. Face off against evil. Look it squarely in the eye and send it away. Dissipate it by not allowing it to have power over you. …There is no place for darkness to hide. You fight the darkness with the light…do not get lulled into a false sense of security…I was shown in this meditation that one force of light offsets two forces of darkness. This ratio keeps the world in balance. To tip the world toward overall good, if the number of dark-side people stays the same, even one more person in the light helps tip the balance to overall good.*

You live in God-time. God-time is nonlinear, nonsequential. It is where miracles take place. God-time exists for everyone at all times. God-time exists within you as a field of ultimate possibilities. Be afraid not to use this—to operate within this field. Take a leap of faith into ultimate and unlimited possibilities. Tarry not for this is the path to your best end.

God consciousness is implicit in Christ consciousness because what Christ knew is that he was one with his Father in heaven.

The reason Jesus didn't manifest for people all the time is because people needed to know they have the power within themselves (to manifest).

She who wears God in her heart wears love. There is no better garment.

You must walk alone to the Light. No one can lead you. They can only show you the way.

Be love now. By being love, you are the pebble in the pond sending out the vibration of love to humanity.

Your higher Self is the merging of your perfect Self with God. It's like heaven on earth. It's not purely God—it's you with God. You're meant to be part of the equation. You are here on earth, and you are meant to be integrated. Who you are is meant to merge with God.

Not judging yourself is the same as loving yourself unconditionally. That is what unconditional love means—no matter what, you love yourself, and that is how God loves you…There is no judgment that resides in your heart. Judgment comes from your ego. Your mind has become a slave to the ego. Let your mind work for your heart; let it be entrained with the vibration of your heart. The heart only knows love for yourself and love for others. You want your mind to walk, to march in lockstep behind your heart, and in that way you will see the world the way God sees the world. When you are looking at the world through your ego, you are looking at the world through the lenses that have been defined by others…Your heart is so powerful that it knows only love. Your heart knows not of judgment or condemnation. Let your heart lead the way…Until you have compassion for yourself, no one can have compassion for you… Have mercy on yourself. As you judge yourself, you judge others. As you judge others,

you judge yourself. These are universal truths…Don't put limits on your Love; God has put no limits on his Love for you.

❧

Be afraid not. For in your fear, you condemned yourself to fear. In every situation, you choose love or fear, and when you do not choose love, you choose pain. Let go of your fear, and know that God is with you. It is okay to feel the pain of loss, but (somehow) *it is supposed to make its way through you, and not be held on to.*

Acceptance is the key to non-suffering. Through the suffering we are meant to learn non-judgment. Give your pain and suffering to God by accepting His will. Never, ever believe that you are alone because you are not.

❧

Ask that God's Love infuse all of you and give you the strength and power you need to persevere because what is true is that there has never been so much love on the planet at one time, and that makes all of you stronger.

❧

Being a servant of God is not the same thing as the earthly master and servant relationship. It is more of a Teacher and student relationship where the student possesses all the attributes of the Teacher and is looking to "serve" the Teacher by actualizing all those attributes. The student is becoming the Master or Teacher by becoming LOVE.

❧

The absence of the ego allows you to recognize your unity with the Divine and with one another. What you do to others, you do to yourself. In the unified state, you are at peace.

❧

Go nowhere your heart doesn't lead you. Always love yourself first because in that action all else follows. You cannot give to another what you don't have. For only firmly rooted in love can you give love. Give love to yourself and you give love to others.

Withhold love for yourself and you withhold love from others. Go nowhere where love does not grow...and it will grow everywhere you are if you know first how to love yourself.

All of humanity is on one team. We need all 7 billion of you playing against the ego team. If even one of you drops out or stops playing, then who is there to carry the ball of love that I pass? Who will score another point for love and compassion against team ego? Don't drop out of the game. Don't sit on the sidelines. We need everyone playing on the side of Love. It is how we will win the game. I need you there and ready to catch the ball of love when I pass it to you. Catch it and carry it to the end zone. Catch it, and score a goal for Love. Get a point closer to winning over team ego.

If you want to set yourself free, you must open your heart and follow its lead.

Spiritually speaking, pure love is the only thing that heals. Faith in God is the only thing that gets it where it needs to go.

Never has love failed. No matter what the questions, love is the answer.

You are the only one who stands between you and your happiness. It is all how you choose to react to a situation.

Life is at its beginning and its end at the same time. It begins and ends with you. It begins and ends with love.

Enlightenment is not a linear progression. It is a process that turns back on itself to burnish the piece of coal that is you into the diamond that God knows you to be.

It does no one any good for you to undervalue yourself. You can only be valued by others as much as you value yourself. So it is incumbent upon you to value yourself as God values you, which is the same as saying to love yourself as God loves you.

The emphasis is on value—value for yourself. So much emphasis in the finance world is placed on valuing an asset, and you are to look at yourself in the same way. You are the asset, and you don't want to undervalue yourself. An asset that is worth unconditional love—that is your value.

I got a message a long time ago about the new currency being love, peace and joy. And if you were to value yourself in the new currency, you would be worth unconditional love, unconditional peace and unconditional joy. And that is how God values you, and that is how others will value you when you value yourself that way. It starts with you. It actually starts with God, but He's already done His piece. He's waiting for you to do yours. And your piece is just to recognize what He already knows. And when you do your piece, everything else falls into place.

So waste time not—in loving yourself. Let it begin now because the world needs you. The world doesn't need you as half a person; it needs you as wholly loved by you. It's like the friendship necklace. A heart you give to your best friend and you have the other half and when you put them together, they fit like the pieces of a puzzle. So here's the deal: It's like God is one half of the friendship necklace, and you are the other half, except you can't fit with his half until you recognize your divinity and love yourself unconditionally. That's the key. That's the key that enables you to fit your piece of the puzzle with His—and then it's perfection. It's like these two pieces come together in this beautiful, bright, divine white light, and this light just shines out in every direction and makes you whole. That is what God is waiting for with each of us. He is waiting for us to recognize ourselves and to love ourselves unconditionally the way He does so that our piece of the puzzle can fit with His, and this divine healing can be born.

Each of us holds the other half of that friendship necklace with God. He wants so badly for us each to recognize ourselves as lovable, as unconditionally lovable, and worth the value of unconditional love, unconditional peace and unconditional joy.

So, the question is, what will you do with your half of the necklace? You are the necklace. You are that half of the necklace. Your whole being—your body, your mind, and your spirit—are half of the necklace but to make it fit you have to love yourself the way God loves you. I don't know how many other ways to say it. It is always the same message for everybody. It's the same message for everybody in the world. For everybody on this planet, it's always the same.

Just live that message, and you won't have to think about anything else. Just focus on that message and do it. Everything else will fall into place. There is nothing else to do. There are no other questions to answer.

Mother Teresa is here because she loved the world so much. She loved even the most unlovable of God's children—at least in the eyes of the physical world. She was here to show the world that they are not unlovable. She, like Jesus, came to show unconditional love.

She says: Dear child, you are not the least of God's children. You have been blessed so many times over. Take those blessings and spin them into the gold that is you. God's love knows no boundaries. He is with you always. He resided inside of you. He resides through you, and He resides outside of you. You cannot be separated from His love.

To be a bride of Christ means to be married to his ways.

I had a request to teach a client's children Reiki. The client knew I no longer practiced Reiki but understood its usefulness, as do I, as a self-healing modality. Her husband, however, was not comfortable with it. The Holy Spirit presented this solution to me in meditation.

Teach them what Jesus said (…whoever believes in me will do the works I have been doing, and they will do even greater things than these…) and tell them that you are taking Jesus at his word, and they should too. But they must do this with all humility and knowing that it is the Christ within them who makes healing possible, and further, that all healing decisions be left to the will of God. You are but an instrument in His (God's) toolbox. Make yourselves available at all times, and know that you and He (God) are one.

Jesus did not come here to be worshipped. He came here to show us how to live.

Christ is alive in you; you need to remember that. He's alive in you in all his glory. You must walk with that confidence. That's the kind of confidence ... it's like confidence and humility at the same time. It's a natural combination when it comes from Christ—when that confidence comes from Christ. And it's in that knowing that he's in you that gives you that co-creative power...Because God can create, and so can you because you are one with God.

That is the travesty of religion. It is that it has hidden that truth not only from you but from all of God's children. What God can do, you can do—just do it with love. When you know your unity with God, the love comes naturally. There is never any danger in what you create when you create with God.

Priests were the first ones to abuse the creative power, which is why they recognized the danger. They saw the danger in themselves—that is what has scared priests through the centuries. Throughout history priests were so hungry for power, they thought everybody would be hungry for power; and they didn't want to give up theirs—so they hid the truth. They hid the co-creative power for so long that they lost the knowledge of it. It's time to reclaim the truth for yourself. Just live it in your own life. Start living it. The best you can do is start living that truth of your co-creative power with God in the knowledge that not everybody is hungry for power. You are hungry to know your union with God and to know all that's rightfully yours that comes from that union. And what's rightfully yours is the ability to create...Go in the knowledge of your unity with God, and there will be nothing you cannot do. Always ask for the humility to carry it out.

...Don't regret time lost because the grounding of the humility is very important as the foundation for that power to come. For that power can only rest on a very solid foundation of humility. Without that foundation of humility...you become afraid to use it like the priests of the past. They worked in fear. Only the humble can survive this power. Only the humble become co-creative forces with God and are not afraid to share that. So don't be afraid to let your light shine, and don't be afraid of the power that's yours...of being unified with God.

...that is what is meant by "the meek shall inherit the earth." Because it's the meek... or humble—it's the humble who will inherit the earth because it's the humble people that will finally recognize their co-creative power with God. Don't forget this ... This is a very important lesson for you and for everybody. Don't say no to God. Accept His invitation to be His co-creator.

Tell Him now what you want ... in doing so you are going to be co-creating what you say. The difference is that now not only are you asking, but you are allowing it to come in. It's like making a cake. It's like you do your part, and then you put it in the oven, and you allow it to bake—you allow it rise. That's God's part. You've set your intention as the co-creator with God, and then you have to give it to Him so that you allow your creation to bake. If you keep opening the oven door, it is not going to bake. You just have to trust God, just like you trust the oven to bake your cake. Trust that God is doing his part.

God married His divine nature to our humanity so that you would live in love, peace and joy. You are meant to fully accept both your humanity and your divinity. You are not meant to deny either aspect of yourself. Allow this marriage within you, and you will experience the love, peace and joy God intends for you.

We have lost our connection between our humanity and our divinity. Divine magic + the brilliance of our humanity = Balance

As you recapture the magic of being Divine and human at the same time, you are recapturing it for many people. It is magic, not in a mysterious way, but in a beautiful marriage of the earthly and spiritual. It is not about heaven on earth; it is about heaven as earth and earth as heaven. Heaven and earth, the material and the Divine Essence are joined in the creation of Love. Earth and the physical (plane) is Love made tangible. Everything that is created when you bring the physical and material aspects of earth and the Divine together is Love. When a person is created it is the material aspect of the earth with the Divine Spark. Humans are the marriage of the material energy of the earth and God's love. A baby is not just a series of bio-chemical reactions building upon one another. There is something else going on and that is the Divine Spark. You are given a window into this marriage of the Divine with the material world every time a child is born and you are messing it up. It is up to humans, married to the Divine at all times…If you don't instill in the child the nature of its Divine Spark, it will never be as powerful as it can be. Jesus showed us what the marriage of the Divine Spark and the human looked like…you have to be fully grounded in the human and fully transcendent in the divine magic ...

Christ consciousness is a step most must go through on their way to recognizing God consciousness. Jesus pointed you in this direction. He tried to explain and show you your divine unity, but you refused to listen. And now you must know that the consciousness that makes you Divine is so much more powerful than you ever imagined…You can co-create. He is pointing the way to God consciousness…You too reside within the consciousness. Never doubt your place in this eternal landscape. You must know that you are wrapped in the arms of Love. So where you go, Love goes.

You must reach for the impossible while things are still possible.

When you let go of everything, you gain everything.
In death you are forced to let go of everything. Now (in this lifetime) you have a choice.

The problem is people give up too soon. The lesson of faith is intertwined with everything. That is why sometimes things don't happen right away. Faith is not a separate thing. It is intertwined in everything. Visualize what you want, and hold this vision of faith. These things will be reflected back to you in God's hands.

Forgiveness is how you get from here, back to love. It is the path, the road you must follow.

You are being told there are no certainties on this journey except your love for God. Let that guide you…if you want God to catch you, you have to be willing to fall into His hands. The paradox is that when you do that you hold the earth in your hands.

You are being asked to know that you are already loved. Just rest in the knowledge that you are loved, that you and love are one in the same thing.

As I did energy work on Linda, I saw two sets of hands—two entities peeling back the skin to reveal a thin layer of gold foil. They were working very delicately, trying not to tear the gold foil as they separated the skin from the foil that was underneath it. As the skin was peeled off, it revealed "the person" underneath. As the sun hits this gold foil, there is an explosion of golden light reflected—the true person is exposed. God as the Sun hits you, and you reflect God back to Himself. The sunlight, in this case, is God's light. The gold is who you are. When you are purely that gold, you can't do anything but reflect God's light back, and it is not just to God, it is a reflection of His light outward.

That's what you are moving toward. You carry the power of the Sun and Son. That is where your power comes from—in being able to reflect God's light back out onto the world. As He shines it on you, you shine it back out. "Don't ask why."

Love yourself. All love starts with self-love. Don't look outside yourself for what you yourself don't have.

When you surrender, you surrender not in ambivalence but in the knowledge that God will choose that which is for your greatest good.

Be in a state of grace and be one with the depths of your soul.

It is like the deep part of the ocean. If you are at the bottom there can be a huge storm brewing on top with enormous waves, but in the deepness there is perfect stillness and peace. The storm above is not your concern. And so it is when you find that depth within yourself. It is about getting used to being in that stillness—in that space of deep peace.

Here I saw my client's spirit rising to the surface of the ocean, which was like glass with the sun shining upon it. *When these storms come you know to go back to this place of deep peace, to dive back under and sit by this rock at the bottom of the ocean. That rock is your God, and the still water around you is His peace and His love. And the waves and the storm at the top (on the surface) are the will of men. And every now and then, they stop their saber rattling and screaming, and the surface gets calm. Then they start up again, and they stir the surface of God's peace until it is not recognizable as His love and peace, anymore. And so it is truly that what we witness on the surface is that which is in the minds of men.*

*Spiritual intelligence is what links…intellectual intelligence to the Divine. When your intellect is open to the Divine, there is more compassion in everything you do—compassion for yourself and more compassion for others. It is the rebranding of "no one left behind." No child left behind is really NO ONE left behind. When you have spiritual intelligence, you have **no one** left behind.*

MESSAGES FROM JESUS

Jesus appeared clear as day with his heart visibly surrounded by a crown of thorns. He pulled me across the veil separating my world from his. I felt myself fill with an ethereal, white light. He showed me, and more importantly allowed me to **feel**, how beautiful and simple life is. Completely unaware of the people in the gymnasium around me, my body felt as if it were emanating white light, and tears filled my eyes. Jesus answered a question I hadn't asked, at least not at that particular moment. He communicated without words: *It is so simple. It is all about love.* He was talking about the meaning of life.

~

I am in you, and you are in me.

~

I want you to recognize me in everyone.

~

Proceed with me, not ahead of me.

~

You have much yet to give that you have not even begun.

~

Me: How do we reconcile free will with fate or the idea that "you can't miss your calling?"

Jesus: *You wrote the script. You wrote in all the "wrong" choices and your fated choice. There is free will even in spirit. I am here to support you no matter what choices you make—the ones that bring you closer, and the ones that bring you farther from your goal of complete union with the Father and with all creation.*

~

Walk not in fear or sorrow, my children, for I have always been at your side, and I will continue to guide you and to cherish you. I ask only that you cherish me. Not your jobs, not your belongings, not just the things that are right with your life but everything. For in cherishing everything, you cherish me. My life was a guide to you, an example of how I want you to live.

~

May the peace that resides within be yours without. May the peace that is me within you be reflected onto all of life around you. For it is in that reflection that you will see a new world—a world free of suffering.

Look for me in everyone you meet. For when you see me there, I will be reflected back to you. You will see not that person's "faults," you will see only me—this is as it should be. I give you these opportunities to bring "heaven to earth"—seize them—they are all around you.

I leave you with love and the knowledge that you and I are one—now and forever. Amen.

~

Love has no boundaries—my love for you (has no boundaries). Spread my love. Spread my words. I love you without end, and so you must love my other children. They are all your siblings and were created by me for you. They are in your life to help you to learn. Love them as I love you. My love for you is without conditions, and so must be your love for others. They are my gift to you. Do not shun my gifts with fear or anger or judgments—you will miss the point (lesson).

~

The light that shines in me also shines in you; and so it is with all of God's children.

~

How can others be what you yourself do not yet believe you to be?

~

(Complete) humility presages enlightenment. Humility leads you to me. Take thy steps away from power and illusion. Look for me not through illusions. The "Lady of the Lake"[47] is an illusion—she is a temptress. Do not yield to her power. She holds not the answers, nor the power. Follow her, and you fall into a vast body of falsity—illusion built upon illusion. It is my light you must follow—my light and simple robes—not the glory of the "Lady of the Lake." She will lead you to emptiness. There is a struggle going on between your ego and me. My way has no glamour. My way has no fame. My

way is simple—it is real and needs no props. It needs no fancy container. Do not try to clothe me in robes I do not wear.

The new world order starts from within. It is an internal revolution. In the new world order, you are ruled by your soul not by your mind.

*Fly my child, fly. Spread your wings and fly. Burst through the wall (of fire) to the other side. You cannot walk timidly through the wall. You must charge through, and you will find on the other side, stillness. You will be safe. The world you know will no longer exist for it is the reflection of your current illusion. Come. See the world as I see it. Experience the world as I experience it—through stillness. Lift up your heart, and give it over fully to me for I will not mishandle it. You are safe in my world. Leave the world you created behind. You will not find me by peeking under rocks. You will find me by **knowing** that **I am** the rock. I am everything that surrounds you. It is time to release the pain, so you may lift your arms in flight. In the name of the Mother and the Father, I release you from this pain, and I release you from past hurts. Fly, my child, fly.*

St. Thérèse of Lisieux—Can you clarify the above message? *Yes, my child. Jesus wants (your client) to be free of doubt and pain so she may soar to the next level.* What does the next level entail? *Seeing through the eyes of God.*

It is a tough lesson in recognizing Divinity in another when those who hurt you the most are where I ask you to look for Divinity. I would not ask this of you if I thought you couldn't do it. You can. Release those who anger you, and you release me. You release me, and you have released yourself from bondage. It is you who holds yourself in bondage by holding others accountable. No one is accountable other than to me. This (judgment) is not your job. For when I assess, even I don't judge. I see purity and I ask that you do the same. Put your mind to it and it shall be done.

Do not let personal will cloud intuition. My advice has been given for millennia and whether or not it is followed has always been and always will be a matter of their free will. …Holy art thou, and holy are they. Forget this not. The path is not one of pain

or pleasure. It is simply the path they choose, and though I may choose otherwise—it is not my choice. …Choose not to see the pain (of their choices) for that is a judgment and judgment is of the ego. Your choice would not be better (or worse)—simply your choice.

Perceive only what is true to me, and you will know the way (to enlightenment). See through my eyes, my children, for therein will be "clear sight." Clear sight leads to clear action. Clear action leads back to me, and so you have created a circle of peace within which you exist. For to exist in that circle of peace is to exist in the inner chamber. Fear not where you are going. The path is clear and waiting. The doors are open and awaiting your arrival. Amen.

The eyes of the Lord look down upon you where you lay. See not the shadows but the reality that created them. For thine is the kingdom and the glory. What is mine is yours, and what is yours is mine. The beauty (abundance) of my kingdom lies at your feet if only you are willing to see. You stand on a pile of gold, but you see it not. Clear your eyes—clear them of the illusion. I am there. I have always been there, and I will always be there.

Ah, the heavens bestow blessings upon you. Lift your eyes to the Light, and see what gifts await you. For these gifts are not of silver and gold but something more dear— radiant love. There is nothing more powerful in all God's kingdom. Minimize it not. Walk the walk of love. Talk the talk of love.

The dawn of a new world order awaits your call. Open your arms to receive these gifts I give to you.

There is nothing so dear as love. Tell this to everyone "who has ears to hear." For my eyes don't lie, and I see in all of you love. No role is "special" as St. Thérèse showed with the field of flowers. The violet and the rose are of equal value in my kingdom (garden).

I take many forms, and you will never know what I may look like (earth too!) I am in the ground you refuse to walk on. I am in the dirt and the bugs. I am in the homeless. I am in those who do not "shine." **Know** *this to be true.*

Be fooled not by the many forms death takes: death of the past, death of the future, death of old habits, death of the ego. Honor them, and embrace them all. Invite them in, and fear them not. For it is in these deaths that you truly live. Each time you "die," you live more fully in me. It is the beginning. Amen.

Lead them out of the darkness. How? *Be my light.*

Be my light on earth, and all else will follow.

I was not meant to be idolized. That was a mistake. I was here to show you what is your "right."

What is my purpose?
Your purpose is to follow me.

Your power comes from me. Don't question your capacity to heal.

Hold the Light for those who cannot see it. Be the Light for those who cannot feel it.

You must look at others so they can see the divine image of themselves. This is how they will heal. This is how Jesus healed.

Glory belongs to God.

Heal thyself with the Christ within. The Light is within you. The Light never leaves you. You must pay attention. He who carries the Light carries me. He who carries the Light performs miracles. Be my light on earth. Carry my heart—my Sacred Heart.

The first mistake of mankind was thinking I (Jesus) was special.
The second mistake of mankind was forgetting his (own) divinity.

...All I want is for you to love one another. What happens in Revelation you do to yourselves. The war, the famine—is already upon you. This story is not about a point in time. It is a lifestyle choice that my children are making, (and) have been making for thousands of years. There are always those with more and those with less. You have yet to figure out how all can have what is needed. I have given you tools and technologies, yet you exploit them for the beneficial gain of the few, not the many.

Close your eyes, and see what the world could look like. Would you ever imagine a world where a group of people had not? Where you set aside hundreds of thousands who you said would get no food, no clean water and no shelter? Of course not; yet that is what you have done. It pains me to see my children fight...I am all of you made manifest in all your potential glory.

Blessed are ye who walk among my flock.
Blessed are ye who serve me for you shall know heaven.
There was never a time when I did not walk with you.
There was never a time that you did not walk with me.
There comes a time when all men are meant to be known to themselves.
The time is here to discard the "masks" and to discard the "clothing" that cloaks you in illusion.
Know thy true self.
Know thy true Father and thy true Mother.
Know not the kingdom you have made but the kingdom my Father has promised you; only then will you be free.
You will shed the veil of persecution.
I await you all at the gates of heaven.

Open those gates within yourself, and walk right through!
You need suffer no more. All this (suffering, war and famine) can be over in a holy instant.
Blessed be, thy divine children.
Amen.
Heaven awaits.

Come children to the hem of my garment. No one who comes unto me will be lost. Your faith should come as easily as your breath...Fear not. What comes will come. Always know that I am here to guide you. You will never be lost.

Humble. Be humble. Love needs no adornments.

Just as a river runs to the sea, each soul is on its journey back to the sea that is God.

*...you fight the darkness with the Light. **Never** hold back the Light. ...Show them the feminine face of God. Show them my face, which is both male and female. How can I be one or the other? I am neither, and I am both at the same time. Do not be fooled by appearances of your brothers and sisters on earth. For they too are both and are neither.*

There is no world that cannot be saved. The shift to a higher level of consciousness has already begun. Everything you see as a small step is a large energetic step.

This is the Age of Light. This is the Age when the light of the heart and the light of the soul shine brighter than the light of the mind.

It's all about love; don't get sidetracked. Focus on the love that exists in each one of you—and shines out in all its glory. No explanations are needed. Become the Light. That Light shines in all of my children. By recognizing yours, you are helping them to recognize theirs. Go out into the world with that Light shining forth; that Light should precede you no matter where you go. There is an unlimited amount of energy. This is the bottomless well. There is so much love that exists everywhere. Only fools believe in the power of the darkness—that darkness has more power than love. There is never a time when the devil has more power than love. And when people ask you what energy you are working with, you tell them LOVE—it is the energy of love. That's it. It is easy to understand...And then they will not be afraid.

*Go with the energy of love in your hearts, and know that is all you will ever need. There is nothing that will protect you more in a battle than love—**love** for your enemy. This is what is meant by turning the other cheek. It is showing them the face of love. Always show them the face of love. This is how they will know that God is in you. So little is known of true love in this world. Yet truly that is all there is. Go now to that place of love that exists in each of you. See it and feel it. This is your center. This is who you are. Remember this and only this as you walk forward into the world. People think they carry the weight of the world on their shoulders, but you know that you carry the world in your hand. When the world is full of love, it is weightless and floats above the palm of your hand. That is how we heal the world—through love.*

I love the world as it is, as it will be, as it is becoming.

Love rules. Let love rule your heart. Let love rule your mind.

*He who sees me as his path is saved, but I am not the **only** path. There are many paths that lead to my Father's Garden. Choose the path that is right for you. Then walk it until you reach the Garden. You will know the path that is right for you because it will bring you peace. It will bring you joy. It will bring you love. The closer you get to the Garden, the more stable these states will become. Once in the Garden, you will **BE** peace, joy and love. It is the only state you will know. Trust me when I tell you this is who you are already; but you do not yet know that. Peace is what grows in my Father's*

Garden—inner peace, love and joy. Why stay away when you can have it now? Begin your journey—do not delay. The Garden is the earth itself, and it is in your heart. Ask yourselves, "What have we done to our Father's Garden?" Reclaim the garden. Weed out sorrow and pestilence. Tend to the seeds of harmony and forgiveness. This Garden was given to all the inhabitants of earth. Think not that you have dominion over any of it. It was meant to be shared.

~

When you judge you are so condemned. You are not made to carry the weight of that judgment.

~

God loves you.

~

How can I be of service today?
Love my children.

~

…Every thought, every intention brings you closer to peace. Wager not your bet against me. For I am your savior, your guide and your light. …Fear not this coming contraction. For all life will become one. Life is at its beginning and its end at the same time. Do not look for the "start" of peace for it is already here. For thine is the kingdom and thine is the glory. (This is Jesus saying the kingdom and the glory is ours as well as his.) *There is too much to mention, but know that you will see peace in your lifetime and the lifetimes of your children.* (Do you mean inner peace?) *All peace. They are one in the same. There is no one who dies unnecessarily. Peace is upon us. Don't look back, and don't ask how. For when thine peace comes, you will know only in hindsight. Fear not the details of how my world comes to fruition. For there is only one way—by the Hand of God. So too you will know peace in my garden…You all live in my Father's Garden if only you have eyes to see. Open your eyes, … For only through your eyes can others see. Life is a course in the miraculous if only you have eyes to see! Life is miraculous. Miracles abound when you are looking through me— through my eyes, which can't leave anyone out.*

There is so much done and so much still to do. Honor yourself, ...and your ways of knowing—for never has there been so much courage and so much power in the world at one time. You know because I Am, so do not let another day pass where you do not love yourself because it starts there. It starts within as the seed of knowing...It is all about LOVE. ...

Men and women need to take back the co-creative force of the divine feminine. Women were never meant to be demeaned. God loves both men and women equally. See not the differences before you but the wealth that comes from joining forces. Embrace the divine feminine and the divine masculine within each of you. It is through the divine feminine that you gain cooperation and veneration for all living things. (I do not know who was speaking to me here, but Jesus and Mary were both visible to me).

Someone has to be a guest at my table. I prepare a feast, and everyone thinks they have to prepare their own feasts. Be a guest, ...and learn to feast at my table. It is always bountiful, and there are so many empty chairs around my table because so few choose to respond to my invitation. Don't be one of those people, ... Respond with open arms, an empty stomach and an open heart. For at my table you feast on love. You feast on so much more than what you see on the table.

There is no division in my world, only unity...You with me (Jesus). You with God. That is what you want to remember.

You first have to be unified with God before you can be unified with another. You first have to accept your imperfections before you can accept theirs.

You must love yourself as much as God loves you. Self-respect will then be implicit in self-love. Self-respect is of the ego unless it arises implicitly from self-love

(God speaking)...And therefore I Am, and you are. You exist in love and because of love.

Love yourself. It is through self-love that everything else falls into place. No sooner do you love yourself then all the dominoes stand back up in place. For everything that heretofore fell will be righted. Do not underestimate the power of love.

God's name has a powerful energy. It has the power to transform us when said with reverence.

I am the living God. I am in you. And when my children learn their unity with me, there will be no more darkness.

Be the rain of love that falls down upon the parched earth. There is no element the earth needs more.

I used my life as an example in a final glorious act of surrender and unselfishness. I sacrificed my own life to teach you true love and forgiveness. When will you learn? The point is not that you have to suffer. The point is that you have to love so much that you are willing to give your life.

Don't let another shine before thee. Jesus, I don't understand this message. *First, don't wait for permission to shine my light, and second, don't wait to see another's light before shining your own. You are all equal in your ability to carry my light.*

Let go of your fear. Fear is your ego trying to control things.

To know Christ is to be Christ.

FORGIVENESS RELEASES ALL KARMA. (Translating a vision) *That's why Jesus' last words on the cross were: Forgive them Father they know not what they do. When Jesus spoke his last words, "Forgive them Father, they know not what they do," he wiped the karmic slate clean for all those present at the crucifixion. He did not intend for you to carry the cross. Put down the cross. You are forgiven. Forgive everyone in your life right now, including yourself! You cannot carry unforgiveness any longer. The unforgiveness in your heart is magnified; the world cannot take it any longer. It has to go. Jesus spent his whole life talking about love, and his last words were about forgiveness. Why? Because when people don't understand that forgiveness is implicit in unconditional love, they need to hear it as a separate, last and final statement—his last words. Forgiveness is so important that Jesus used His last breath to give us the secret code, the answer to the test, the key to the puzzle. Forgiveness. If you missed his messages about Love that he spent his life spreading, then you needed to get the message about forgiveness. He was giving everyone another chance. He wiped everyone's karmic slate clean, and he is asking you now to put down that cross you have been carrying. Forgiveness releases all karma.*

∾

Jesus, how can I be of service today?
Own me. Embody me. ... Hold (my ways) back not, any longer.
(To me, "own me" meant to own the Christ within, to own the qualities we ascribe to Christ for they are within us too.)

∾

MESSAGES FROM GOD

Do you really think the decisions I make will be worse than the ones you've made for yourself?

~

What is unity but to be one with God. When My children are one with Me, they will be one with each other. For truly if you are one with Me, you cannot be anything but one with each other.

~

It's so simple—it's all about love. Don't judge who you should love. Love all those you see. Love those that are easy to love and those who make it difficult to love them. My love for you knows no bounds as your love would know no bounds. Go forth into this world carrying My light—the light of love and compassion. ...You have only to look inside yourselves to find it. Once again I ask you to close your eyes. See the light that is you. You are Me personified. We are one, and in so being, you are one with each other. Love Me, and you love yourself. Love yourself, and you love one another. There is no place for judgment or exclusion. I have not asked you for that. One of you is not more or less worthy than the other. ...Remember our unity, and it will set you free. Blessed are the children who walk in My Light.

~

*Life is not a pyramid with God at the top (or you at the top of your circle). God's organization is **flat**. He is in everyone equally, making everyone on earth equal to everyone else.*

~

...This is not a game with rewards and penalties. There is only abundance, peace, joy and love for those who know to recognize it. Recognize the peace that existed "in the beginning" when people still knew Me.

~

What is this about Jesus being THE Messiah?

Tell them I (GOD) am God. No matter what they call Me. They can call Me "tree," but I will still be God. It doesn't matter how they reach Me as long as they reach Me. They can get to Me through a tree.

~

What is my purpose?
To live My purpose. To spread love. Live your life with the heart of a child.

~

Who lays claim to a miracle is God.

~

Join with Me to sow the seeds of love.

~

If I love God so much does that mean I create an out-of-balance situation with my children?
Love Me. Love them. It is one in the same.

~

Me: I surrender. You win.
God: It is in your surrender that you also win.

~

I have chosen a woman because a woman is indispensible to My plan. There is no man without woman. Woman is My flesh made manifest. So I asked God, "What about woman being begotten from Adam's rib?" and God replied: *God created man and woman. They are both a manifestation of Me. I AM both and neither. I AM you and your brother. Do not assign Me a gender for I AM above and beyond that. It is asked of you not to focus on the duality. One (male or female) was never made to represent Me more than the other. Take this to heart: men and women are in My eyes equal. They are different aspects of Me. Never has it been said that women and men are not equal. Their unequal stature has come from you. Only when men recognize their strength will they recognize the strength of women. Until then they live on the false idea of superiority.*

Humanity is at a tipping point, and it is weighted toward love.

You are able to cope with the lessons that this life brings you. This is now a time that humanity truly has the ability to transcend to higher levels of consciousness, to higher levels of love, and you are an important part of that—everybody has a part. But know that your own healing is entangled with the accomplishment of those goals. You are not alone, nor is your journey for the benefit of (only) you. None of you are on a journey that is solely for your (own) benefit. You are all tied to My universal plan, the achievement of which will be a life of unconditional love above all, for all, by all of us. Go now and hope and pray for the salvation of everyone because never has there been such an opportunity for Divine Love to prevail.

When you fear you question My will for you.

Fear is what keeps people trapped in dogma…fear of hearing what God might actually have to say to them.

This was in response to why people so blindly follow the dogma of religious institutions. They would rather exist within the framework built for them and approved for them by another. In the vision that accompanied this message, I was shown the superstructure of a skyscraper and people voluntarily confining themselves to the interior of the structure even though in a superstructure there are no walls keeping one inside. They look around at the structure and think they must stay within the confines of the steel beams because that is what has been built and approved of by (insert the name of any religious institution). That structure tells them what they know about God. It tells them what is possible with God. It sets out all the guidelines like whether God can talk to them directly, whether or not they can have visions, whether or not they can hear Jesus, etc. The vision did not suggest that all structures are inherently faulty. The vision suggested the structures may be sound but that the individual is free to walk outside of them. They are free to walk around them and to climb on them, to look up and under them. In other words, test them out.

This is where dogma fails people—when it prevents them from self-exploration, and in the context of this book, when it prevents them from exploring their own relationship with God. We encourage you to climb in and around the structure. Try to push it over. If it falls, it is not real. Love is real; it won't fall. It will withstand all your poking and prodding, pushing and pulling, climbing and jumping. What God is saying in the above quote is that people willingly follow dogma because it is safer than actually walking outside the structure and listening for themselves to what God might be saying or showing them directly.

Your job is to be love and to send love to all you meet.

... And it is My love that flows through you, and it flows through me and makes us one. It's that thread that unifies and joins us with all humanity. It is that thread that has been lost.

When your love for yourself matches My love for you, you will have achieved the kingdom of heaven within you.

*...My Light is within you now. What you have asked for has been given. And what has been given cannot be taken away. I do not give half a gift, so you can see that you and My son are whole in Me. This is true for everyone. I await their recognition. They do not have to come through My son, but they have to come to Me. They have to come to Me with full abandon. They have to abandon all else they hold dear. That doesn't mean they will lose all else they hold dear. It simply means that to enter into union with Me they must be **willing** to let go of all they hold dear. That willingness allows you and I to form the complete whole.*

...Go to that place in yourself where love lives, and there you will find heaven; there you will find the Promised Land—the Land so many have been searching for has always been within your reach. Push aside your judgment, your preconceived notions; these are the brambles that hide the garden where My Love grows in its infinite glory. Go there now. Be a part of that landscape. Whether you live in the Promised Land or the land of your own making is your choice. Choose wisely.

Let no opportunity for love of yourself or love of another pass you by. You can't change another who trespasses against you, but you can love them unconditionally, and you can forgive them (which is implicit in unconditional love). Paradoxically, when you do this, the other person may change because you have freed him from his jail—the jail your judgment contained him in.

It takes a lot of love to run the world.

No one can love you better than (you love) yourself.

*...The transformation they are looking for will not come about by tearing things down but by building things up—by building bridges of love between all people. This is so easy. All people must do is extend a hand to another, and say "how can I help?" But then they must act. They cannot just ask how they can help. They must help the best they can. The bridges will be built in this way. ...the only thing that will heal is **love**. It is not democracy or autocracy. It is anything done with **love**. It is not the form of government. It is what is in the hearts of the people both in and out of government. Don't cry. Be the Light.*

Me: If there is 7 billion of us hearing God, what happens if we all hear a different message?

God: *...there is only one message and it is LOVE.* (This message can be delivered in 7 billion ways, but if it is from God or Jesus, it will always have LOVE at its core—unconditional love of all, for all).

No one should see themselves as less valuable than another.

First step is thinking. Second step is thinking with your heart. Third step is not think-ing at all (this is not about losing your mental faculties. It is about opening up a new doorway.) Align yourself with God's will and surrender.

We ask, after we fall, why God didn't catch us. He answers: *Because you didn't trust that I would catch you. You had no faith in Me. You put your faith in yourself and blame Me when you fall.*

Like a child, you must trust that your Father will meet your every need. You do so exactly as a young child, trusting your Father not only in your mind but also with your whole being. A young child, who has always been unconditionally loved, nur-tured, protected and cared for, does not know there is another alternative. That is how your relationship with God must be. But, you must willingly let go of any notion that He will not take care of you, that He will not provide for you or take away your every burden. He cannot take from you your burdens without your complete willingness to let them go.

*Heaven is in a rose. Look upon the rose until you see heaven. I am in the shadow and in the light. Look upon **everything** and say, "God what do you see here?" Do that with everything until you can look upon any person and say, "God what do you see here?" and He will say, "I see Me." Go in peace and the knowledge that I am in you, with you and around you; and that you are in Me, with Me and around Me. It can be no other way.*

God, what do you see in the rose I am holding?

I see everything I have asked it to be. The rose does not resist Me. It contains its begin-ning (the center is still unfolding) *and its end* (the outer leaves are beginning to age and shrivel at the edges) *at the same time. There is beauty you can only see by beholding the rose, but not by being the rose. Climb from the dark crevasse where the petals cling to each other. Climb up and out, and look upon it as I do, and you will see the beauty that comes from the light and the dark. As you gaze upon the rose, I gaze upon all of you. I see the living and the dying, the old and the young, the light and the dark. I look and I see Me. I am all of those things. I see the galaxies swirling. I see the microcosm of the macrocosm.*

People aren't meant to weight their pockets down with gold.

All God wants is to be reflected back to Himself. It completes the circle. He gives to you, and you give back to Him everything that you are, and everything that He is.

Reflect God back to the people. Reflect Him back in all His glory because His glory is their glory. And their glory, unencumbered, is His glory. Go forward simply, because truly His gold I have shown you. It is reflective no more than sand. And that's what Jesus knew. He walked in the sand and in the dust, and he reflected God back to the people. Gold is a crutch. Vestments are a crutch. Staffs are crutches. The glory of man imposed upon himself by man is a crutch. God found himself in a fisherman and a carpenter...He finds Himself equally in the lowest of the low and the highest of the high, but He recognizes not the crutch. Walk down your path whether it be on sand or on water knowing that God is with you.

The notion of Me as you is nothing if it is not reflected back to all you see.

There are so few mystics not because they can't, but because they won't.

Do not fall prey to your own sense of justice. You try to rescue others when you believe love is not enough. Love is always enough. Have nothing in your heart but your love for Me, and all else will follow. Your journey starts by stepping into My heart. Look not behind you, beside you or ahead of you, but only into My eyes, and there you will find yourself. You are not alone in your struggle for I will always be there for you. Focus your eyes on Me, and together we will bring heaven to earth for it is done by each and every one of you.

Let not your eyes be blinded by material goals. For through My eyes, whether you be rich or poor, you will only see abundance. Go not to the desert without Me for without Me you will only find desert. Go into the desert with Me, and you will find the cornucopia of life. The choice is yours. So as one heals, we all heal. As one sees, we all see. Your nest at the edge of the desert will not protect you. Go to the desert with just a flask of water to start, and everything will be provided. There is so much there for those with eyes to see.

They pile up gold coins as if that will feed them, as if that will protect them. You have tried your way, now try Mine. Too many die in tombs with their gold piled beside them. The entry fee to heaven is free, and it has always existed in your heart. All you need is love. Turn the key, and you enter My palace.

PRAYERS & MEDITATIONS

Words of God Prayer

Let my voice speak the words of my heart.
Let my heart speak the words of my soul.
Let my soul speak the words of God.

∼

I Am Yours Prayer

God, I love You
God, I trust You
God, I find You in my heart.
God, when I am lost, find me.
When I am blind, help me see.
God, I am Yours to do with what You please.
May it please You to have me serve You.
For without Your love, I am nothing.

∼

Surrender Prayer

God, I owe my life to You, and I give my life to You.
God, I give this day to You.
Help me to fulfill Your will.
I will live my life with faith, humility and alignment with God's will.

∼

Surrender Affirmation

God I surrender. I have faith in You and in Your divine plan for me and the world.

∼

Unconditional Love Prayer

Ask to love the way that God loves.
Ask to love yourself the way that God loves you.
Ask to love all God's children the way that God loves them.

Ask to love the earth and all that lives upon it the way that God loves the earth and all that lives upon it.

~

Our Father Who Loves Me Prayer
Our Father
Who loves me so much
Bring me abundance in all ways:
Abundance in unconditional love for myself and others,
Abundance of joy,
Abundance of compassion,
Abundance of knowing,
Abundance of courage to follow Your will,
Nurture me.
Guide me.
Protect me.
I am Yours now.
And like a child needs his or her father,
I need you.

~

Faith Prayer
I have faith in God.
I have faith in miracles.
I am God's servant.
He has shown me to put up my hand to stop the oncoming tsunami.
I will stand at the shore, hand raised against the tide and
I will trust that He who asked me to do this will deliver the miracle He promised.
I do that now. There will be no fear because my relative smallness belies the God that exists in my heart.

~

Prayer of Acceptance
God, allow me to be used to fulfill Your Will.

I accept everything that is mine.
I accept everything that I am.

∾

Unity Meditation

This meditation is intended for groups of two or more: Close your eyes, and imagine yourself as Divine white light. After one minute, open your eyes, and look at the person sitting next to, and the people around, you. See each other as the same light you just saw as you. Recognize your unity with one another. Feel the love that builds from this recognition. This is who you truly are, and this is who your neighbor truly is. The outline that forms your body is an illusory separation between you and your true essence. You are all ONE, but you must look past the physical to know this.

∾

The Light Within Meditation

Begin by envisioning a square building with no windows and no doors, a building with no light source so that it is completely dark. Now imagine a circular hole in the roof; see the sunlight shining in, illuminating every corner of the room. And so it is when you open yourself to Divine Love—it illuminates your entire being, filling you with light. The difference between you and the square building is that when you are filled with the Light of Love, you become Love. The Light burns within you—it **is** you. Repeat the meditation, but this time, see yourself standing in the middle of the building as it fills with the light of the Sun—the Light of the Divine. Begin to see yourself as the physical manifestation of the Divine. Continue to meditate from this place of love.

∾

Love vs. Fear Meditation

Close your eyes. Place your feet flat on the floor, your hands on your lap and breathe deeply. See your physical body and mind as recording devices—they have no other function but to record and express your emotions. At any point in time, they are the sum total of all you have said, thought or believed. And everything you have said, thought or believed stemmed from one of two emotions—LOVE or FEAR. All of your words, thoughts and beliefs that arose from LOVE brought you STRENGTH.

Your body and mind recorded these as life-supporting, bringing optimal function to every cell, to every organ of your body. All of the words, thoughts and emotions you have ever had that arose from FEAR have been recorded by your mind and body as life-threatening. Fear based words, thoughts and emotions weaken your cells, your organs, and your natural bodily functions, which are designed to be in a state of optimal health at all times. Release them now.

Release every word, thought and emotion you have ever had that was based on fear. There is no need to enumerate them. Simply setting the intention will release the fear-based energy you carry. Ask that, as you release this fear based energy, it be instantly transmuted to the light and taken by our angels and spirit guides back to the I AM who knows that all fear is an illusion. There was never anything to be fearful of. Fear arises when you trust not in the Divine plan—when you forget, after taking all possible earthly steps, to let go and let God. Do you need to remind your heart to beat? Do you need to remind your body, after taking one breath, to take another? No. You do your part to nourish the body, and you are then forced to trust that the Divine plan that created you will take care of the rest. The plan is designed with co-creation is mind. You do not feed yourself out of FEAR that your heart will stop beating or that your lungs will stop breathing. You feed yourself because it is your part in the co-creation of your health. You relinquish your next breath to God. You do not live in a constant state of fear that your next breath will not come. And so it is with ALL events in your life. Do your part; then let go and don't worry. Trust in the Divine plan as you trust that one breath will follow another, as you trust that one heart beat will follow the last.

Now, take this time to breathe in TRUST. Breathe in LOVE. Breathe in FAITH in an ordered, Divine plan, and breathe out FEAR. Continue until you feel, see or hear your body fill with the light of LOVE. See your body fill with light—the light of your Divine self. In this state, recognize your unity with God. Trust Him. Have faith in His plan. In this state, there is no room for FEAR. Let it go, and let God consume you with love.

Enjoy the vibration of this higher level of consciousness, and know that this is your natural state. All lower levels of consciousness are brought on by FEAR—recognize them not. You are Divine. You are one with each other and with the I AM. Be at peace. Amen.

∽

Meditation for World Peace

The power of peace lies within. It is a state of being that already exists. It is up to you to see it and as you see it, you project it into or onto the world. The current world is the projection of the global hologram—it is the world that people think it must be, even though they'd like to have it otherwise. It is up to you to see it anew. Envision the world as it can be—as it is under the blanket of scarcity and fear that you have lain upon it. The state of peace and unconditional love of all, for all, is already there. Pull back the blanket. Uncover the world as I know it—as I see it. See with My eyes. See the beauty—the love—the peace and the joy. Live in this world. Project your perception out into this room—into this city, state, country and world. You alone have the power to create the world you are now seeing.

Do you see people shaking hands, enemies embracing, lovers hand in hand? Do you see races, religions, ethnicities coming together in love and peace? Do you feel the joy? Do you see a world without borders where there are resources aplenty? Walk with Me in this world. You are not limited by space or time so walk freely around the earth. Look in every corner, and see what you have manifested. See this new earth. You are the givers of birth to a new world order. You are manifesting the world anew, in My image.

The world doesn't reach this point on its own. It gets there through you. You are what makes the world complete. Your projection of love makes it whole in love. You have come back to a time before time, where there is harmony, peace and joy, where no one is better or worse than the next, where we exist as one. And so as one heals, we all heal. As one loves, we all love. As one experiences joy we all experience joy. Peace happens for us all, or for no one; but it must start with you—with your vision, which cannot leave anyone out. It comes from the deepest recesses of your heart and soul. It is the dream of the creation that you live anew. Embrace your power to create the world in My image, for it is through you that My world comes to fruition.

See the spinning earth and the love vibrations that emanate into the cosmos. For as you see peace on earth, you also bring peace to the entire universe. May you be blessed to live the life you are now manifesting, in a world that reflects back to you unconditional love, peace and joy.

May peace reign upon you. Namaste.

∾

Oneness Meditation

I breathe in love.

I breathe out conflict between my mind and the mind of God.

My mind and the Divine mind are one.

Field of Love Meditation

I was shown in a vision how all around us and in us there exists a beautiful field of LOVE. *It is an energy that is everywhere, and all we have to do is stop and "look up." Everything is already here. There is nothing we have to do but stop and feel this Love—sense it all around us. It is so simple. People tend to think life is much more complicated than this, but Love is all there is. If we would just recognize this, the world would just disappear because our lessons would be done. It is all about Love. The field of Love is so beautiful. We need to remember this—what it looks and feels like, so we can help others to know and feel it as well…People need to know what we saw … that this Love also flows through us—through our veins and through our nervous system. The only thing that prevents us from seeing it or feeling it is our mind. It gets in the way.* The last message I received was, *Nothing exists but that which is in the minds of men—change your mind.* The feeling was that the "nothing" referred to nothing other than Love. The "men" referred to all of humanity.

The Every Day of an Everyday Mystic

Communicating with the Divine: Seeing, Sensing, Feeling and Hearing

To help you to see and to hear the Divine more clearly, it might be helpful to understand the different ways in which I "see" sacred visions and "hear" sacred messages. When Jesus came to me in a vision on December 2, 1996, he did not so much visit me as he took me to visit him—wherever it is that he exists. I, like many others, refer to that place as heaven, although I believe we all have different ideas of what heaven is. Having been in heaven with Jesus, I can tell you that I felt it to be a place of pure, unconditional love—a place where although I had some vague sense of a form, my body no longer had any significance or function. I can also tell you that it is not "up there" somewhere. Heaven, for lack of better nomenclature, is right here. It exists **alongside** our own physical world. All I had to do to see it was to be pulled across the divide that separated me from heaven. I believe that we could create that place right here on earth if we could love enough—if we could truly love ourselves, and one another, unconditionally as Jesus asks us to do. On the heavenly side of the divide, there was so much white light everywhere. Jesus, surrounded in white light, was radiant. He spoke to me without words, as if his thoughts were placed directly into my consciousness so that I could understand his message at the deepest part of my being. So, when he communicated to me the meaning of life saying, *It is so simple. It is all about love,* I was able to not only understand the words, but I could also **feel** the meaning of his message. I could feel what he meant by the word **love**. I will tell you this, that even having been immersed in that love, it is very difficult for me to live it in my own life. Although I come closest with my children whom I love unconditionally, it does not match the love in which Jesus embraced me—the love, according to this sacred vision, that exists parallel to our own physical world.

More frequently, Jesus chooses not to pull me across the divide into that heavenly place, but instead he appears in my world. In these instances, I am still able to function somewhat, unlike in the instance above, where I could not. My ability to function in his presence varies. There are times when his presence is so strong that I can barely stand. Here is an example taken from an email I sent to my friend Marie:

Sent: Wednesday, September 16, 2009 6:32:50 PM

Subject: Your visit to church

Marie, I went to (an empty) church today and just sat in gratitude in front of the statue of the sacred heart of Jesus. Earlier in the day I was doing energy work on Kim and the Christ consciousness took me over. It was so powerful. I actually collapsed to the floor when Jesus was done. I could barely get up on the Reiki table for Kim and Linda to work on me. …I think all this started with my first visit to the church as per your suggestion. I can't even describe the feeling when I am fully awakened to his Light inside of me. Marie, I know we can't suffer when he is within us, and I know he is within you. You may feel pain but you will not suffer—his Light is too bright. …

Sometimes the love from his presence is so powerful that water streams from one or both of my eyes. Sometimes my heart rate escalates to a point where I feel my heart will beat right out of my chest, and other times both my heart rate and breathing slow down so much that I feel as though I may not take another breath. During one of these instances, Linda and Kim became so frightened they thought they had to resuscitate me, and maybe they did when they prayed for my heart to keep beating.

There was another period when each time Jesus appeared to me, his profound love would fill my throat and chest making it feel as if I would explode. Each of these phases was temporary, lasting only until I became accustomed to the new level of energy coming through me. When Jesus first started to work through me, he would cause my arms to rise up (involuntarily) at an angle to my body where they would remain for and hour and never tire. This is significant because I am not strong, and holding my arms up for a few seconds when he is not working through me causes extreme discomfort. Most times while in his presence, or in the presence of Mother Mary, I would go into a trance where surrounding noises or activities could not break our bond.

In every instance I could see either Jesus' face or his entire body, usually dressed in a simple white tunic, longish brown hair and brown eyes. Personally, I think he appears to me in a way he knows I would recognize him, given my upbringing.

He frequently appears when I do healing work on clients as well as when I am in meditation. He oftentimes speaks to me in these visions. There was one instance when he told me to kiss the feet of a client so that she'd know it was he who was present and speaking. I did not want to do this, and Jesus and I went back and forth a few times before I relented and did as he asked. After the healing session ended and I delivered Jesus' message, which explained why I'd kissed her feet, she was completely unfazed. I, however, was feeling Christ's love for her so deeply, and his love was so overwhelming, that it brought me to tears. Feeling the love of Christ for a woman who sat looking at me with no emotion was quite an awkward situation.

The presence of Mother Mary is different. The first time I saw Mother Mary and heard her speak, I could see her entire body expanding into the enormous space above the sleeping figure of a male friend of mine. It was many years later that she showed up in client healing sessions and when she did, she not only appeared, but I could also see her spirit come into my body. When she did this my body began to shake and my hands and arms rapidly shook back and forth in my client's energy field. It was a beautiful experience, and although it was temporary, Mother Mary would continue to appear to me both in client sessions and in meditations. She speaks to me and to my clients, and her messages can be found in the section dedicated to her and in Part III. When she appears she is always beautiful and gentle. Her form often seems to fill a rather large space. Looking back on the first time she appeared to me, I wish I hadn't resisted her presence by thinking I was just over-tired. I wished I hadn't rationalized her away.

When St. Thérèse of Lisieux appeared, I did not have the same feeling as when Jesus pulled me across the veil separating my world from his or as when Mother Mary appeared. In St. Thérèse of Lisieux's presence, as well as in the presence of St. Teresa of Avila and Archangel Michael, there was, and still is, a feeling of deep contemplation, reverence and peace.

St. Rita's presence was slightly different. She first appeared to me on April 21, 2011, but at the time, I didn't think much of it because I didn't know that there was a St. Rita. As usual it was only in hindsight that I could see the significance of my vision. I hadn't been able to sleep well with my husband's snoring, so I went up to the room in which I channel grace, which doubles as a guest bedroom. No sooner did I lie down than Jesus appeared, along with Mary and St. Thérèse of Lisieux. Then a faint figure appeared, not at all clear, along with a "knowing" that this was St. Rita. Years of these "knowing" feelings not withstanding, I ignored the vision and the message, as I am prone to do when they are meaningless to me. I am not one to make something out of nothing—and as far as I was concerned St. Rita didn't exist, so the vision was probably nothing—maybe I simply misunderstood. Months later I told a friend about the vision, and she guided me to a movie about St. Rita's life, which she'd just watched. Luckily, it was on Netflix so I watched it and was blown away. This was not your ordinary saint. She was a regular person who just happened to be capable of extraordinary feats of compassion, love and forgiveness. Not only was she a real saint, but she became my latest role model.

She started to show up in my channeled grace healing sessions and in some cases would ask me to step aside while she performed all the necessary healing work. Being asked to step aside was new to me and left me feeling a bit useless, but I did as I was told and everyone she worked on reported healings. I have since learned she is considered the saint of the impossible and if you don't know about her already, you may want to make her acquaintance.

I have never seen God, but I do hear His voice or more accurately, there is an unmistakable **knowing** when it is God that is speaking. God somehow puts the knowing directly into my consciousness.

I have no control over when God, Jesus, Mother Mary or any of the others appear or speak. It is entirely up to them. They use me as they see fit. When I channel grace, I empty my mind, and I go into a meditative state of union with the Divine. I feel God's love in me and His presence fills the room in which I am working. It should also be noted that once I became accustomed to hearing from Divine beings, I heard from them even when not in quiet meditation. I would hear from them while I was driving or talking with friends—the instances are endless.

Sometimes when I am in the presence of Jesus or Mother Mary, and they speak to me, intending for me to deliver their messages to my client, I cannot raise my voice above a whisper. Linda has reported that on some of these occasions even the sound and cadence of my voice changes, although I can't hear the difference. What I can feel is that my voice is coming from near the base of my throat as opposed to deeper down, where it seems my normal voice originates. When Jesus or Mary are present, my breathing can be so shallow that I have very little air flow with which to project words. It is difficult to operate in this physical plane while in the presence of Jesus or Mary. Conversely, when the Holy Spirit is delivering messages through me, the words can sometimes come as though the air is being pushed out of me making each word sound as if it were an exclamation as opposed to being part of a sentence. Overall, it can be difficult to condense the higher vibration of the messages being delivered to me into the primordial sounds of our limited language as expressed through the physical speech organs of our tongue, larynx and mouth. I would love it if I could somehow bypass language and place into people the entire thought forms and feelings that are being presented to me.

Fortunately, I am sometimes given messages word for word, a few words at a time, albeit without any idea where the sentence is going. Other times I am given full sentences or full thoughts, which in the past, I had to write very fast to capture; now if my client so desires, I allow them to record the channeled grace session. I always conduct my personal meditations with pencil and paper at hand so that I can capture messages as they are revealed to me. In yet another method of communication, the Divine speaks to me through feelings that I must then translate into words. However, I have found our vocabulary to be woefully inadequate. It is like trying to describe love to someone who has never felt it. This may be why the channeled messages seem a bit awkward. Oftentimes, I am given multiple messages that I store up in my mind while I wait for a story line to develop or while I ask the Divine for verification that what I am hearing is correct. In this case, I might deliver the resulting messages out of sequence. Although they may read awkwardly, the veracity of the messages remains intact. You may also have noticed that the messages in this book sometimes seem as if God, Jesus, or the entity speaking, is speaking in the third person. This was not the case. The words in the client sessions and meditations, in which God, Jesus or another entity spoke to me, were written for the benefit of my client or were written with the intention of sharing the message with my friends and students. To avoid confusion with the pronoun "I" that God or Jesus was using, I oftentimes changed the pronoun to "he" or, alternatively, I might include myself in the message so I'd write "us" or "we." In the second edition of this book I changed some of the pronouns in the messages back to the first person to avoid confusion to the reader.

Vision vs. Imagination

It is important to distinguish between a vision and your imagination. A vision draws you in so that you become a part of the experience. You can feel the presence of the entity in the vision, and you can at times become one with that entity. In a vision you are not just seeing but you are also **feeling** the entity's presence. If it is your imagination, the "vision" will be flat or more two-dimensional. My imagination does not include a feeling component. In the case of a vision, unlike the dream state, you are not asleep. While having a vision you can still hear the dog barking, the phone ringing, people talking, etc.—you will however have no inclination to react to them. The other important difference for me is that visions stay with me for long periods of time. My imagination fades. Visitations are with you for as long as the entity wants to hang out. I had one instance in which I prayed to Jesus to have our plane land safely in New York during a storm. The pilot had just announced as we circled the airport that we might have to turn around and land in another state. I saw Jesus appear outside the plane's window. He told me we would land safely in New York and we did. The thing was, I kept seeing Jesus with me everywhere I went for weeks after that incident. I know how **my** imagination works, and I can tell you, I can't make an imaginary vision stay with me. Jesus stayed with me. That's how I know he is real and that he is here for us now. Another distinguishing feature between a vision and my imagination is that the vision is usually accompanied by a verifiable message about which I had no prior knowledge.

I would encourage you to keep a journal of your experiences as you begin your serious spiritual practice. Over time you will learn to distinguish between what is imagined and what is a Divine message or vision. Never be afraid to question.

APPENDIX II

Using the Power of Intention:

Practical Applications of Consciousness

Global Coherence Initiative	http://www.glcoherence.org
Global Peace Movement	http://www.globalpeacemovementnow.com
HeartMath	http://www.heartmath.com
Institute of Noetic Sciences	http://noetic.org
The Intention Experiment	http://theintentionexperiment.com
Monroe Institute	http://www.monroeinstitute.org

Learn to Meditate*

Theresa Joseph	*Meditation for World Peace*
Brian Weiss	*Meditation: Achieving Inner Peace and Tranquility in Your Life*
Jon Kabat-Zinn	*Guided Mindfulness Meditation*
Herbert Benson, M.D.	*The Relaxation Response* (basis for Transcendental Meditation; more information on learning and practicing TM may be obtained through The David Lynch Foundation)
Jack Kornfield	*Meditation for Beginners* *Guided Meditation: Six Essential Practices*

* This is a very abbreviated list meant only as a sample of the many techniques available. If you are interested in meditation there are many styles and teachers that you will find upon further investigation.

Recommended Reading

The Alchemist by Paulo Coelho

A Course in Miracles

And Then There Was Heaven by Roland Comtois

AngelSpeake: How to Talk with Your Angels by Trudy Griswold

Anatomy of the Spirit by Caroline Myss

"Behind the Selma March" in *A Testament of Hope: The Essential Writings and Speeches of Martin Luther King, Jr.* by Martin Luther King, Jr. and James M. Washington (editor)

The Bhagavad Gita translated by Eknath Easwaran

The Biology of Belief: Unleashing the Power of Consciousness, Matter & Miracles by Bruce H. Lipton, Ph.D.

Blessings of the Cosmos by Neil Douglas-Klotz

Click: The Girl's Guide to Knowing What You Want and Making it Happen by Annabel Monaghan and Elisabeth Wolfe

Closer to the Light: Learning from the Near-Death Experiences of Children by Melvin Morse, M.D. with Paul Perry

The Divine Matrix: Bridging Time, Space, Miracles and Belief by Gregg Braden

Entering the Castle: An Inner Path to God and Your Soul by Caroline Myss

The Gnostic Gospels by Elaine Pagels

God Spoke to Me by Eileen Caddy

The Gospel of Thomas by Elaine Pagels

The Gospel of Mary Magdalene by Jean-Yves LeLoup

Healing Beyond the Body by Larry Dossey, M.D.

The Hope: A Guide to Sacred Activism by Andrew Harvey

I am Malala: The Girl Who Stood Up for Education by Malala Yousafazi

I Heard God Laughing: Poems of Hope and Joy Translated by Daniel Ladinsky

The Interior Castle by St. Teresa of Avila

The Isaiah Effect: Decoding the Lost Science of Prayer and Prophecy by Gregg Braden

John of God, The Brazilian Healer Who's Touched the Lives of Millions by Heather Cumming

Joshua by Joseph Girzone

Left to Tell: Discovering God Amidst the Rwandan Holocaust by Immaculee Ilibagiza

Love for No Reason by Marci Shimoff

Love Without Conditions by Paul Ferrini

Love Wins by Rob Bell

"Loving Your Enemies" in *A Testament of Hope: The Essential Writings and Speeches of Martin Luther King, Jr.* by Martin Luther King, Jr. and James M. Washington (editor)

Many Lives, Many Masters by Brian L. Weiss, M.D.

A Message of Hope from the Angels by Lorna Byrne

Power vs. Force: The Hidden Determinants of Human Behavior by David R. Hawkins, M.D., Ph.D.

A Return to Love: Reflections on the Principles of A Course in Miracles by Marianne Williamson

Revelations: Visions, Prophecy, & Politics in the Book of Revelation by Elaine Pagels

Saint John of the Cross (Devotions, Prayers and Living Wisdom) by Mirabai Starr (Ed.)

Son of Man: The Mystical Path to Christ by Andrew Harvey

The Story of a Soul: The Autobiography of St. Thérèse of Lisieux by John Beevers

APPENDIX V
Resources

Rev. Diane Berke	http://onespiritinterfaith.org
Roland Comtois	http://blessingsbyroland.com
Heather Cumming	http://www.healingquests.com
Dr. Jude Currivan	http://www.judecurrivan.com
Deirdre Corcoran Foote	https://www.facebook.com/SuperDogSocial
Trudy Griswold	http://www.angelspeake.com
Steven Gottlieb	http://www.stevenghealing.com
Andrew Harvey	http://www.andrewharvey.net
Luciana Walker	http://www.lucianawalker.com
JoAnn Wolff	joannwolff1111@gmail.com

APPENDIX VI

What I Like About Atheism

Two dear friends who are atheists, one a self-described orthodox atheist, inspired this Appendix. I love them both and given the opportunity, I would not change a thing about either of them including their views on God. I don't expect either of them to read this book, and I wouldn't ask them to, but in the unlikely case an atheist does find himself or herself reading this book, there are a few further clarifications I would like to make.

First, I don't believe Jesus is coming back to save us. We must save us. If there is a God then He is in us and we are in Him. We are the ones we have been waiting for.

Second, I did not raise my children in any religion because although I do believe in God, a term I try to explain in the Introduction to this book, I don't understand the religious traditions. I feel as though my messengers, Jesus in particular, have been co-opted by religion. The messages he sends to me are about taking responsibility for ourselves and those people and situations around us. We are to extend our caring and compassion out into our local, national and global community to the extent we are able to do so. I know it sounds absurd since this book is about living in alignment with God's will, but what I really like about the atheist view is that without a belief in God, they are the ones who save themselves. They are the ones who save the world. Whether one chooses to work with God or not, life still critically depends on us. I believe that joined with God, we are a powerful force, but I don't believe that without God we are not capable of the same things because it all boils down to one thing: love. Not everyone needs God to know how to love. I trust that after reading the messages in this book, you will find that, regardless of their source, the messages of love and forgiveness are timely and universal.

ACKNOWLEDGEMENTS

I thank God, in the many forms He chooses to appear or speak to me.

I thank my mom for her insistence that I document the Divine revelations I was receiving. Without that documentation there would be no messages and no story to share with you.

I thank my friend Linda Fallo-Mitchell for all the time and patience she showed in making this book a reality. Without Linda there would be no book.

I thank Donna Poile, Linda Fallo-Mitchell and Kimberly Allis for their undying love, friendship and teachings.

I thank my husband Peter for his patience as I spent precious free time writing in our home office, which I facetiously named "Ravello."

I thank my daughter Danielle, who always asks a deeper question.

I thank my son Mitchell, who keeps me humble by making fun of my work.

I thank Roland Comtois for his channeled messages over the years.

I thank Andrew Harvey, who said I must, must, must write the messages I received in a book.

I thank Annabel Monaghan for her ongoing encouragement and support.

I thank my early readers: Kimberly Allis, Nancy Bischoff, Lee Bryant, Joan & Bill Burgess, Kathy Evertsberg, Anne Harris, Diane Insolia, Flora Insolia, Danielle Joseph, Lesley King, Sheryl Leach, Annabel Monaghan, Janice Richards, Marie Posthumus and Allison Wolowitz.

I thank Ellen Mosher.
I thank Diane Insolia.

I thank Elizabeth Wellington, who as God's scribe, expertly copyedited this book.

I thank Polly Simpkins, who was the first to ask me to tell my story,
my Reiki Teachers: Margareth Ornitz, Carol Warren and
Heather Cumming—
And all the people who believe in me when I don't believe in myself.

I thank all of my friends and family.
I thank all of my clients.
I thank all of humanity without whom there would be no one to love.

Everyday Mystic: Finding the Extraordinary in the Ordinary
is now available in print and digital format at
Amazon.com and other retailers as well as at
the Global Peace Movement website
http://www.globalpeacemovementnow.com

For inquiries please email us at
Info@GlobalPeaceMovementNow.com

ENDNOTES

1. Reiki is a Japanese technique for stress reduction and relaxation that also promotes healing. It is administered by "laying on hands" and is based on the idea that an unseen "life force energy" flows through us and is what causes us to be alive. Reiki is a simple, natural and safe method of spiritual healing and self-improvement that everyone can use. A treatment feels like a wonderful, glowing radiance that flows through and around you. Reiki treats the whole person, including the body, emotions, mind and spirit creating many beneficial effects that include relaxation and feelings of peace, security and wellbeing. Source: www.Reiki.org. Reiki is currently used in hospitals, hospices, spas and wellness centers.

2. Spirit or the Holy Spirit as I use it, is one method, but not the only method, by which God communicates with me.

3. Pay attention to those tears that seemingly spring from nowhere. They are the result of the enormousness of your heart energy trying to speak to your mind. It is so vast and overwhelming that you get "all choked up." Oftentimes, that is how you know it is your heart speaking to you.

4. Because I see Jesus as working on God's behalf, I use God interchangeably with Jesus.

5. Although often associated with Native American culture, according to Mircea Eliade, a scholar of religion, the word shaman comes from the language of a tribe in Siberia. A shaman is a man or woman who "journeys" in an altered state of consciousness in order to encounter and interact with the spirit world. The shamanic journey is the most common practice of the traditions and is usually induced by rhythmic drumming or other percussion sound, such as a rattle. Shamans typically journey with their power animal.

6. Some people believe that there are energetic lines in the earth called ley lines.

7. Dr. Jude Currivan is a cosmologist, planetary healer, international award-winning Hay House author, visionary and educator based in England.

8. It needs to be noted that I continue to be unenlightened enough not to allow my young adult children to encounter apparently dangerous situations when I can help

it. I will continue to attempt to delay those lessons and they will continue to push me past my comfort zone.

9. Often called Kirlian photography, aura photography provides a visual representation of the human energy field.

10. Shamans believe that pieces of our soul or spirit can split off due to traumatic, or perceived traumatic experiences. For children, a traumatic experience can be as simple as leaving a beloved home or friends.

11. It should be noted that people with certain mental illnesses sometimes manifest similar occurrences which can be confused with mystical experiences. I do not advocate opening to divine visions or messages for those with certain diagnosed mental illnesses unless the practice is approved by a mental health professional.

12. Although my spiritual interactions are primarily with Jesus and Christian mystics that does not mean that I am a proponent of Christianity over other religions or over having no religion at all. I have also seen the Buddha, Quan Yin, Hindu gods and goddesses, and others. I do not have a religion. So please, as you read, if the messengers do not resonate with you, try to focus on the messages themselves. If you can do this, you will see that the messages transcend the presence or absence of religion.

13. As mentioned I did not start charging clients until they began bringing me gifts in exchange for the Reiki sessions. Even though I did not want to charge, I realized that people were not comfortable with receiving and not being able to give in return. I overcame my hesitance and began charging a fee, although not without being very clear that money should not be an obstacle to receiving a Reiki treatment (I was, and still am, seeing people who cannot pay, free of charge). To my surprise, my clients started coming to see me more frequently. Regardless of my reasons for not charging, namely that it was not **my** energy that was helping people, my clients were uncomfortable with not being able to exchange something of value for my time. Setting a price freed them to call me as often as needed.

14. It was Linda's idea to teach. I had already taught Reiki to one student and found that I didn't have the patience for all the words it took to convey ideas that experientially could be conveyed in a nanosecond. I had been practicing Reiki long enough to know that what Jesus could communicate through a feeling or by imparting a direct

knowing to me, took pages of explanation. For Linda, who had been a college professor, written and verbal explanations were not a problem.

15. I left my corporate job 16 months later; although when this message was delivered I didn't know I would be leaving.

16. The angel who was speaking to me at that time.

17. Mirabai Starr (Editor), *Saint John of the Cross (Devotions, Prayers & Living Wisdom)*. Boulder, CO: Sounds True. 2008. p. 58.

18. This is slightly paraphrased because I wasn't writing as I channeled. I got further clarification on the "not thinking" in a later meditation: *This is not about losing your mental faculties. It is about opening up a new doorway.*

19. The seventh chamber is a reference to St. Teresa of Avila, a 16th-century saint and mystic who had a vision of a crystal castle with seven mansions, each representing a different stage in spiritual development. *The Interior Castle* is a guide through each stage of development until the soul's final union with the Divine. I was familiar with the concept of the mansions of St. Teresa's *Interior Castle*, as I had started but never finished reading her book early in 2006. I hadn't remembered her using the term "chamber." So when the meditation ended, I looked in the Fount Classics edition of her *Interior Castle* and found that when she gets to the seventh level, instead of calling it a mansion, she refers to it as the seventh chamber.

20. As a full trance medium, John of God incorporates many different Entities. Among them are St. Ignatius, St. Francis Xavier, King Solomon and St. Rita of Cascia.

21. I founded the *Global Peace Movement* www.GlobalPeaceMovementNow.com to raise consciousness and manifest peace. This is discussed in more detail in Chapter 7.

22. Based on my experiences, I believe heaven is a state of being; not a place.

23. See Chapter 7.

24. Based on a channeled message I received in meditation.

25. See Appendix II for information on more recent, ongoing studies, including The Global Coherence Initiative, HeartMath and The Intention Experiment.

26. *The Meditation for World Peace* can be found, for free, at my website: http://www. globalpeacemovementnow.com/meditations.php. Other meditations and ways to participate are listed in Appendix III.

27. Linda Tucker, *Mystery of the White Lions: Children of the Sun God* (Carlsbad, CA: Hay House, 2010), 257.

28. The aura is the electromagnetic field of energy (light) that emanates from all matter. The human energy field or aura extends beyond the body and has been shown to have definite frequencies or vibrations that correspond to the colors of the visible light spectrum. It should be noted that the size, shape and color of auras change with our state of consciousness and will be seen differently by different people and equipment.

29. Martin Luther King, Jr., *The Strength to Love.*

30. I suspect this metaphor was used because the client to whom this message was delivered worked in finance.

31. Refers to the *Meditation for World Peace*, which Linda and I host.

32. As stated earlier, to me God/Him is the same as Love. The nomenclature is meaningless to me. God is a **feeling** that exists that transcends the mind and body, and is all LOVE and nothing else. It is unconditional love of all, for all. To me God is the ineffable.

33. The day before going to St. Catherine's church, someone made reference to Revelation, so I thought that I should read that part of *The Bible* to find out what they were talking about. Years later, I read a fascinating historical account of *The Book of Revelation* by Elaine Pagels entitled *Revelations: Visions, Prophecy, & Politics in the Book of Revelation*, Penguin Group 2012. John of Patmos, writing at a time after Jesus' crucifixion and while Christians were being persecuted, was immersed in the prophetic writings of Isaiah and other prophets. John essentially reshapes their visions, and using metaphor to avoid persecution, he characterizes the persecution of Christians by Roman forces. He declares Jesus to have been victorious via his ascent into heaven. "John's Book of Revelation...evokes the horror of Jewish war against Rome...John's vision and monsters are meant to embody actual beings and events."(p.33) Today the players have changed but the wars continue to be waged.

This I believe is what Jesus is referring to when he says: *This story is not about a point in time.*

34. Neil Douglas-Klotz, *Blessings of the Cosmos,* Sounds True, 2006, p. 28.

35. Several months later, when I explained to a client what had happened at Roland's healing circle, she said I had received **shaktipat**, which, in Hinduism, is the descent of grace. I hadn't even told her that the message I received a week later was that I was channeling grace. She knew from the description of what happened that I had received the grace of God and then said, "Lucky you." God knows I always need confirmation, and he always provides it.

36. David R. Hawkins, M.D., Ph.D., *Power vs. Force: The Hidden Determinants of Human Behavior.* Carlsbad, California: Hay House, Inc. 1995, p.23

37. Roland had no idea that Linda had received a message telling me to write a book. He had no idea that I was proceeding, albeit reluctantly, on that book. He also had no idea that I was working for years on my own humility or that Mother Mary had entered me to work on my clients.

38. If you are wondering how I knew if it was Jesus speaking to me, other than the fact that I could see and hear him clear as day, I am not in the habit of deliberately humiliating myself like that—especially when I have time to think about it!

39. According to Robert Schwartz, in *Your Soul's Plan: Discovering the Real Meaning of the Life You Planned Before You Were Born*, each soul plans all that it will encounter after it incarnates into the physical world.

40. That part of ourselves that we do not recognize, but is capable of living up to our highest ideal. Psychiatrist Carl Jung called our submerged creative potential the "Golden Shadow."

41. John of God Crystal Bed Treatment helps balance one's energy through specialized quartz crystal lamps used in conjunction with the entities of the Casa de Dom Inacio in Abadiana, Brazil.

42. The ineffable. The **feeling** that exists that transcends the mind and body that is all LOVE and nothing else—unconditional love of all, for all.

43. Beevers, John (translator), *The Story of a Soul, The Autobiography of Thérèse of Lisieux*. Garden City, New York: Image Books, A Division of Doubleday and Company. 1957. p.157.

44. Beevers, John (translator), *The Story of a Soul, The Autobiography of Thérèse of Lisieux*. Garden City, New York: Image Books, A Division of Doubleday and Company. 1957. p. 157.

45. ibid. p. 158.

46. ibid. p. 158.

47. In Arthurian legend the Lady of the Lake tricked Merlin into giving her his power. I believe this reference was made because of my client's life-long fascination with Arthurian legend.